ENVIRONMENTAL AIR POLLUTION

ENVIRONMENTAL AIR POLLUTION

By

Dr. P.R. Yadav

Lecturer
Dept. of Zoology
D.A.V. College
Muzaffarnagar (U.P.)
(India)

DISCOVERY PUBLISHING HOUSE PVT. LTD.
NEW DELHI-110 002

First Published - 2009
Reprinted - 2017

ISBN: 978-81-8356-443-4

Environmental Air Pollution

Published by:
DISCOVERY PUBLISHING HOUSE PVT. LTD.
4383/4B, Ansari Road, Darya Ganj
New Delhi-110 002 (India)
Phone: +91-11-23279245, 43596064-65
Fax: +91-11-23253475
E-mail: discoverypublishinghouse@gmail.com
sales@discoverypublishinggroup.com
web: www.discoverypublishinggroup.com

Printed at:
Infinity Imaging Systems
Delhi

Preface

The present title has been written especially to fill the need for a one volume general discussion of the *Environmental Air Pollution*. We are degrading our environment and consuming resources at unsupportable rates. Biodiversity is disappearing at a pace unequaled since the end of the age of dinosaurs sixty-five million years ago. Priceless topsoil is washing off farm fields, ancient forests are being destroyed to make newsprint and toilet paper, and rivers and lakes are polluted with untreated sewage and industrial waste, and pollution obscures the skies and appears to be altering our global climate. As modern communications and travel bring us into closer contact with every part of the world, we have come to recognize that our common environment is shared with other humans and nonhuman neighbours. Unless we all learn to live more sustainably and with less impact on our environment, the prospects for future generations are increasingly grim.

Throughout the text, complexities have been sorted out into a logical progression and technicalities have been boiled down to give clear, straightforward emphasis to basic trends and directions. Each important point is illustrated with an example to help clarify the idea; the numerous line drawings have all been chosen or created to help convey particular points. However, the use of superfluous numbers and references has been avoided, because it is felt that at the introductory level these often tend to clutter rather to clarify issues. The result is a text that is easy to read, without resorting to verbal gimmicks or talking down to readers.

To make the work more comprehensive and informative, the author has consulted many authoritative books, research journals, abstracts, monographs etc., so there can be no claim to originality except in the manner of treatment.

The author expresses his thanks to his friends and colleagues whose continue inspirations have initiated him to bring out this book.

The author expresses his gratitude to Mr. Wasan and staff of M/s Discovery Publishing House Pvt. Ltd. for their whole hearted co-operation in the publication of this book.

Author

CONTENTS

1

INTRODUCTION

The physiologist Lawrence J. Henderson remarked in his book *The Fitness of the Environment* that "Darwinian fitness is compounded of a mutual relationship between the organism and the environment. Of this, fitness of environment is quite as essential a component as the fitness which arises in the process of organic evolution; and in fundamental characteristics the actual environment is the fittest possible abode of life." It is difficult to imagine life evolving under conditions other than those found at the surface of the earth. Indeed, could we imagine life in any form other than our own?

Biologists before and after Henderson have argued that certain physical and chemical conditions and properties must be met for any sort of life to evolve and that only a limited range of these suitable conditions exist on the earth. Any imaginable form of life must have a liquid basis; gases are too diffuse and structureless, solids too rigid. The basic medium of life on the earth is water; thus, life processes occur only at temperatures between the melting and boiling points of water, those that prevail at the surface. Henderson argued that of all compounds only water has all the qualities necessary to support life. In this chapter, we shall discuss the many serendipitous properties of water and the other features of the environment important to life: temperature, carbon and oxygen, inorganic nutrients, salts, and light.

WATER

All organisms are composed mostly of water, whether they dwell in oceans, lakes, or rivers, or on land. Water is generally abundant on the earth's surface and, within the temperature range usually encountered, it is liquid.

Water has many thermal and solvent properties favourable to life. One must add or remove a large amount of heat energy to change its temperature, and because water conducts heat rapidly the temperatures of organisms and aquatic environments tend to be relatively constant and homogeneous. Water also resists change of state between solid (ice), liquid, and gaseous (water vapor) phases. To evaporate a quantity of water requires an input of over 500 times more energy than that needed to raise its temperature by 1 degree Celsius. Freezing requires the removal of 80 times as much heat as that needed to lower temperature by 1 degree. Another curious thermal property of water is that whereas most substances become more dense when they are cooled, water becomes less dense as it cools below 4°C. Consequently ice floats, not only making ice-skating possible but also keeping the bottoms of lakes and oceans from freezing, thus providing refuge for aquatic plants and animals during winter.

Table 1.1. Thermal properties of water

Specific heat is the quantity of heat energy required to raise the temperature of 1 g of water 1°C: 1 calorie (cal) or 4.2 joules (J).

Heat of melting is the quantity of heat energy that must be added to ice to melt 1 g of water at 0°C: 80 cal or 335 J.

Heat of vaporization is the quantity of heat energy that must be added to evaporate 1 g of water: 597 cal or 2498 J at 0°C, 536 cal or 2243 J at 100°C.

Thermal conductivity is the flux of heat through a 1 cm^2 cross-section at a gradient of 1°C cm^{-1} (units are J cm^{-1} sec^{-1} °C^{-1}): 0.0055 at 0°C, 0.0060 at 20°C, 0.0063 at 40°C, and 0.022 for ice at 0°C.

Density is the mass per unit volume:

water at 30°C	=	0.99565 g cm^{-3}
20°C	=	0.99821
10°C	=	0.99970
4°C	=	0.99997 (maximum density)
0°C	=	0.99984
ice at 0°C	=	0.917

Water has an immense capacity to dissolve inorganic compounds, making them accessible to living systems and providing a substrate within which they can react to form new compounds. The formidable solvent properties of water derive from the strong attraction of water molecules for other compounds. Molecules are composed of electrically charged atoms or groups of atoms called ions. Common table salt, sodium chloride (NaCl), is made up of a positively charged sodium atom (Na^+) and a negatively charged chlorine atom (Cl^-). When salt is placed in water, the attraction of the water molecules for the charged sodium and chlorine atoms is so great, compared with the bonds that hold the molecule together, that the salt molecule readily dissociates onto its component atoms -another way of saying that the salt dissolves. The dissociation of sodium chloride into its component ions may be written

$$NaCl \rightleftharpoons Na^+ + Cl^-$$

or, portraying the role of the water molecules as a solvent, as

$$NaCl + H_2O \rightleftharpoons H_2ONa^+ + Cl^-$$

The arrows indicate that even in solution ions continually rejoin as well as dissociate. The absolute magnitudes of the dissociation and association rates determine how fast a substance dissolves. The magnitudes of these rates relative to each other determine the solubility of the substance at equilibrium.

Soil Water

Most terrestrial plants obtain the water they need from the soil. The amount of water that soil holds and its availability to plants vary according to the physical structure of the soil particles. Soil consists of grains of clay, silt, and sand, and particles of organic detritus. Grains of clay, produced by the weathering of minerals in certain types of bedrock, are the smallest; grains of sand, which are the quartz crystals that remain after minerals more susceptible to weathering are removed from rock, tend to be the largest; silt particles are intermediate. Collectively, these particles are known as the soil skeleton; as the name implies, these comprise a stable component that influences the physical structure of the soil and its water holding ability, but do not play a major role in its chemical transformations.

Water is sticky. The capacity of water molecules to cling to each other and to surfaces they touch accounts for the familiar phenomena of surface tension and the rise of water against gravity in capillary tubes. Water clings tightly to surfaces of the soil skeleton. Because the total surface area of particles increases as their size decreases, silty soils hold more water than coarse sands, through which water drains quickly.

Water capacity is not equivalent to water availability. Plant roots easily take up water that clings loosely to soil particles by surface tension, but water near the surface of sand and silt particles is bound tightly by stronger forces. These forces are called the water potential of the soil. Soil scientists measure soil water potential and the strength with which the cells of root hairs can absorb water from the soil by equivalents of atmospheric pressure. Capillary attraction holds water in the soil with a force equivalent to a pressure of 1/10 to 1/5 atmosphere (76-152 torr or 0.01-0.02 megapascals [1 MPa = 1,000,000 Pa]). Water attracted to soil particles with less force than atmosphere (water in the middle of interstices between large soil particles, hence at great distance from their surfaces) drains out of the soil under the pull of gravity and joins the groundwater in the crevices of the bedrock below. The amount of water held against gravity by forces of attraction greater than u to s atmosphere is called the field capacity of the soil.

A force equivalent to 1/10 atmosphere is sufficient to raise a column of water nearly 1 meter. We know that plant roots can exert a much greater pull on water in the soil, because water rises in the tallest trees to leaves more than 100 meters above the ground. In fact, plants can exert a pull of about 15 atmospheres (1.5 MPa) on soil water. Once plants under drought stress have taken up all the water in the soil held by forces weaker than 15 atmospheres, they can no longer obtain water and they wilt, even though water remains in the soil. Thus, a soil water potential of 15 atmospheres is referred to as the wilting coefficient, or wilting point, of the soil.

As soil water is depleted, the remainder is held by increasingly stronger forces, on average, because a greater proportion of the water is situated close to the surfaces of soil particles. For a typical soil with a more or less even distribution of soil particle sizes from clay (up to 0.002 mm) through silt (0.002–0.05 mm) to sand (0.05–2.0 mm). Such soils are called loams. When saturated, a loam holds about 45 grams of water per 100 grams of dry soil (45 per cent water). The field capacity is about 32 per cent, and the wilting coefficient about 7 per cent. The difference between the field capacity and the wilting coefficient, about 25 per cent in this case, measures the water available to plants. Of course, plants obtain water most readily when the soil moisture is close to the field capacity.

In soils with predominantly smaller particles the soil skeleton has a relatively large surface area; such soils hold a larger amount of water at both the wilting coefficient and the field capacity, and a correspondingly larger proportion of soil water is held by forces greater than 15 atmospheres. Soils with predominantly larger skeletal particles have less surface area and larger interstices between particles. More of the soil water is held loosely and is thus available to plants, but such soils have lower field capacities. Plants can obtain the most water from soils having a variety of particle sizes between sand and clay.

Temperature

Life processes, as we know them, are restricted to the temperatures at which water is liquid: 0 to 100°C at the earth's surface. Relatively few organisms can survive body temperatures above 45°C. Some bacteria occur in hot springs close to the boiling point of water, and the photosynthetic cyanobacteria tolerate temperatures as hot as 75°C. The properties that permit existence at high temperatures are not well understood. Compared to most bacteria, the proteins of thermophilic bacteria have subtly different proportions of amino acids; as a result, the structure of these proteins remains stable at temperatures up to 95°C.

While temperatures on the earth rarely exceed 50°C, except in hot springs and at the soil surface in hot deserts, temperatures below the freezing point of water are common over large portions of the surface. When living cells freeze, the crystal structure of ice disrupts most life processes and may damage delicate cell structures, leading rapidly to death. Many species successfully cope with freezing temperatures either by maintaining their body temperatures above the freezing point of water, or by activating mechanisms to resist freezing or to tolerate its effect. The freezing point of water may be depressed by dissolved substances that interfere with the formation of ice. For example, the freezing point of seawater, which contains about three-and-a-half per cent dissolved salts, is –1.9°C.

The blood and body tissues of most vertebrates contain less than half the salt content of seawater and thus may freeze at a higher temperature than the freezing point of the ocean. Saltier blood could enable vertebrates to live in polar seas, but protein structure and function are too sensitive to salt concentration to make this a practical solution. Many organisms reduce the freezing points of their body fluids with large quantities (up to 30 per cent in some terrestrial invertebrates) of glycerol and glycoproteins, which act like antifreeze; their presence in the blood and tissues allows antarctic fish, for example, to remain active in seawater that is colder than the normal freezing point of the blood of fish in temperate or tropical seas.

Supercooling provides a second solution to the problem of freezing. Under certain circumstances, fluids can fall below the freezing point without ice crystals forming. Ice generally forms around an object, called a seed, which can be a small ice crystal or some other particle. In the absence of seeds, pure water may be cooled more than 20°C below its melting point. Supercooling has been recorded to -8°C in reptiles and -18°C in invertebrates.

Finally, some organisms can tolerate freezing of most or all of the water in their bodies. Such organisms employ some unknown mechanism to restrict ice formation to the spaces between cells rather than within them; hence ice does not destroy cell structure. But because salts are excluded from ice and are therefore concentrated in the liquid water within cells, freezing-tolerant organisms must also cope with extremely high salt levels in their tissues during the winter.

Temperature has several opposing effects on life processes. First, heat increases the kinetic energy of molecules and thereby accelerates chemical reactions; the rate of biological processes commonly increases between two and four times for each 10°C rise in temperature throughout the physiological range. Second, enzymes and other proteins become less stable and may not function properly or retain their structure at high temperatures. Third, the level of heat energy in the cell influences the conformations of proteins, which are balanced between the natural kinetic motions induced by heat and the forces of chemical attraction between different parts of the molecule. The physical properties of fats, which are important components of cell membranes and are accumulated by many animals as a reserve of food energy, also depend on temperature. When too cold, fats become stiff like the fat on a piece of meat taken from the refrigerator; when warm, they become fluid.

Enzymes function well only when they assume the proper shape. Too hot, the molecule may open its structure and tend to unfold; too cold, the molecule may close up so that substrates do not fit properly to active sites. The combination of these factors results in an optimum temperature range for the occurrence of biological systems. The structures of enzymes and other molecules enable them to function best within the normal range of body temperature of the organism.

Energy Transformations

Plants and animals consist of many elements joined together into organic molecules that form the structure of the individual. Such organic compounds also provide the energy needed to maintain the organism in the form of chemical bonds between atoms and molecules. These energy-containing bonds arise from chemical changes in the atoms of various elements. In biological systems, one of the most prevalent of these transformations is the chemical reduction of carbon, accomplished when electrons are added to the atom. An oxidized form of carbon is carbon dioxide (CO_2). During photosynthesis, plants reduce the carbon atom in carbon dioxide. This altered atom forms new compounds, such as the carbohydrate glucose ($C_6H_{12}O_6$), within which its energy level is greatly increased. The added energy comes from light, of course. To release this stored energy for other purposes, both plants and animals undo the results of photosynthesis by oxidizing carbon back to carbon dioxide. During this transformation energy is released, a portion of which organisms harness; the rest escapes as heat.

Photosynthesis and respiration involve the complementary reduction and oxidation of carbon and oxygen. Oxygen's common oxidized state is molecular oxygen (O_2), which occurs as a gas in the atmosphere and dissolved in water. In a reduced state, oxygen readily forms water molecules (H_2O). Thus, as carbon is reduced during photosynthesis, oxygen is oxidized from its form in water to its molecular form. During respiration, inhaled or absorbed oxygen is reduced to its form in water as carbon is oxidized to its form in carbon dioxide. Why, then, does the coupling of an oxidation reaction to a reduction reaction result in a net release of energy? Because the reduction of oxygen is thermodynamically more favourable (requires less energy input) than the reduction of carbon, the oxidation of carbon releases more energy than the reduction of oxygen requires. (This is why oxygen is such a good oxidizer.)

Plants reduce more carbon than they oxidize (otherwise they would not grow), and they therefore require an external source of carbon. The only practical source of inorganic carbon, carbon dioxide, has an extremely low concentration in the atmosphere (about 0.03 per cent, or a partial pressure at sea level of 0.2 torr). As a result, gradients of CO_2 concentration between the atmosphere and the interior of plant cells are very low, certainly much lower than gradients of water vapor pressure between the plant and the surrounding atmosphere. This creates special problems for water conservation by plants, especially in arid environments, and accounts for the fact that plants transpire 500 grams of water, more or less, for every gram of carbon assimilated.

Carbon availability poses less of a problem for aquatic plants than for terrestrial plants because of the high solubility of carbon dioxide in water. When carbon dioxide dissolves, some of the molecules react with water to form carbonic acid (H_2CO_3) and associated compounds, which provide a reservoir of inorganic carbon. The concentration of carbon dioxide in the atmosphere is about 0.0003 cm^3 cm^{-3}; its solubility in fresh water and under ideal conditions is nearly the same, about 0.0003 cm^3 cm^3. Depending on the acidity of the water, carbonic acid molecules dissociate into bicarbonate (HCO_3) and carbonate (CO_3^{2-}) ions; within the range of acidity of most natural waters (pH 6-9) bicarbonate ion is the most common form. Bicarbonate ion dissolves readily in water (69 g of $NaHCO_3$ per liter of water, for example). As a result, seawater normally contains concentrations of bicarbonate ion equivalent to 0.03 to 0.06 cm^3 of carbon dioxide gas per cm^3 of water, over 100 times the concentration of the dissolved gas.

Whereas carbon dioxide poses difficulties for plants in terrestrial environments, it is oxygen that limits animals in aquatic habitats. Compared to its concentration of 0.21 cm^3 cm^3 in the atmosphere, the maximum solubility of oxygen (at 0°C in fresh water) is 0.01 cm^3 cm^{-1} only 14 parts per million (ppm) by weight. Furthermore, below the limit of light penetration in deep bodies of water and in waterlogged sediments and soils, where aquatic plants are absent, and no oxygen is produced by photosynthesis, animal and microbial respiration may severely deplete dissolved oxygen. Deeper layers of water in lakes and the mucky sediments of marshes frequently become totally deprived of oxygen (anaerobic, anoxic). Similar conditions in waterlogged soils of swamps pose problems for terrestrial plants, whose roots need oxygen for respiration just as animals do.

Inorganic Nutrients

Organisms assimilate a wide variety of chemical elements. After hydrogen, carbon, and oxygen, the elements required in greatest amount are nitrogen, phosphorus, sulfur, potassium, calcium, magnesium, and iron. Many other elements, such as boron and selenium, are known to be required in smaller quantity even though their physiological functions are not well understood. As techniques for measuring quantities of elements in the parts-permillion and parts-per-billion ranges develop, the importance of these trace elements to ecological relationships of plants and animals will emerge more clearly.

Plants acquire mineral nutrients other than oxygen, carbon, and some nitrogen from water. They obtain nitrogen in the form of ammonia ion (NH_4^+) or nitrate ion (NO_3^-), phosphorus in the form of phosphate ion ($P0_4^{3-}$), calcium and potassium in the form of their elemental ions (Call, K^+), and so on. The availability of each of these elements varies with their chemical form in the soil, and with the temperature, acidity, and presence of other ions in the soil water. A comparison of the amounts of elements in the soil and accumulated by vegetation suggests that certain elements are likely to be scarcer than others. Phosphorus, in particular, often limits plant production because even when abundant most of the compounds it forms in the soil do not dissolve easily.

Table 1.2. Major nutrients required by organisms, with some of their primary functions

Element	*Function*
Nitrogen (N)	Structural component of proteins and nucleic acids
Phosphorus (P)	Structural component of nucleic acids, phospholipids, and bone
Sulfur (S)	Structural component of many proteins
Potassium (K)	Major solute in animal cells
Calcium (Ca)	Structural component of bone and of material between woody plant cells; regulator of cell permeability
Magnesium (Mg)	Structural component of chlorophyll; involved in function of many enzymes
Iron (Fe)	Structural component of hemoglobin and many enzymes
Sodium (Na)	Major solute in extracellular fluids of animals

All natural waters contain some dissolved substances. Although nearly pure, rainwater acquires some dissolved minerals from dust particles and droplets of ocean spray in the atmosphere. Most lakes and rivers contain 0.01 to 0.02 per cent dissolved minerals and roughly $\frac{1}{20}$ to $\frac{1}{40}$ the average salt concentration of the oceans (3.4 per cent), in which salts and other minerals have accumulated over the millennia.

Dissolved minerals in freshwater and saltwater differ in composition as well as in quantity. Seawater abounds in sodium and chlorine, with significant amounts of magnesium and sulfate. Fresh water contains a more even distribution of diverse ions, but calcium is usually the most abundant cation (an ion carrying a positive charge) and carbonate and sulfate the most abundant anions (those carrying a negative charge). The composition of freshwater and saltwater differs owing to the different rates of solution and solubilities of substances. Few compounds reach their maximum solubilities in fresh water; their concentrations reflect the composition and rates of solution of materials in the rock and soil that the water contacts. Limestone consists primarily of calcium carbonate, which dissolves quickly; thus, water in limestone areas contains abundant calcium ion, making it "hard." Granite contains such minerals as quartz and feldspar, which do not contain calcium and which dissolve slowly; water flowing through granitic areas contains few dissolved substances and is "soft."

Table 1.3. Typical concentrations of elements in soils and annual uptake by plants

Element	*Soil content (weight %)*	*Annual plant uptake (kg ha^{-1} yr^{-1})*	*Soil content/ annual plant uptake (years)*
Silicon (Si)	33	20	21,000
Aluminum (Al)	7	0.5	180,000
Iron (Fe)	4	1	52,000
Calcium (Ca)	1	50	260
Potassium (K)	1	30	430
Sodium (Na)	0.7	24	600
Magnesium (Mg)	0.6	4	2000
Titanium (Ti)	0.5	0.08	62,000
Nitrogen (N)	0.1	30	40
Phosphorus (P)	0.08	7	150
Manganese (Mn)	0.08	1	1000
Sulfur (S)	0.05	2	320
Fluorine (F)	0.02	0.01	26,000
Chlorine (Cl)	0.01	0.06	220
Zinc (Zn)	0.005	0.01	6500
Copper (Cu)	0.002	0.006	4200
Boron (B)	0.001	0.03	400
Molybdenum (Mo)	0.0003	0.0003	13,000
Selenium (Se)	0.0000001	0.0003	40

The oceans are like large stills, concentrating minerals as pure water evaporates from the surface and nutrient-laden water arrives via streams and rivers. Here the concentrations of some minerals, particularly calcium carbonate, are limited by their maximum solubilities. Calcium carbonate dissolves only to the extent of 0.000014 grams per gram (ca. 1 cm^3) of water. Its concentration in the oceans reached this level eons ago, and the excess calcium ion entering oceans each year from streams and rivers precipitates to form limestone sediments. At the other extreme, the solubility of sodium chloride (0.36 g per g of water) far exceeds its concentration in seawater; most of the sodium chloride washing into ocean basins remains dissolved.

Table 1.4. Percentage composition of dissolved minerals in rivers (freshwater), in seawater, and in the blood plasma and cells of frogs

Mineral ion	*Delaware River*	*Rio Grande River*	*Seawater*	*Frog plasma*	*Frog cells*
Sodium (Na^+)	6.7	14.8	30.4	35.4	1.3
Potassium (K^+)	1.5	0.9	1.1	1.3	77.7
Calcium (Ca^{2+})	17.5	13.7	1.2	1.2	3.1
Magnesium (Mg^{2+})	4.8	3.0	3.7	0.4	5.3
Chlorine (Cl^-)	4.2	21.7	55.2	39.0	0.8
Sulfate (SO_4^{2-})	17.5	30.1	7.7	—	—
Carbonate (CO_3^{2-})	33.0	11.6	0.4	22.7	11.7

Osmotic Problems

Organisms obtain nutrients from the soil, water, or their food. Often these are much more concentrated in the tissues than in the surroundings, and organisms must therefore assimilate these nutrients against the prevailing gradient. But organisms also must exclude from their bodies many abundant substances in the environment that are metabolically useless or even toxic at high concentration. When a surface permits the flux of desirable substances, it can keep out others only by selective permeability (if wanted and unwanted substances differ greatly in size or electrical charge) or by actively pumping unwanted substances out across the surface.

Left to their own devices, ions diffuse across the surfaces of organisms from regions of high to low concentration, thereby equalizing their concentrations. Water also moves across permeable membranes (the process is called osmosis) toward regions of high ion concentrations (that is, low water concentration), tending to equalize concentrations of dissolved substances on both sides of the membrane. This tendency of a solution to attract water is known as its osmotic potential. The osmotic potential of seawater is high, that of freshwater is low, and that of the body fluids of vertebrate animals is intermediate. Gradients of osmotic potential pose different problems for freshwater fish, which tend to gain water and lose solutes, and saltwater fish, which tend to gain salt and lose water. Most organisms solve their osmotic problems by pumping ions in one direction or the other, expending considerable energy in the process, across various body surfaces (skin, kidney tubules, and gills).

Certain environments pose special salt and osmotic problems. Aquatic environments with salt concentrations greater than that of seawater occur in some landlocked basins, particularly in and zones where evaporation is great. The Great Salt Lake (20 per cent salt) in Utah and the Dead Sea (23 per cent salt), lying between Israel and Jordan, are well-known examples. The osmotic potential of such environments would suck the water from most animals and plants; but a few aquatic creatures, such as brine shrimp (*Artemia*), can survive in saltwater concentrated to the point of crystallization (300 g per liter, or 30 per cent). Brine shrimp excrete salt at a prodigious rate to maintain their body fluids hypotonic to (less concentrated than) their surroundings.

The small copepod *Tigriopus* lives in pools high in the splash zone along rocky coasts. The pools receive fresh seawater infrequently and, as the water evaporates, the salt concentration rises to high levels. Unlike *Artemia*, *Tigriopus* solves its water loss problem by increasing the osmotic potential of its body fluids. It accomplishes this by synthesizing certain amino acids abundantly. These small molecules increase the osmotic potential of the body to match that of the habitat without the deleterious physiological effects of high levels of salt.

Terrestrial plants living at the edge of the sea have special salt problems. As we have seen, plants transpire hundreds of grams of water for every gram of dry-matter production. Salts in the water that move from the roots to the leaves stay behind in the leaves as water evaporates from their surfaces. Although this poses relatively little problem for plants when the source of water in the soil is fresh, mangrove trees and salt marsh grasses actively excrete most of the salt they take in with water.

Ultimate Driving

Light is the primary source of energy for the ecosystem. Green plants absorb light and assimilate its energy by photosynthesis. But not all light striking the earth's surface is useful in photosynthesis. Rainbows and prisms show that light consists of a spectrum of wave lengths that we perceive as different colours. Wave lengths of light are generally expressed in micrometers (,um) (one-millionth of a meter [10^{-6} m]) or nanometers (μm) (one-billionth of a meter [10^{-9} m]). The visible spectrum extends between wave lengths of about 400 nm (violet) and

700 nm (red). The energy content of light varies with wave length and hence with colour; short wave length blue light has a higher energy level than longer wave length red light.

Light that reaches the upper part of the earth's atmosphere from the sun extends far beyond the visible range: through the ultraviolet region toward the short wave length, high-energy X-rays at one end of the spectrum, and through the infrared region to such extremely long wave length, low-energy radiation as radio waves at the other end of the spectrum. Because of its high energy level, ultraviolet light can damage exposed cells and tissues. As light passes through the atmosphere, however, most of its ultraviolet components are absorbed, primarily by a molecular form of oxygen known as ozone (O_3), which occurs in the upper atmosphere. The atmosphere thus shields life at the earth's surface from the most damaging wave lengths of light.

Vision and the photochemical conversion of light energy to chemical energy by plants occur primarily within that portion of the solar spectrum at the earth's surface containing the greatest amount of energy. Absorption of radiant energy depends on the nature of the absorbing substance. Water only weakly absorbs light whose characteristic wave lengths fall in the visible region of the spectrum of energies; as a result, a glass of water appears colourless. Dyes and pigments are strong light absorbers of some wave lengths in the visible region and reflect or transmit light of definite colours that become identifying characteristics. Plant leaves contain several kinds of pigments, particularly chlorophylls (green) and carotenoids (yellow), which absorb light and harness its energy. Carotenoids, which give carrots their orange colour, absorb primarily blue and green and reflect light in the yellow and orange regions of the spectrum. Chlorophyll absorbs red and violet light while reflecting green and blue. When chlorophylls and carotenoids occur together in a plant, green light is absorbed least, hence the leaves appear greento us.

Photosynthesis in Aquatic Environments

Water absorbs or scatters enough light to limit the depth of the sunlit zone of the sea. The transparency of a glass of water is deceptive. In pure seawater, the energy content of light in the visible part of the spectrum diminishes to 50 per cent of its surface value within 10 meters depth, and to less than 7 per cent within 100 meters depth. Furthermore, water absorbs longer wave lengths more strongly than shorter ones; virtually all infrared radiation disappears within the topmost meter of water. Short waves of light (violet and blue) tend to be scattered by water molecules and thus also do not penetrate deeply.

As a consequence of the absorption and scattering of light by water green light tends to predominate with increasing depth. The photosynthetic pigments of aquatic plants are adapted to this spectral shift. Plants near the surface of the oceans, such as the green alga *Ulva* (sea lettuce), have pigments resembling those of terrestrial plants and best absorb light of blue and red colour. The deep-water red alga *Porphyra* has additional pigments that enable it to utilize green light more effectively in photosynthesis.

Because photosynthesis requires light, the depth at which plants exist in the oceans is limited by the penetration of light to a fairly narrow zone close to the surface, in which photosynthesis exceeds plant respiration. This range of depths is called the euphotic zone. The lower limit of the euphotic zone, where photosynthesis just balances respiration, is called the compensation point. It may be defined by either depth or light level. When algae in the phytoplankton sink below the compensation point or are carried below it by currents, and do not soon return to the surface on upwelling currents, they die.

In some exceptionally clear ocean and lake waters, the compensation point may lie 100 meters below the surface. But this is a rare condition. In productive waters with dense phytoplankton, or in water turbid with suspended silt particles, the euphotic zone may be as shallow as 1 meter. In some polluted rivers, little light penetrates beyond a few centimeters.

Thermal Environments

Much of the solar radiation absorbed by objects is converted to heat. The earth warms each day and cools by night. As the days lengthen and the sun rises higher in the sky toward summer, the surroundings become warmer; more heat is added each day than is lost. The warmth of the sun heating the atmosphere drives the winds. Light absorbed by water provides the major source of heat for evaporation.

Each object and each organism continually exchanges heat with its environment. When the temperature of the environment exceeds that of the organism, the organism gains heat and becomes warmer. When the environment is cooler, the organism loses heat and cools. The heat budget of an organism includes avenues of heat gain and avenues of heat loss. When temperature reaches an equilibrium, gains equal losses. When gains exceed losses, energy is stored or accumulated in the body and temperature rises. When losses exceed gains, temperature drops.

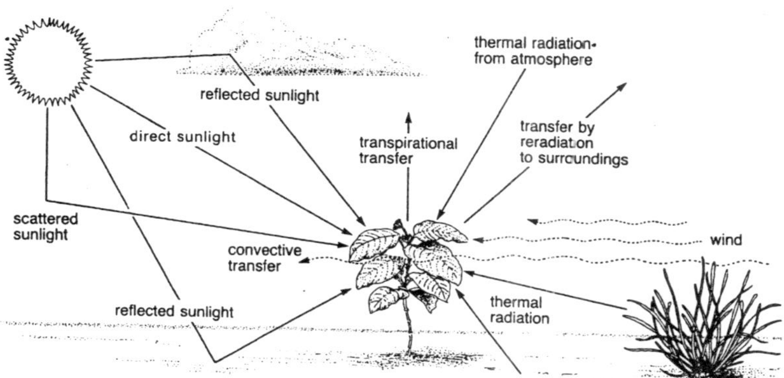

Fig. 1.1. Pathways of exchange of energy between a plant and its environment by radiation, convection, and transpiration.

The major categories of heat transfer between an organism and its environment may be described as follows:

Radiation (gain or loss) is the absorption or emission of electromagnetic radiation. Sources of radiation in the environment are the sun, the sky (scattered light), and the landscape, including vegetation. At night, although we cannot see the infrared radiation, objects that have warmed up in the sunlight radiate their stored heat to colder parts of the environment and, eventually, to space. The bodies of organisms, especially warm-blooded birds and mammals, often are the brightest objects in the night. Because radiation increases with the fourth power of thermodynamic temperature (°K), we radiate tremendous quantities of energy to the clear, black night sky. We can also receive radiation from atmospheric water vapor and from vegetation, which balances much of our radiation loss.

Conduction (gain or loss) is the transfer of the kinetic energy of heat between substances in contact. Thermal conductance (k) is expressed in watts (joules per second), normalized by the cross-sectional area (cm^2), the inverse of the distance traversed (cm^{-1}), and the temperature gradient (°C). Thus, the units of conductance are W cm^{-1} cm $°C^{-1}$, or W cm^{-1} $°C^{-1}$. No heat is conducted to a vacuum ($k = 0$); water ($k = 0.006$) conducts heat better than air (0.00026), owing to its greater density. Some metals, such as silver (4.3) and copper (4.0), conduct heat very rapidly. The rate of conductance between two objects, or between the inside and the outside of an organism, depends on insulative properties of the surface (the resistance to heat transfer, a function of k and surface thickness), surface area, and temperature gradient. An organism may either gain or lose heat depending on its temperature relative to that of the environment.

Convection (gain or loss) is the movement of liquids and gases of different temperatures, particularly over surfaces across which heat is transferred by conduction. Air conducts heat poorly. In still air, a boundary layer of air forms over a surface. A warm body tends to warm this boundary layer to its own temperature, effectively insulating itself against heat loss. A current of air flowing past a surface tends to disrupt the boundary layer and increase the rate of heat exchange by conduction. This convection of heat away from the body surface is the basis of the "wind-chill factor" heard on the evening weather report.

Evaporation (loss) requires heat. The evaporation of 1 gram of water from the body surface removes 2.43 kJ of heat at 30°C. As plants and animals exchange gases with the environment, some water evaporates from respiratory surfaces. Rate of evaporative heat loss depends on the amount of water exposed on the surface of the organism, the relative temperatures of the surface and of the air, and the vapor pressure of the atmosphere. Like heat, moisture can be trapped in the boundary layer of air that forms around bodies, and so convection increases evaporative as well as conductive heat loss. Warm air holds more water than cold air (51 g m^{-1} at 40° C, 17.3 g M^{-3} at 20°C, and 4.8 g m^{-1} at 0°C); hence, it has greater potential for evaporating water than does cold air. Where water is plentiful in hot climates, animals evaporate water from their skins and respiratory surfaces to cool themselves. For warm-blooded animals in cold climates, evaporation can become an unavoidable problem as cold air containing little water is warmed in contact with the body surface. We visualize such water loss on winter days when water evaporated from the warm surfaces of the lungs condenses as our breath mingles with the cold atmosphere.

Aquatic and Terrestrial Environments

Life arose in the sea. Conditions in shallow coastal waters were ideal for the development and diversification of the first plants and animals. Temperature and salinity varied little; sunlight, dissolved gases, and minerals were abundant. Water itself is buoyant and supports both delicate structures and massive bodies with equal ease.

Several hundred million years elapsed between the time modern life began to flourish in the sea and the appearance of life on land. Yet in spite of the harshness of some terrestrial environments, life has generally attained a higher degree of organic diversity and productivity on the land.

To appreciate fully the distinction between aquatic and terrestrial environments, we should contrast the properties of water and air rather than those of water and earth. The density of water (about 800 times that of air) and its ability to dissolve gases and minerals largely determine the form and functioning of aquatic organisms. Water provides a complete medium for life. In contrast, both the atmosphere and the land make essential contributions to the environment of terrestrial life: air provides oxygen for respiration and carbon dioxide for photosynthesis, while soil is the source of water and minerals. Air offers less resistance to motion than does water, and thus constrains movement less, but it also offers less support against the pull of gravity.

WATER IN BUOYANCY AND VISCOSITY

Because water is dense, it provides considerable support for organisms that, after all, are themselves mostly water. But organisms also contain bone, proteins, dissolved salts, and other materials that are more dense than salt or freshwater. These would cause organisms to sink were it not for a variety of mechanisms that reduce their density or retard their rate of sinking. Many fish have a swim bladder, a small gas-filled structure whose size can be adjusted to make the density of the body equal to that of the surrounding water. Some large kelps, a type of seaweed found in shallow waters, have analogous gas-filled organs. The kelps are attached to the bottom by holdfasts, and gas-filled bulbs float their leaves to the sunlit surface waters.

Fats and oils have densities of between 0.90 and 0.93 g cm^{-1} (90 to 93 per cent of the density of pure water). Many microscopic, unicellular plants (phytoplankton), which float in great numbers in the surface waters of lakes and oceans, contain droplets of oil that compensate for the natural tendency of cells to sink. Fish and other large marine organisms also accumulate lipids to provide buoyancy.

Aquatic organisms further lighten their bodies by reducing skeleton, musculature, and perhaps even the salt concentration of body fluids. It has been argued that aquatic vertebrates maintain low osmotic concentrations in their blood and body fluids (about one-third to one-half that of seawater) to reduce density.

The high viscosity of water lends a hand to some organisms that would otherwise sink more rapidly, but hampers the movement of others. Tiny marine animals often have long, filamentous appendages that retard sinking, just as a parachute slows the fall of a body through air. The wings of maple seeds, the spider's silk thread, and the tufts on dandelion and milk-weed seeds provide a similar function and increase the dispersal range of terrestrial species. But to reduce the drag encountered in moving through a medium as dense and viscous as water, fast-moving animals must assume streamlined shapes. Mackerel and other swift fish of the open ocean closely approach the hydrodynamicist's body of ideal proportions. Of course, air offers far less resistance to movement, having less than 1/50th the viscosity of water. But the atmosphere provides little buoyancy. To provide lift against the pull of gravity, birds and other flying organisms expend prodigious energy. The mechanics and aerodynamics of animal flight, involving the conversion of the movement of the muscles and appendages to lift and forward thrust, are described by Pennycuick.

Allometic Change

The relationships of organisms to their environments change with the size of the organism owing to nonproportional scaling of various physical processes with respect to size. In ecology, relationships between rates of processes and dimensions of objects are often described by the allometric relationship

$$\Upsilon = aX^b$$

where ϒ is being compared to X and *a* and *b* are constants pertaining to the relationship. ϒ, for example, might be the frequency of the heartbeat and X the body mass. The constant *b* is referred to as the allometric constant. When *b* is 1, ϒ is directly proportional to X. When *b* is greater than 1, ϒ increases proportionately more rapidly than X, and so the ratio of ϒ to X increases with larger X. When *b* is less than 1, the ratio of ϒ to X decreases with larger X; when *b* is less than 0, the absolute value of ϒ decreases with larger X. Because the equation describing the allometric relationship is a power function, it is often transformed to its logarithmic form

$$\log(\Upsilon) = \log(a) + b\log(X)$$

which is an equation describing a straight line.

The relationship between heart rate and body mass for mammals ranging over many orders of magnitude in size. The equation for the line that best fits the points has an allometric constant less than 0 ($b = -0.23$), in accordance with the slower heart rates of larger species. In contrast, the resting metabolic rates (RMR) of mammals increase with larger size, but less rapidly than mass itself; the allometric constant of the relationship between RMR and body mass is 0.73.

Because allometric constants usually differ from 1, the properties of organisms of different sizes are not directly comparable. Thus, the life span of an albatross may be 10 times that of a sparrow, but this difference is related in part to physiological consequences of size over and above differences in their environments or adaptations. But environment is important, too - albatrosses live longer than geese of similar size - and its effect appears as variation above and below the allometric line of relationship for all species together.

The allometry of certain relationships arises from simple physical or geometrical considerations. For example, the volume of a sphere increases in proportion to the cube of its diameter, but surface area increases in proportion to only the square of the diameter. Hence the relationship between surface (S) and volume (V) has an allometric constant of 2/3, or

$$S = aV^{0.67}$$

Therefore, larger organisms have relatively smaller surfaces compared to the bulk of their bodies. A sphere of radius r has a surface area of $4\pi r^2$ and a volume of $4\pi r^3/3$; the ratio of surface to volume is $3/r$. Thus a sphere having a diameter of 1 millimeter, comparable in size to a small water flea, has 1000 times as much surface per unit of volume as a bear-sized sphere 1 meter in diameter. This makes the uptake of oxygen relatively easy for the smaller organism but heat and water loss pose severe problems. Larger organisms elaborate larger interior surfaces (lungs) to obtain enough oxygen, and employ circulatory systems to move things around inside; conversely, heat and water conservation pose less severe problems. In general, because large animals

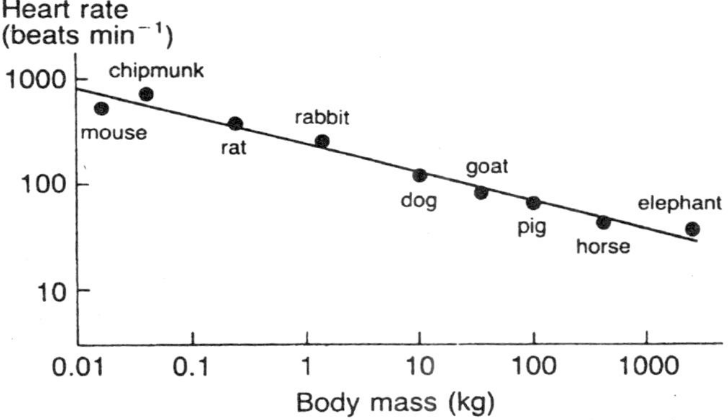

Fig. 1.2. Allometric relationship between heart rate and body mass in a variety of mammals ranging in size from mouse to elephant.

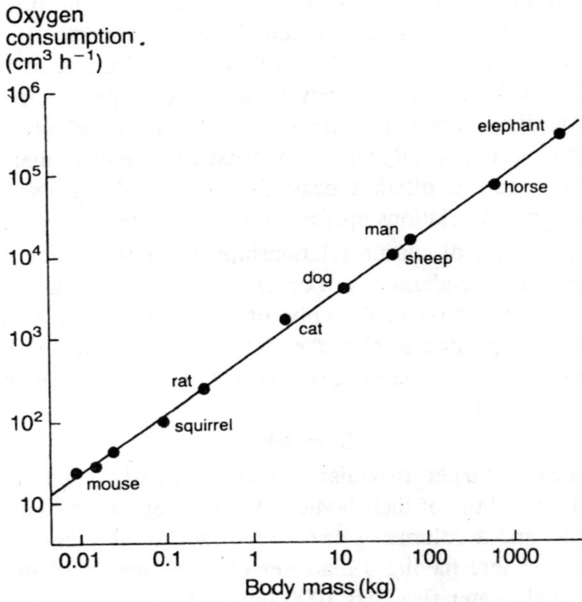

Fig. 1.3. Allometric relationship between resting metabolic rate and body mass in mammals.

have great bulk per unit of surface compared to smaller animals, they have greater capacity to resist change imposed by changes in the environment.

Size changes everything in ecology. In aquatic habitats, drag on the body depends on size and speed. Whereas a whale can coast on its momentum, a copepod stops dead in the water as soon as its power stroke ends; its momentum isn't sufficient to break through the viscosity of water. On land, size scales the movement of appendages and greatly affects locomotion. All these considerations influence the manner in which plants and animals adapt to the conditions of the environment.

We often contrast the living and the nonliving as opposites: biological versus physical and chemical, organic versus inorganic, biotic versus abiotic, animate versus inanimate. While these two great realms of the natural world are almost always distinguishable and separable, they do not exist in isolation from each other. Life depends upon the physical world. Living beings also affect the physical world. Their impact is often subtle, but soils, the atmosphere, lakes and oceans, and many sedimentary rocks owe their characteristics in part to the activities of plants and animals.

Living systems require the purposeful expenditure of energy to keep the organism out of equilibrium with and distinct from its physical surroundings. In this chapter, we shall explore how organisms maintain their integrity as open systems, continually exchanging materials and energy with the physical environment.

UNIQUE PROPERTIES

Motion and reproduction are the two most evident of the properties that distinguish living organisms from inanimate objects. Motion expresses a fundamental property of life, the ability to perform work directed toward a predetermined goal; biological reproduction derives its need from the mortality of the individual and ensures the continuation of life. Although distinct from physical systems, living beings nonetheless function within constraints set by physical laws. Like internal combustion engines, they transform energy to perform work. The automobile engine's burning of gasoline is chemical; its transmission of power from the cylinder to the tires is mechanical. The organism's metabolism of carbohydrates and its movement of appendages follow related chemical and physical principles. The biological world is therefore not an alternative to the physical world, but an extension of it.

While biological systems operate on the same principles as physical systems, there is an important difference. In physical systems, energy transformations act to even out differences in energy level throughout the system, always following the path of least resistance. But in biological systems, the organism purposefully transforms energy to keep itself out of equilibrium with the physical forces of gravity, heat flow, diffusion, and chemical reaction. The goal of keeping itself distinct from the physical world applies whether the organism is pursuing prey, producing seeds, or maintaining basic body functions.

In a sense, the organism's use of energy is the secret of life. A boulder rolling down a steep slope releases energy during its descent, but it performs no useful work. The source of the energy—in this case, gravity—is external, and as soon as the boulder comes to rest in the valley below, it is once more in equilibrium with the forces in its physical environment. A bird in flight, on the other hand, constantly expends energy to maintain itself aloft against the pull of gravity. The bird's source of energy the food it has assimilated is internal, and the bird uses that energy to perform useful work-to pursue prey, to escape from predators, or to migrate.

The ability to act against external physical forces is the one comm-on property of all living forms, the source of animation that distinguishes the living from the nonliving. Bird flight supremely expresses this property, but plants just as surely perform work to counter physical forces when they absorb soil minerals into their roots and synthesize the highly complex carbohydrates and proteins that make up their structure.

The ultimate source of energy for life is light from the sun. Pigments in the green tissues of plants absorb light and capture its energy; that energy is then converted to food energy through the manufacture of carbohydrates from simple inorganic compounds—carbon dioxide and water. This energy-trapping process is called photosynthesis—literally, a putting together with light. Energy locked up in the chemical bonds of sugars—and thence of proteins, fats, and other organic compounds—is used by plants and by animals, which either eat plants or eat other animals that eat plants, and so on, to fire the engines of life.

Interdependence

Life depends totally on the physical world. Not only do organisms ultimately receive their energy from sunlight, they must also tolerate the extremes of temperature, moisture, salinity, and other physical factors of their surroundings. The heat and dryness of deserts exclude most life forms, just as the bitter cold of polar regions turns back all but the most hardy. The form and function of plants and animals must obey the rules of the physical world. The viscosity and density of water require that fish be streamlined according to restrictive hydrodynamic design principles if they are to be both efficient and swift. The concentrations of oxygen in the atmosphere and in lakes, streams, and oceans place upper bounds on the metabolic rates of animals and microorganisms. Similarly, the limited ability of plants and animals to dissipate body heat-accomplished by the purely physical means of evaporative cooling, thermal conduction, and radiation of heat from the body surface to the surroundings -determines their rate of activity and their safe exposure to direct sunlight.

While organisms depend totally on the physical world, they also affect the physical world, sometimes in a profound manner. The oxygen we take for granted with every breath is the by-product of photosynthesis by bacteria that lived eons before the appearance of most forms of life. Before photosynthetic bacteria evolved in primitive seas, metabolism was accomplished slowly by anaerobic fermentation of organic molecules. The atmosphere of the earth consisted of strongly or mildly reduced gases, perhaps methane (CH_4) or carbon dioxide (CO_2), ammonia (NH_3) or molecular nitrogen (N_2), water vapor (H_2O), and hydrogen (H_2); geologic evidence points quite strongly to the absence of free oxygen (O_2) (Berkner and Marshall 1965). As bacteria began to utilize sunlight as a source of energy, photosynthesis liberated oxygen, some of which escaped from the oceans and accumulated in the atmosphere. Over the past 31 billion years, the known span of life, photosynthetic bacteria and plants have assimilated carbon and nitrogen; they have been partly replaced in the atmosphere by oxygen produced during photosynthesis.

Plants and microorganisms play an equally influential role in the development of soil from rock. Plant roots invade tiny crevices and pulverize rock as they grow and expand. The "rotting" of plant detritus by bacteria and fungi produces organic acids, which dissolve minerals out of rock, thereby weakening the rock's crystalline structure and speeding its weathering. Fragments of detritus eventually alter the physical structure of the soil. Certain bacteria and cyanobacteria are responsible for the biological fixation of nitrogen from the atmosphere. Animals play a part in the development of soil by burrowing, trampling, and defecating. Burrowing rodents, for example, create a striking mound topography where drainage is poor and the climate is seasonally dry.

The Dust Bowl that developed in the American Midwest during the 1930s provided a vivid example of what can happen when the environmental roles of plants and animals are disrupted. The Dust Bowl region is normally dry and windy, but the roots of the native perennial grasses were extensive enough to hold the soil in place. When the prairies were brought under the plow, annual crops having less extensive root systems replaced the perennial grasses. A series of dry years reduced crop growth and turned the soil surface to fine dust.

Plants also influence the movement of water. Rain does not accumulate where it falls. If it did, New York State would be under 60 meters of water within a lifetime. Some water flows over the soil or through the underlying earth to enter rivers, lakes, and, eventually, the ocean. The remainder escapes by evaporation from the ground surface and by transpiration from vegetation. In such places as the eastern United States, where the leaves of deciduous trees have about four times the surface area of the ground underneath, vegetation provides the major pathway for water escaping from the soil to the atmosphere. When a forest is cut, much of the water that would have evaporated from the leaves flows instead into rivers. Without provision for extensive replanting, deforestation causes flooding, increased erosion, downstream silt deposition, and removal of mineral nutrients from the denuded soil. In the humid tropics, where vegetation holds most of the nutrients in the system, deforestation can decrease soil fertility tragically.

Vegetation absorbs sunlight more efficiently than does bare ground. Because it also has a humidifying effect on the atmosphere, vegetation alters local heat budgets and fosters precipitation, thereby contributing to local weather. In vast regions of Africa just south of the Sahara Desert, the removal of most native vegetation a consequence of overgrazing and the collection of wood for fuel-greatly intensified the devastating drought of the 1980s.

TRANSFORMATIONS

Physical and chemical processes usually lead to transformations that release energy; those that require energy are highly improbable. As a result, the energy level of any bounded physical or chemical system decreases with time as the system loses energy to its surroundings; in other words, such a system spontaneously changes from a higher to a lower energy state. The oxidation of a carbohydrate—for example, the burning of a piece of paper—releases energy in the form of light and heat, and the products of this oxidation (carbon dioxide and water, in this case) contain less energy than the reactants (oxygen and carbohydrate).

Physical systems also dissipate energy. A swinging pendulum contains a certain amount of energy that is periodically transformed between the kinetic energy of the weight moving at the bottom of its swing and the potential energy stored at its highest point. In a frictionless environment, a pendulum would continue to swing forever without loss of energy. But in an atmosphere, the weight sets molecules of oxygen and nitrogen in motion and thereby transfers some of its energy to its surroundings. As it loses energy, the weight swings through smaller and smaller arcs. In this way, energy initially residing in the pendulum becomes more evenly distributed throughout the larger system.

If we could perceive energy density as values of light, organisms would appear to us as beacons against the dim background of the physical world. Animals and plants represent immense concentrations of energy -energy derived from the brightest light in the surroundings, the sun. To prevent physical and chemical processes from dispersing its energy more evenly throughout the system in which it exists, the organism performs work on the system in a manner designed to maintain its own integrity. By way of analogy, imagine yourself as a high mound of sand piled steeply on a flat landscape. Little avalanches of grains tumble down from your sides, the wind blows others away, and rain erodes your stature and carries your substance off in milky rivulets. To maintain your prominence, you continually scoop up nearby sand and pile it on top of your head. You may even reach across to another pile, where sand is easier to get, to maintain or perhaps add to your own substance. If you are clever, you build walls at your base to help retain your sand. In many ways living forms elaborate this theme, with the sand representing their energy and substance.

While each organism maintains a highly improbable concentration of energy in its body, it continuously expends energy to preserve its integrity. The energy expended must be balanced by energy gained, either by the assimilation of sunlight directly or by the assimilation of food. The energy released upon the metabolism of carbohydrates to carbon dioxide and water equals the net energy a plant assimilates to manufacture that amount of carbohydrates from raw inorganic materials. This assimilation of energy runs counter to the tendencies of physical and chemical processes, and it requires the expenditure of energy to build and maintain the individual's structure. Plants and animals also need additional energy, over and above this amount, because biochemical transformations are not perfectly efficient. The metabolism of carbohydrates is like a slow burn, but the organism cannot harness all the energy released; much is lost as heat, a form of energy that neither plants nor animals can use. Through the many biochemical transformations of the living organism, and because of the inefficiency of these transformations, all assimilated energy eventually is dissipated to the physical system -that is, energy is only transient in biological systems.

Thermodynamic Steady State

A uniform sphere of metal in space provides a simple illustration of a physical thermodynamic system. Completely lifeless, the sphere passively intercepts light emanating from the sun, or from some more distant star, and radiates energy into the black depths of space. Energy is assimilated, transformed, and lost from the system. When the sphere absorbs light, its temperature rises as molecules are caused to move more rapidly; the energy in the light is transformed to heat energy. But the hotter an object, the more rapidly it loses energy to its surroundings, and so the sphere radiates more and more energy to empty space. Eventually, the sphere heats up so much that it loses energy as rapidly as it absorbs it, and at this point the temperature of the sphere comes into equilibrium with its environment. This equilibrium is a dynamic steady state, in which the thermal characteristics of the system remain constant but the system sustains a continual flux of energy.

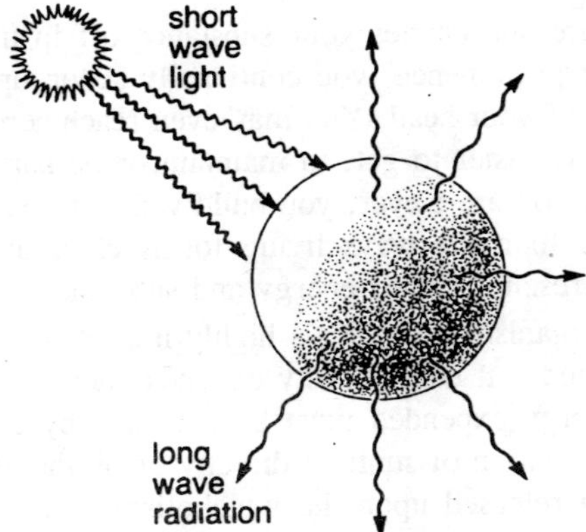

Fig. 1.4. Thermal model of a solid sphere, which receives energy as it absorbs sunlight and loses energy by radiation to space.

Simple physical principles allow us to characterize the steady state quantitatively and predict how the equilibrium temperature will vary with the conditions of the physical environment and the qualities of the sphere. The rate of change in the sphere's heat energy content (H) is the difference between its rate of absorption of radiant energy from the sun (A) and its rate of radiation of energy from the sphere to the environment (R). Thus, $dH/dt = A - R$.

Absorption depends on

F, the radiation flux through the sphere's environment, expressed as energy per unit of time per unit of area perpendicular to the source

C, the cross-sectional area of the sphere, which determines how much energy is intercepted

a, the absorptivity of the surface, which determines how much of the intercepted light is absorbed rather than reflected

Energy in units called joules (J) and rate of energy flux in units of joules per second, or watts (W), the common electrical power rating (see the endpapers for the International System of Units; for comparison, 1 joule = 0.239 calories). The intensity of the energy flux through the environment can be expressed as watts per square meter ($W\ m^{-1}$). (The flux of radiant energy from the sun at the distance of the earth is about 1350 $W\ m^{-1}$.) The cross-sectional area of a sphere can be expressed in square meters (m^2). Absorptivity is a dimensionless proportion of the total incident radiation. Hence, multiplying the flux density by the cross-sectional area by the absorptivity gives the rate of absorption in watts $(W\ m^{-2})(m^2) = W$; that is, $A = aFC$.

Radiation varies in direct relation to

T^4, the temperature of the system, measured in degrees Kelvin (°K) raised to the fourth power (°K = °C + 273; that is, absolute zero, 0°K, is –273°C)

S, the area of the surface of the sphere (m^2)

e, the emissivity of the surface, a property akin to absorptivity

In fact, good absorbers are also good emitters. Because radiation is measured in watts per unit of surface area, emissivity must have units of watts per area per fourth root of thermodynamic temperature (W m^{-2} $°K^{-4}$) to make radiation come out in watts.

Absorption and radiation can now be combined in a single equation of the form dH/dt = A – R; namely,

$$\frac{dH}{dt} = aFC - eST^4$$

The system comes into equilibrium when $dH/dt = 0$; that is, when

$$eST^4 = aFC$$

radiation equals absorbance. The temperature of the sphere at its steady state can be found by rearranging the condition for equilibrium to obtain

$$\hat{T} = \left(\frac{aCF}{eS}\right)^{1/4}$$

Because the surface area of a sphere is four times its cross-sectional area, the ratio *C/S* in this expression can be replaced by 4. Thus, equilibrium temperature (*T*) depends only on the absorptivity, the emissivity, and the radiation flux. Spheres having the same surface

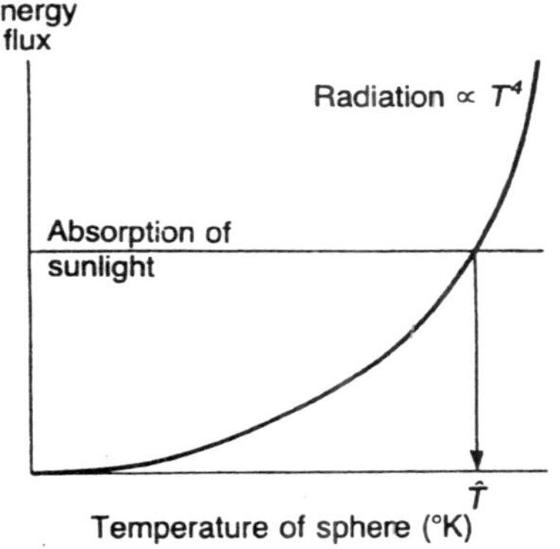

Fig. 1.5. Relationship of radiation to temperature of the radiating surface.

qualities but different sizes equilibrate at the same temperature; those closer to the sun (higher *F*) achieve higher temperatures than those more distant. All other things being equal, radiation flux varies inversely with the square of the distance from a heat source (that is, $F \propto D^{-2}$). Equilibrium temperature therefore varies inversely with the square root of the distance from the source ($T \propto (D^{-2})^{1/4} = D^{-1/2}$) Temperature may be adjusted by changing the surface properties of absorptivity and emissivity—for example, by covering a satellite with a reflective surface to prevent the interior from overheating in the full sunlight of space.

Control the Flux of Energy

The flux of energy or material across the surface of an organism can be described in general terms

$$\text{flux} = \text{surface area} \times \text{gradient} \times \text{conductance}$$

The gradient is the difference between the levels or concentrations of energy or material inside the organism and those in its surroundings. Conductance is the ease with which the energy or material crosses the surface barrier. In electrical terms, which are often used in analogies of ecological systems or to construct analog models, flux is current (amperes), gradient is electrical potential (volts), and conductance is the inverse of the electrical resistance (ohms per square meter of surface or cross-sectional area of wire).

Organisms can control flux by altering any of its three components. A mammal's thick winter fur reduces the conductance of heat (thermal conductance) from its body to its surroundings. The hard, waxy cuticles covering the exoskeletons of insects increase the resistance of the body's surface to water flux. Because pale colors reflect more light than do dark colors, desert organisms frequently adopt them to reduce radiational heat load. Biological surfaces may also actively transport materials either from inside out or from outside in. Many ions are moved into and out of cells in this way by membrane-bound molecular "pumps" that maintain suitable concentrations of physiologically important ions (for example, sodium or potassium). Such active transport requires the expenditure of energy.

Surface area can be manipulated in many ways. Organisms can reduce exchange areas by sealing off some portion of the surface, thus restricting flux to smaller regions that may be highly specialized. The exterior surface of a leaf is protected from water loss by a wax cuticle not unlike the surface of an insect. Gas exchange form the interior of the leaf takes place through stomates, tiny holes whose size can be controlled precisely in accordance with concentrations of water within the leaf. Surfaces can also be increased by elaborate folding, as in the external gills of salamander larvae or in the interior lungs of mammals.

The gradient between an organism and its surroundings depends, of course, on the internal and external environments. The internal environment is dictated in part by the ranges of body temperature, ion concentrations, and other conditions suitable for life processes. Moreover, the biochemical transformations often exaggerate gradients and thereby maintain high fluxes. For example, as our tissues consume oxygen, internal concentrations are reduced, enhancing the outside-inside gradient and encouraging oxygen flow across the lung surface. Conversely, metabolism produces carbon dioxide and, as its concentration builds up within tissues and the blood, its outward flux increases.

The gradient between internal and external environments may also change when organisms move through a heterogeneous environment. Shady and sunny spots present dramatically different radiative environments to an organism concerned with regulating its temperature. When humidity, ion strength, pH, soil nutrients, dissolved oxygen, prey abundance, disease organisms, and other factors vary over distances that are small compared to an individual's daily range of movement, choice of environment has a direct bearing on flux. The responses of plants and animals to many of these factors will be considered in the following chapters, but all may be understood in terms of the components of flux across the organism-environment boundary.

Finally, we must distinguish between passive (physical) and active (biological) flux. The first is the natural thermodynamic tendency of material or energy to move from areas of high concentration to areas of low concentration. Passive fluxes across a surface occur in direct proportion to the gradient or difference across the surface. Given time, and in the absence of other processes, passive flux continually reduces a gradient until flux drops to zero. Thus, in the absence of an energy input, a hot sphere gradually cools to the temperature of its surroundings.

Active flux allows biological systems to accumulate substance against a physical gradient as, earlier, we were accumulating sand into unstable piles of self. Active flux requires the expenditure of energy because it opposes the energy-releasing tendencies of physical fluxes. Therefore, in terms of the flux equation, active flux has a negative conductance.

ORGANISM-ENVIRONMENT FLUX

A bird's egg contains all the nutrients that the embryo needs to grow to hatching. The incubating parent generally maintains the egg's temperature within narrow limits, about 34 to 38°C. Its only exchanges with the outside world during the period of embryonic development are the influx of oxygen for metabolism and the effluxes of carbon dioxide, produced by respiration, and water. These exchanges are essential for growth, for if the egg surface were completely sealed, the embryo would suffocate. Exchange occurs through tiny pores that penetrate the eggshell and bring the surrounding atmosphere into contact with the respiratory membranes of the embryo. Gases pass freely through these pores by physical diffusion. But while the egg must gain oxygen from the environment and rid itself of carbon dioxide, loss of water by the same route is undesirable because it might lead to dehydration. The egg therefore is challenged to accomplish necessary gas exchange while limiting water loss to a tolerable level.

Gas exchange is a flux, determined by surface, gradient, and conductance according to the general relationship just outlined. In the early 1970s, O. Douglas Wangensteen et al. discovered that the movement of gas through the pores of an eggshell obeyed simple laws of physical diffusion. Hermann Rahn and C. V. Paganelli, in whose laboratory at the State University of New York at Buffalo much of this research was conducted, tell how the investigation got started:

The beginning of our interest in the gas exchange of avian eggs can be quite clearly documented. It occurred in 1968 after the arrival of O. Douglas Wangensteen as a Postdoctoral Fellow from the University of Minnesota. One day he asked us how eggs breathe. Since none of us had ever thought about this problem, we suggested that he might find out. Using shell fragments and an O_2 electrode he established that gas transport across the eggshell is essentially limited to gas phase diffusion and obeys Fick's law in contrast to gas exchange of man and other animals, where transport is dominated by convection.

Fick's law concerns the diffusion of a gas across a constant concentration gradient. Accordingly, the rate of diffusion (V) of gas across an eggshell, measured in cubic centimeters per second ($cm^3\ s^{-1}$), is the product of

1. pore area, A (cm^2)
2. the diffusion coefficient of the gas, D($cm^3\ cm^{-1}\ s^{-1}$)
3. the inverse of the length (L) of the pore (cm), that is, shell thickness

4. the difference in the concentration of gas (C) between the egg and the surrounding air (cm^3 cm^{-3})

Because gases occur in an aqueous phase inside the egg, the difference in vapor pressure, between the inside and outside of the egg can be substituted for the concentration difference (*C*) with an appropriate conversion factor. Therefore, gas exchange may be described by the equation $V = (A/L)\ DP$. Experimentally determined values of D(cm^3 cm^{-1} S^{-1}) in air at 38°C (the incubation temperature of chicken eggs) are 0.27 for water, 0.23 for oxygen, and 0.18 for carbon dioxide; the heavier gas molecules of CO_2 diffuse more slowly than the lighter molecules of O_2 and H_2O.

The idealized chicken egg has a pore area of 0.023 cm^2 and a shell thickness of 0.030 cm. The vapor pressure of water at 38°C is 50 torr. That is, the tendency of water to evaporate from a liquid surface at 38°C is exactly balanced by the tendency of water to move from the gas to the liquid phase when the pressure of water vapor at the surface is 50 torr, or about 7 per cent of the total pressure of the atmosphere at sea level (760 torr).

Table 1.5. Units of pressure

Pressure is a force (weight) per unit area. In the English system of measurement, the usual unit of pressure is the pound per square inch (lb in^{-2}). The pressure of the atmosphere at sea level—that is, the total weight of atmosphere above a square inch of surface—is 14.7 lbs in^{-2}. This value is often expressed in terms of the height of a column of mercury (Hg) having the same weight (29.9 in or 760 mm). A pressure of 1 mm Hg is sometimes referred to as 1 torr. In the International System of Units (see the endpapers), the unit of pressure is the pascal (Pa), which is the weight of 1 newton (N) per square meter.

Expressed in these various units, sea-level atmospheric pressure is equal to:

1	atmosphere of pressure (atm)
14.7	pounds per square inch (lbs in-2)
29.9	inches of mercury (in Hg)
760	millimeters of mercury (mm Hg)
760	torr
101,325	pascals (Pa)
0.101	megapascals (MPa)
1.01	bar (1 bar = 100,000 Pa)

Rahn et al. used a simple device, called an "egg hygrometer," to determine the vapor pressure in the immediate environment of the egg under the incubating parent. An egg hygrometer is constructed in the following manner. First, the conductance of water vapor across an eggshell is determined by placing the egg in a dessicator, an airtight container in which the water vapor pressure is kept close to zero by using silica gel to absorb water from the air. Under these conditions, the external water vapor pressure is zero and the internal pressure is a simple function of temperature. Therefore, the conductance per torr of a known vapor pressure gradient can be calculated from the weight loss of the egg, which can be measured simply by change in weight. Then the contents of the egg are removed through a small hole and replaced with silica gel, thereby reducing the vapor pressure of water *within* the egg hygrometer close to zero. The hole is sealed and the egg is replaced in a nest with the rest of the clutch. Under these circumstances, the weight of *water gained* by the egg indicates the vapor pressure of water in the nest environment. For example, suppose a chicken egg kept in a dessicator at 25°C (vapor pressure of water equal to 24 torr) loses 240 milligrams of water per day. This is equivalent to 10 mg d^{-1} $torr^{-1}$. If the same egg filled with silica gel and placed in a nest gained 200 mg d^{-1}, the vapor pressure of the nest would be 20 torr.

By placing calibrated egg hygrometers in the nests of many species of bird, Rahn and his co-workers determined that the vapor pressure of water in the nests of most species is maintained between 18 and 26 torr regardless of the temperature and water content of the surrounding air. This regulation is achieved by the parent's adjusting the water permeability of the nest and the parent's temporal pattern of sitting.

Because the pressure gradients of oxygen and carbon dioxide are controlled primarily by the metabolic activity of the embryo, they therefore change during the course of incubation. The pressure of oxygen in sea-level atmosphere is about 150 torn, and that of carbon dioxide is close to zero. In an unincubated chicken egg, the partial pressures of oxygen and carbon dioxide equilibrate with the air surrounding the egg. As the embryo approaches hatching, however, it metabolizes energy rapidly and partial pressures of gases within the egg decrease to 104 torr for oxygen and increase to 37 torn for carbon dioxide (Rahn et al. 1974). Note that as the requirement for oxygen increases, the pressure gradient also increases, enabling oxygen to enter the egg more rapidly. Conversely, as the embryo produces carbon dioxide more rapidly, the concentration of the gas within the egg increases, causing a rise in CO_2 flux from the egg. But gas conductances ultimately do place an upper limit on the embryo's rate of metabolism; above this limit, levels of carbon dioxide would become toxic for the embryo. Increasing the gas conductance of the shell to alleviate this problem would result in excessive water loss.

The different environments in which birds breed place different demands on gas exchange. At high altitude, atmospheric pressure is reduced; at 3800 meters, for example, it is 60 per cent of sea-level value. Atmospheric oxygen pressure drops from 150 torr at sea level to 90 torr at 3800 m; within the egg, the partial pressure of oxygen drops accordingly to far below the level in the egg at sea level. Wangensteen et al. found that chickens kept at 3800 m elevation adapt to the reduced oxygen concentration in the egg by reducing embryonic metabolism and prolonging the incubation period slightly. Although one might think that the problem of delivering oxygen to the embryo could be solved by increasing pore area, the limitation at high altitude is not the rate at which oxygen moves across the shell; rather, it is the low absolute level of oxygen. In fact, gas conductances increase with altitude because gas molecules move through thinner air and therefore experience fewer collisions. Because air pressure (hence density) at 3800 m is 60 per cent lower than at sea level, gas conductances are 60 per cent higher. To prevent excessive water loss at high altitude, bird eggs actually have reduced pore area.

Wedge-tailed shearwaters, seabirds that breed on remote oceanic islands, have reduced the pore area of their eggs to prevent excessive water loss resulting not from high altitude but from a greatly prolonged incubation period. Although the egg of the wedge-tailed shearwater is about the same size as a chicken egg, its incubation, for some unknown reason, takes 52 days as compared with 21 days for the chicken. If the shearwater egg lost water at the same daily rate as the chicken egg, the embryo would die of dehydration before the end of the incubation period. Because water vapor pressures in the nests of the shearwater and the chicken are similar, the only solution to this problem of excessive water loss is to reduce the pore area, and hence the gas conductance, of the eggshell, and this the shearwater has done.

The water vapor conductance of the shearwater egg is 6.2 mg d^{-1} $tore^{-1}$ compared with 14.4 mg d^{-1} $torr^{-1}$ for the chicken egg. As Ar and Rahn have shown, total gas conductance in bird eggs is adjusted so that the amount of water lost per gram of egg over the entire incubation period is approximately the same for all species. For the 60-gram chicken egg with a water vapor conductance of 14.4 mg d^{-1} tore' over 21 days, this value is 5.0 mg g^{-1} $tore^{-1}$; for the 60-gram shearwater egg, it is 6.2 mg d^{-1} $torr^{-1}$ X 52 days/60 g = 5.4 mg g^{-1} $tore^{-1}$.

One problem creates another, however, as the reduced pore area also reduces the embryo's supply of oxygen. To solve this new problem, the shearwater embryo pips (that is, breaks a tiny hole through the eggshell) several days before it hatches and before its oxygen requirements reach their maximum. It then begins to breathe air directly.

One final example involving avian eggs will further illustrate the consistency and inevitability of the responses of organisms to their physical environments. Brush turkeys (*Alectura*) belong to a chickenlike group of Australian birds known as the megapodes. The brush turkey is unique among birds in that incubation takes place within mounds of vegetation built by the male. The eggs are warmed by the heat of the vegetation as it decomposes. This unusual style of incubation creates unusual problems, for within the nest mound, oxygen is scarce and both carbon dioxide and water vapor increase to high levels. Seymour and Rahn measured partial pressures of 48 torr for water vapor, 100 torr for oxygen, and 62 torr for carbon dioxide in brush turkey nests. Water loss is not a problem because the vapor pressures inside and outside the egg are similar. Oxygen is almost as scarce in the mound as it is at 3000 meters altitude. The most critical problem is that to get rid of carbon dioxide, the embryo must tolerate levels of carbon dioxide in the egg in excess of 62 torr. To increase the flux of carbon dioxide without increasing the concentration of the gas within the egg, brush turkeys have greatly increased the gas conductance of their eggs, to 2.6 times as much as that of an egg of similar size of a species that builds a more typical nest.

Dominate Adaptations

Compromise is a consistent theme in the relationship of organisms to their environments. As the avian egg illustrates, terrestrial organisms cannot reduce water loss without reducing access to oxygen or carbon dioxide in the atmosphere. The same thick coat of fur that promotes the conservation of body heat in cold surroundings prevents the dissipation of excess heat when the environment warms up. Modifications of the legs and feet of horses that enable them to run swiftly also produce a built-in stiffness that makes the limbs useless for scratching and swatting flies. Of course, horses have found ways around this problem. They have

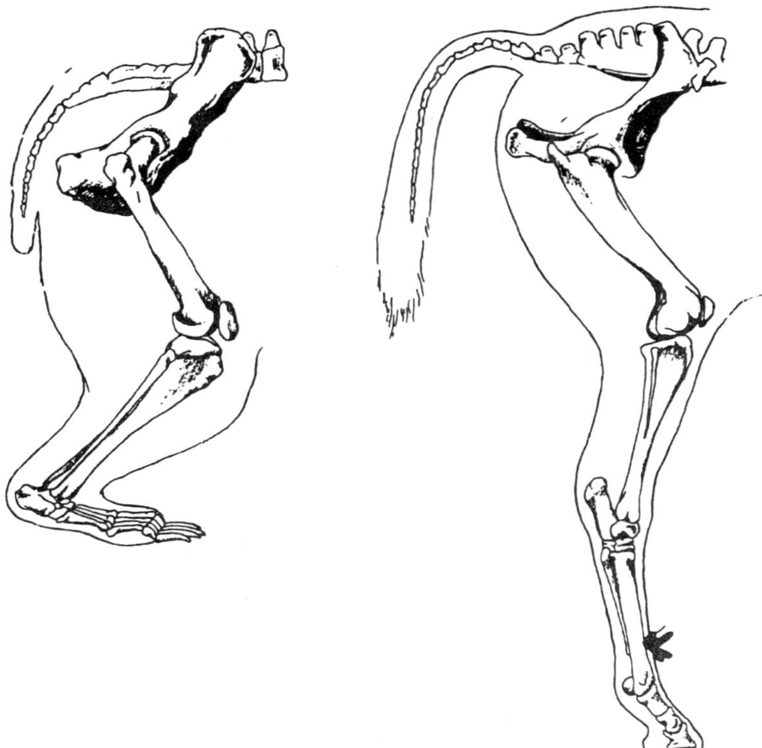

Fig. 1.6. Hind limbs of a bear (left) and a horse, showing the elongated and simplified structure of the horse's foot for rapid locomotion.

long tails to swish flies off their hindquarters, and as for scratching, horses love nothing so much as rolling in the dust.

Still, every adaptation has its costs. No organism has unlimited time, resources, or body tissues. What it allocates to one function, it must take from another. Nothing is free. In the absence of any benefit, even small costs become apparent. The eye, so important to humans, is useless to cavedwelling fish that live in total darkness; the cost of producing eyes and their associated muscles and nerves apparently is sufficiently great that many species of cave organisms have reduced them to tiny, rudimentary structures.

Although the examples in this chapter have concentrated on physical factors in the struggle for existence, organisms must also contend with biological aspects of their environment: predators, prey, pathogens, and even collaborators. These factors, too, impose certain requirements of structure and function for successful living, and they also create conflicts of allocation. Time taken to watch for predators is time taken from feeding. Carbohydrates that a plant devotes to spines as a defense against herbivores are carbohydrates that cannot be packaged in seeds. The bargain that each type of organism strikes among these conflicting needs is determined by the pressures it faces in its environment.

The activities of organisms transform energy and materials, linking the physical and biological worlds into ecosystems.

In the course of maintenance, growth, and reproduction, organisms transform materials and energy, often against the thermodynamic grain. By doing so, they to some extent transform the physical world. Also, many physical and chemical processes transform the environment independently of life; others undo what living forms have done. These transformations shape the physical world in which organisms live, particularly by determining the conditions for life and by influencing the availability of nutrients. The idea that life processes and physical processes are intimately related is the basis of the ecosystem concept in ecology, which encompasses both the biological and physical realms. Materials cycle through both organic and inorganic forms, and their flux through these cycles is determined by biological and by physical transformations. Just as the egg and its developing embryo are only a small segment of the total life cycle of the bird, the exchanges of gases across the shell between the egg and its immediate surroundings are themselves only a small part of a vast machine-the ecosystem, occupying a thin, wet film on the surface of the earth.

2

Physical Contaminants

Small particulates, whether of natural or anthropogenic origin, can pollute air and water supplies. These particles poses a hazard to human health and to the environment in a variety of ways. We will explore the properties of particulate contaminants, the health threats they present, where they come from, and how they behave in the environment.

Particulate sources are divided into those arising from a single, well-defined emission source, which is called *point-source pollution*, and *nonpoint-source pollution*, which is generated from a wide area. Particulate emissions can have natural origins or be of human origin. Naturally occurring particulates may become a threat when mobilized by human activities, such as agriculture, logging, and construction, or they may arise from natural processes such as volcanoes or soil erosion. Human-made particulates include those created by industrial processes; combustion in power plants, wood stoves, fireplaces, and internal combustion engines, rubber particles from tire, wear; and other sources.

Particle Size

Particle behaviour is, to a large extent, determined by size. Many particle properties, as well as their environmental and health impacts, are related to their size. In general, smaller particles pose a greater health threat than do larger particles.

Nanoparticles

Nanotechnologies refers to "technology of the tiny," with dimensions in the range of nanometers (SI unit prefix for 10–9 or one-billionth, 0.000000001, of a meter). As an illustration of the scale of interest, a chain of 5 to 10 atoms is about 1 nm long, the helix of

DNA has a diameter of about 2 nm, and the average human hair is about 80000 nm in diameter.

Nanotechnology and nanoscience research represent a key aspect of the development of innovative materials and new productive sectors. Nanomaterials (nanoparticles, nanospheres, nanotubes, and nanostructured surfaces) are used in ceramic, textile, cosmetic, optic, and chemical industries. In addition, they are applied in biomedicine as nanobiomaterials, nanospheres for drug release, and nanotubes for gene therapy. Most nanoparticles that are currently used today are made form transition metals including silicon, carbon, and metal oxides.

Human exposure to nanoparticles can occur as environmental (e.g., elemental Pt^0 on larger Al_2O_3 carrier particles emitted from automotive catalytic converters, ultrafine TiO_2 in cosmetic ingredients such as sunscreen), occupational (e.g., large-scale preparation of nanoparticles), and biomedical (e.g., ultrafine TiO_2 for tumor tissue targeting and delivery of killing compounds for cancer cells by UV light). At the occupational level, there are four main groups of nanoparticles production processes; gas-phase, vapor deposition, colloidal, and attrition, all of which may potentially result in exposure by inhalation, dermal, or ingestion routes. All processes may give rise to exposure to agglomerated nanoparticles during recovery, powder handling, and production processing. In spite of the potential occupational and public exposure to nanomaterials that is dramatically increasing, information on the human health impact of nanoparticles is severely lacking.

Particles in Air or Aerosols

Particles suspended in air are called *aerosols*. These pose a threat to human health mainly through respiratory intake and deposition in nasal and bronchial airways. Smaller aerosols travel further into the respiratory system and generally cause more health problems than larger particles. For this reason the United States Environmental Protection Agency has divided airborne particulates into two size categories: PM_{10}, which refers to particles with diameters less than or equal to 10 μm (10,000 nm), and $PM_{2.5}$ which are particles less than or equal to 2.5 μm (2,500 nm) in diameter. For this classification, the diameter of aerosols is defined as the *aerodynamic diameter*:

$$d_{pa} = dps\ (\rho_p/\rho_w)^{1/2} \quad \ldots(1)$$

where

d_{pa} = aerodynamic particle diameter (μm)

d_{ps} = Stokes' diameter (μm)

ρ_p = particles density (g cm^{-3})

ρ_w = density of water (g cm^{-3})

Atmospheric particular concentration is expressed in micrograms of particles per cubic meter of air ($\mu g/m^3$). The U.S. EPA established a *National Ambient Air Quality Standard* (NAAQS) for PM_{10} of 150 $\mu g\ m^{-3}$ averaged over a 24-hour period, and 50 $\mu g\ m^{-3}$ averaged annually. More recently, separate standards for $PM_{2.5}$ of 65 $\mu g\ m^{-3}$ for 24 hours and 15 $\mu g\ m^{-3}$ annually have been introduced.

Symptoms of particulate matter inhalation include decreased pulmonary function, chronic coughs, bronchitis, and asthmatic attacks. The specific causal mechanisms are poorly understood. One well-documented episode occurred in London in 1952, when levels of smoke and sulfur dioxide aerosols, largely associated with coal combustion, reached elevated levels due to local weather conditions. Over a 10-day period, approximately 4,000 deaths were attributable to cardiovascular and lung disorders brought on or aggravated by these aerosols. In addition to the sources, volcanoes and breaking waves also generate airborne particles, sometimes in very large quantities.

Airborne particles can travel great distance. Intense dust storms during 1998 and 2001 in the Gobi desert of Western China and Mongolia elevated aerosol levels to concentrations near the health standard in Wester North America several thousand miles away!

Smaller particles tend to travel greater distances than large particles. Stokes' Law is used to describe the fall of particles through a dispersion medium, such as air or water.

$$V = [D^2 \times (\rho_p - \rho_l) \times g]/18\eta \qquad ...(2)$$

where

V = velocity of fall (cm s^{-1})

g = acceleration of gravity (980 cm s^{-2})

D = diameter of particle (cm)

ρ_p = density of particle (Density of quartz particles is 2.65 g cm^{-3})

ρ_l = density of dispersion medium (air has a density of about 0.001213 g cm^{-3}; water has a density of about 1 g cm^{-3})

η = viscosity of the dispersion medium (about 1.83×10^{-4} poise or g cm^{-1} s^{-1} for air; 1.002×10^{-2} poise for water)

Using Stocke's Law, we can calculate the rate of fall in air. Small particles are thus a greater concern than larger particles for several reasons. Small particles stay suspended longer. Therefore, they travel greater distances. Risk of exposure to small particles is amplified by their extended suspension times. Small particles also tend to move further into the respiratory system, exacerbating their effects on health.

Aerosols of Concern

Asbestos

Asbestos particles are a special case of mineral aerosols that are known to lead to debilitation, disease, and death. They have been defined by the EPA as six naturally occurring minerals with well-defined compositions and their hazardous size mandated. When airborne, these exceedingly small particles can be identified using standard mineralogic analyses employing x-ray diffraction and optical and electron microscopy in transmission, diffraction, and scanning modes. The mineral classified asbestos, and many other silicate mineral species (e.g., talc, erionite, and vermiculite), all may occur in fibrous form. The fibrous structure of these minerals permits the formation of sharp aerosols that can be embedded in the lungs. It is likely that no matter what the environment, at home or outdoors, people have been, and are, continually exposed to particulates and aggregated that are mixtures, and some will contain asbestos or other minerals.

Asbestosis is the disease that results when lungs generate scar tissue (fibrosis) as a result of high exposure. Lung scarring may continue post-asbestos exposure, and although affected portions of the lung can be rejected, the quality of life thereafter is abysmal. Lung cancer, although associated with asbestos mineral exposure, is more frequently directly associated with smoking. Many occupations, for example, construction workers or brake repair technicians, often include individuals who smoke, resulting in multiple opportunities for respiratory trauma and therefore multiplying the risks. Another deadly disease associated with asbestos particles in mesothelioma, a cancer of the pleura rather than of the lung tissues.

Though the public health issues related to asbestos have been aired, the specific mechanisms of fibrogenesis and carcinogenesis related to the exposures, especially at low doses (nonoccupational) are not fully elucidated, and remain under discussion and investigation. Asbestos in the built indoor environment is also a potential source of exposure. Asbestos removal from buildings is closely regulated to prevent exposure to construction workers. The recent terrorist attack on the World Trade Center that generated widespread dust throughout lower New York City is a recent instance where asbestos issues were raised.

Silica

One of the most common natural materials and a major component of beach sand, quartz (SiO_2), may become an offending material causing a particulate-based disease. Silicosis is due to exposure to crystalline silica, and is exclusively occupational, with the size and morphologic characteristics of the particle key to respiratory problems. Construction workers, especially those jack hammering or those blasting dirt off of building surfaces using a stream of silica, without nasal and mouth protection, are at great risk. Often biological as well as mineral materials become airborne in both cases.

There are several crystal forms of SiO_2, including diatoms, the source of diatomaceous earth. The use of these various silica materials is not monitored nor are those at risk necessarily aware of their exposure, but great efforts have been made by some industries and one can anticipate future actions, especially responding to OSHA regulations.

Silicosis is characterized by focal nodular lesions, which can be detected radiologically in the upper lung. This expression of silicosis is distinct form that of asbestosis, where fibrosis is usually diffuse and in the lower portions of the lung. Lung function may not be markedly affected initially although under continuing exposure, the nodules coalesce and fibrosis becomes massive and pervasive for large parts of the lung. The formally pliable lung tissues become occluded by scarring and the deposition of the fibrous protein, collagen, often calcify or harden, further compromising respiration and the transmission of the essential gases in these portions of the respiratory system.

Human-made aerosols

Particulate matter in the atmosphere can be from direct emission or pollution that enters the atmosphere as previously formed particles. These are called *primary particles*. Alternatively, *secondary particles* are formed in the atmosphere from precursor components, such as ammonia, volatile organics, or oxides of nitrogen (NO_x) and sulfur (SO_x). Primary particles may fall into the $PM_{2.5}$ or the PM_{10} size ranges (plumes), whereas secondary particles fall mainly into the $PM_{2.5}$ category.

Industrially generated primary particles arise largely from incomplete combustion processes and high-temperature metallurgical processes. Secondary particles, on the hand, are produced form gases emitted from industrial processing and various combustion processes (including automobiles, power plants, wood burning, and incinerators) that undergo gas-to-particle conversion and then growth and coagulation. In the atmosphere, sulfur oxides are oxidized to form sulfuric acid and fine sulfate particles. Gas condense to form ultra-fine aerosols (less than 0.01 μm), either from supersaturated vapor produced in high temperature combustion processes or through photochemical reactions. These particles grow in size through condensation and coagulation to form larger particles (0.1-2.5 μm). The principal sources of SO_x in the U.S. include coal power plants, petroleum refineries, paper mills, and smelters. In contrasts, NO_x is largely produced by industrial and automotive combustion processes.

Health threats form $PM_{2.5}$ and PM_{10} generated by human activities are much like those from naturally occurring particulates. Adverse health effects are most severe in senior citizens and those with pre-existing heart or lung problems. Recent studies estimate that with each 10 $\mu g\ m^{-3}$ increase in PM_{10} above a base level of 20 $\mu g\ m^{-3}$, daily respiratory mortality is estimated to increase by 3.4% cardiac mortality increases by 1.4%, hospitalizations increase by 0.8%, emergency room visits for respiratory illnesses increase by 1.0%, days of restricted activity due to respiratory symptoms increase by 9.5% and school absenteeism increases by 4.1%. Particles formed from incomplete combustion, such as those formed by wood-burning and diesel engines, contain organic substances that may have additional health effect. Diesel exhaust has been shown to increase lung tumors in rats and mice, long-term human exposure to diesel exhaust may be responsible for a 20-50% increase in the risk of lung cancer.

In addition to human health concerns, $PM_{2.5}$ associated with wood burning, automobile exhaust, and industrial activities is responsible for much of the atmospheric haze in the U.S. Aerosols (particularly $PM_{2.5}$) absorb and scatter light, producing haze and reducing visibility. When severe, this interferes with automobile and aviation navigation, posing safety threats. Atmospheric particulates can also be a nuisance by settling on an in cars and homes and other buildings.

Bioaerosols

Biological contaminants include whole entities such as bacterial and viral human pathogens. They also include airborne toxins, which can be parts or components of whole cells. IN either case, biological airborne contaminants are known as bioaerosols, which can be ingested or inhaled by humans.

Coccidioidomycosis (also known as *Valley Fever*) is one disease caused by inhalation of spores of the fungus *Coccidioides immitis*, which is the indigenous to hot, arid regions, including the Southwestern U.S. The fungus can travel from the respiratory tract to the skin, bones, and central nervous system and can result in systemic infection and death.

Endotoxin, also known as lipopolysaccharide, is ubiquitous throughout the environment and may be one of the most important allergens. Endotoxin is derived from the cell wall of gram-negative bacteria and is continually released during both active cell growth and cell decay. Hence, endotoxin is found wherever Gram-negative bacteria are found. In soils, bacteria concentrations routinely exceed 108 per gram, with a majority of bacteria being Gram negative. Soil particles containing sorbed microbes can be aerosolized and hence act as a source of endotoxin. Farming operations such as driving a tractor across a field has been shown to result in endotoxin levels of 469 *endotoxin units* (EU) m^{-3}. EU units are related to a turbidometric Limulus Amebocyte Assay. These values are comparable to those found during land application of biosolids operations. Daily exposures of as little as 10 EU m^{-3} from cotton dust can cause asthma and chronic bronchitis. However, dose response is dependent on the source of the material, the duration of exposure, and repeated exposures.

When inhaled by humans, endotoxin has demonstrated the ability to cause a wide variety of health effects including fever, asthma, and shock.

Data illustrate that endotoxin aerosolization can occur during both wastewater treatment and land application of biosolids. However, the data also show that endotoxin of soil origin resulting from dust generated during tractor operations results in similar amounts of aerosolized endotoxin. Given that the major source of PM_{10} in the U.S. are unpaved roads, and that these particulates are of soil-borne origin, it is possible that endotoxin associated with wind blow soil particles is a major contributor to respiratory problems.

Mycotoxins are secondary metabolites produced by fungal molds. Fungi such as species of *Aspergillus*, *Alternaria*, *Fusarium*, and *Penicillium* are common soil-borne fungi capable of producing mycotoxins. Most notably, aflatoxin is produced by *Aspergillus flavus*. Aflatoxin is one of the most potent carcinogens known and is linked to a variety of health problems.

3

Chemical Contaminants

It can be argued that all matter in one form or another can become a contaminants when found out of its usual environmental or at concentrations above normal. However, chemical contaminants become pollutants when accumulations are sufficient to adversely affect the environment, or to pose a risk to living organisms. Today, there are thousands of industrial chemicals that can be dangerous to humans and the environment. Fortunately, the vast majority of these chemicals are not produced in large enough quantities to be a human or environmental threat. However, there are more than 3000 natural and human-made chemicals that are toxic enough and are produced in sufficient quantities to be a potential environmental hazard. Thus, the production, storage, transport, and disposal of these chemicals are regulated by government agencies. There are numerous sources of chemical contaminants released to the environment, but these generally fall into a few general categories. This chapter will present an overview of the various types of chemical contaminants and their sources.

Types of Contaminants

There are three basic categories of chemical contaminants: organic, inorganic, and radioactive. In turn, there are several classes of contaminants within each of these categories. Major classes of contaminants are listed in Table 3.1.

Thousands of chemicals are released into the environment every day. Thus, when conducting site characterization studies, it is important to prioritize the suite of chemicals under investigation. For most sites this is done by focusing on so-called priority pollutants, those that are regulated by federal, state, or local governments. The primary such

Table 3.1. Examples of organic, inorganic and radioactive chemical contaminants.

Organic contaminants

Petroleum hydrocarbons (Fuels)—Benzene, toluene, xylene, polycyclic aromatics

Chlorinated solvents—Trichloroethene, tetrachloroethene, trichlorethane, carbon tetrachloride

Pesticides—DDT (dichloro-diphenyl-trichloro-ethane), 2,4,-D (2,4-Dichlorophenoxyacetic acid), atrazine.

Polychlorinated biphenyls (PCBs)—insulating fluids, plasticizers, pigments

Coal tar/creosote—Polycyclic aromatics

Pharmaceuticals/food additives/cosmetics—Drugs, surfactants, dyes

Gaseous compounds—Chlorofluorcarbons (CFCs), hydrochlorofluoro-carbons (HCFCs)

Inorganic contaminants

Inorganic "salts"—Sodium, calcium, nitrate, sulphate

Heavy/trace metals—Lead, zinc, cadmium, mercury arsenic

Radioactive contaminants

Solid elements—Uranium, strontium, cobalt, plutonium

Gaseous elements—Radon

list of priority pollutants is that governed by the National Primary Drinking Water Regulations, which provide legally enforceable standards that apply to all public water systems. These standards protect public health by limiting the levels of contaminants that are allowed to exist in drinking water.

The frequency of occurrence of the contaminants listed in Table 3.2 as well as other chemicals, differs greatly for each specific contaminated site. The contaminants that are most frequently encountered at U.S. Environmental Protection Agency (EPA) designated Superfund sites are presented in Table 3.3. It is quite likely that one or more of these contaminants will be present at most hazardous waste sites.

The U.S. EPA has developed special reporting rules for certain chemicals of concern under the Toxic Release Inventory program. These chemicals, listed in Table 3.4, are classified as *persistent*, *bioaccumulative*, and *toxic* (PBT) chemicals. These compounds pose increased risk to human health not only because they are toxic, but

Table 3.2. National primary drinking water standards

Inorganic chemicals	*MCL or TT (mg L^{-1})*	*Potential health effects from ingestion of water*
Anitmony	0.006	Increase in blood cholesterol; decrease in blood glucose
Arsenic	0.01	Skin damage; circulatory system problem; increased risk of cancer
Asbestos (fiber > 10 micrometers)	7 MFL	Increased risk of developing benign intestinal polyps
Barium	2	Increase in blood pressure
Beryllium	0.004	Intestinal lesions
Cadmium	0.005	Kidney damage
Chromium	0.1	Some people who use water containing chromium well in excess of the MCL over many years could experience allergic dermatitis.
Copper	TT[8]; action level = 13	Short-term exposure: Gastrointestinal distress. Long-term exposure: Liver of kidney damage. People with Wilson's Disease should consult their doctor if their water systems exceed the copper action lavel.
Cyanide (as free cyanide)	0.2	Nerve damage or thyroid problems
Fluoride	4	Bone disease (pain and tenderness of the bones); children may get mottled teeth.
Lead	TT[8]; action level = 0.015	Infants and chidren: Delays in physical or metal development. Adults: Kidney problems; high blood pressure.
Mercury (inorganic)	0.002	Kidney damage
Nitrate (measured as Nitrogen)	10	Methemoglobinemia or "blue baby syndrome" in infants under 6 months—life threatening without immediate

Continue..

		medical attention. Symptoms: Infant looks blue and has shortness of breath.
Nitrite (measured as Nitrogen)	1	"Blue baby syndrome" in infants under 6 months—life threatening without immediate medical attention. Symptoms: Infant looks blue and has shortness of breath.
Selenium	0.05	Hair or fingernail loss; numbness in fingers or toes; circulatory problems
Thallium	0.002	Hair loss; changes in blood; kidney, intestine, or liver problems
Organic chemicals		
Acrylamide	TT[9]	Nervous system or blood problems; increased risk of cancer
Alachlor	0.002	Eye, liver, kidney or spleen problems; anemia; increased risk of cancer
Atrazine	0.003	Cardiovascular system problems; reproductive difficulties
Benzene	0.005	Anemia; decrease in blood platelets; increased risk of cancer
Benzo(a)pyrene (PAHs)	0.0002	Reproductive difficulties; increased risk of cancer
Carbofuran	0.04	Problems with blood or nervous system; reproductive difficulties
Carbonatetrachloride	0.005	Liver problems; increased risk of cancer
Chlordane	0.002	Liver or nervous system problems; increased risk of cancer
Chlorobenzene	0.1	Liver or kidney problems
2,4-dichlorophenoxyacetic acid	0.07	Kidney, liver, or adrenal gland problems
Dalapon	0.2	Minor kidney changes

Continue..

1,2-Dibromo-3-chloropropane (DBCP)	0.0002	Reproductive difficulties; increased risk of cancer
o-Dichlorobenzene	0.6	Liver, kidney, or circulatory system problems
p-Dichlorobenzene	0.075	Anemia; liver, kidney or spleen damage; changes in blood
1,2-dichloroethane	0.005	Increased risk of cancer
1,1-Dichloroethylene	0.007	Liver problems
cis-1,2-Dichloroethylene	0.07	Liver problems
trans-1,2-Dichloroethylene	0.1	Liver problems
Dichloromethane	0.005	Liver problems; increased risk of cancer
1,2-Dichloropropane	0.005	Increased risk of cancer
Di (2-ethylhexyl)adipate	0.4	General toxic effects or reproductive difficulties
Di(2-thylhexyl)phthalate	0.006	Reproductive difficulties; liver problems; increased risk of cancer
Dinoseb	0.007	Reproductive difficulties
Dioxin (2,3,7,8-TCDD)	0	Reproductive difficulties; increased risk of cancer
Organic chemicals		
Diquat	0.02	Cataracts
Endothall	0.1	Stomach and intestinal problems
Endrin	0.002	Nervous system effects
Epichlorohydrin	TT[9]	Stomach problems; reproductive difficulties; increased risk of cancer
Ethylbenzene	0.7	Liver or kidney problems
Ethylene dibromide	0.00005	Stomach problems; reproductive difficulties; increased risk of cancer
Glyphosate	0.7	Kidney problems; reproductive difficulties
Heptachlor	0.0004	Liver damage; increased risk of cancer

Continue..

Heptachlor epoxide	0.0002	Liver damage; increased risk of cancer
Hexachlorobenzene	0.001	Liver or kidney problems; reproductive difficulties; increased risk of cancer
Hexachlorocyclopentadiene	0.05	Kidney or stomach problems
Lindane	0.002	Liver or kidney problems
Methoxychlor	0.04	Reproductive difficulties
Oxamyl (Vydate)	0.2	Slight nervous system effects
Polychlorimatedbiphenyls (PCBs)	0.0005	Skin changes; thymus gland problems; immune deficiencies; reproductive or nervous system difficulties; increased risk of cancer
Pentachlorophenol	0.001	Liver or kidney problems; increased risk of cancer
Picloram	0.5	Liver problems
Simazine	0.004	Problems with blood
Styrene	0.1	Liver, kidney, and circulatory problems
Tetrachloroethylene	0.005	Liver problems; increased risk of cancer
Toluene	1	Nervous system, kidney, or liver problems
Toxaphene	0.003	Kidney, liver, or thyroid problems; increased risk of cancer
2-(2,4,5-Trichlorophenoxy) propionic acid (silvex)	0.05	Liver problems
1,2,4-Trichlorobenzene	0.07	Changes in adrenal glands
1,1,1-Trichloroethane	0.2	Liver, nervous system, or circulatory problems
1,1,2-Trichloroethane	0.005	Liver, kidney, or immune system problems
Trichloroethylene	0.005	Liver problems; increased risk of cancer
Vinyl chloride	0.002	Increased risk of cancer
Xylenes (total)	10	Nervous system damage

also because they remain in the environment for long periods of time, are not readily destroyed and build up or accumulate in body tissue.

Table 3.3. Common pollutants found at superfund sites

Acetone	Lead
Aldrin/Dieldrin	Mercury
Arsenic	Methylene chloride
Barium	Naphthalene
Benzene	Nickel
2-Butanone	Pentachlorophenol
Cadmium	Polychlorinated biphenyls (PCBs)
Carbon tetrachloride	Polycyclic aromatic hydrocarbons (PAHs)
Chlordane	Tetrachloroethylene
Chloroform	Toluene
Chromium	Trichloroethylene
Cyanide	Vinyl chloride
DDT, DDE, DDD	Xylene
1,1-Dichloroethene	Zinc
1,2-Dichloroethane	

In a related development, an international treaty was recently enacted to control the future production of a class of chemicals termed *persistent organic pollutants* (POPs). The Stockholm Convention is a global treaty to protect human health and the environment from POPs, which are chemicals that remain intact for long periods, become widely distributed geographically, accumulate in the fatty tissue of living organisms, and are toxic. There are 12 chemicals currently on the POP list: aldrin, chlordane, DDT, dieldrin, dioxins, endrin, furans, heptachlor, hexachlorobenzene, mirex, polychlorinated biphenyls, and toxaphene. Many of these chemicals are pesticides, are pesticides, and inspection of Table 3.4 shows some of them are also listed in PBTs.

Agricultural Activities

Agricultural systems consist of highly controlled tracts of land that generally receive large inputs of chemical fertilizers and pesticides. The ultimate goal of these chemical additions is to generate optimum amounts of food and fiber. However, fertilizers are often applied in excess of the crop needs or are in chemical forms that make them very mobile in soil and water environments. For example nitrate pollution of groundwater is often caused by excessive nitrogen fertilizer applications that result in leaching below the root zone. Agricultural activities can cause land, water, and air pollution.

Table 3.4. Persistent, bioaccumulative, and toxic chemicals

Chemical categories	*Sources*
Dioxin and dioxin-like compounds	Chemicals manufacturing and processing by-products, waste combustion
Lead compounds	Mining, manufacturing, leaded fuels
Mercury compounds	Mining, manufacturing
Polycyclic aromatic compounds	Petroleum production, combustion, coal tar
Chemicals	*Sources*
Aldrin	Pesticide
Benzo(g,h,i)perylene	Petroleum refining, fuel combustion
Chlordane	Pesticide
Heptachlor	Pesticide
Hexachlorobenzene	Pesticide
Isodrin	Pesticide
Lead	See above
Mercury	See above
Methoxychlor	Pesticide
Octachlorostyrene	Chemical manufacturing by products, combustion
Pendimethalin	Pesticide
Pentachlorobenzene	Pesticide production, combustion
Polychlorinated biphenyl (PCBs)	Transformer fluids, lubricants, flame retardants, water-proofing agents
Tetrabromobisphenol A	Flame retardant
Toxaphene	Pesticide
Trifluralin	Pesticide

Fertilizes which are generally inorganic chemicals, are routinely applied at least once a year and include, in order of decreasing amounts, N, P, K and metals. The annual applications of these chemicals range from 50 to 200 kg ha^{-1}, as N, P, or K. Micronutrient (e.g., Fe, Zn, Cu, B, and Mo) fertilizer addition are also applied regularly to agricultural fields but with less frequency because of lower crop requirements. These chemicals are applied to agricultural lands at average rates of 0.5-2 kg ha^{-1}, in their respective elemental forms, every 2-5 five years. A third group of inorganic chemicals applied to agricultural land consists of soil amendments. These materials are applied to agricultural fields with some frequency for two reasons: (1) to decrease or increase soil pH, decrease soil salinity, and improve soil structure, and (2) to replenish macronutrients like Ca^{++}, Mg^{++}, K^{+}, and SO_4^{-}. To control macronutrient deficiencies, the application rates of these chemicals range from 50 to 500 kg ha^{-1}. To control soil pH and salinity, applications typically range from 2,000 to 10,000 kg ha^{-1}.

The inorganic chemicals act as a nutrient and as a pollutant, depending on the amounts applied, the location of application, and soil-plant-water dynamics. For example, the soil nitrogen cycle, which illustrates the transformations, sinks, and sources of this element. Plants and some soil minerals can act as sinks for the two major forms of N. Conversely, some plants, animals, the atmosphere, and humans (fertilizer additions) can contribute to excessive N (NO^{-}_3) concentrations that lead to groundwater pollution. Groundwater polluted with high levels of nitrate has been shown to cause methemoglobinemia (blue baby syndrome) in infants and some adults. Methemoglobinemia occurs when nitrate is converted to nitrite by the digestive system. Nitrite reacts with oxyhemoglobin (oxygen carrying blood protein), forming methemoglobin. Methemoglobin cannot carry oxygen resulting a decreased ability of the blood to carry oxygen resulting in a decreased ability of the blood to carry oxygen. Consequently, oxygen deprivation in body tissues can occur. Infants suffering from methemoglobinemia develop a able coloration of their mucous membranes and possible digestive and respiratory problems.

Most pesticides are organic compounds and are often applied in agricultural systems at least once a year, albeit in much smaller quantities than fertilizers. However, synthetic pesticides, designed to be very toxic to plants and pests, may have deleterious effects at very low concentrations. Most synthetic pesticides are broadly classified as insecticides, herbicides, and fungicides. While most pesticides are solids, they are usually dissolved in water or oil to facilitate their handling and application. Fumigants are gaseous pesticides typically used to control insects. Less common forms of inorganic pesticides are used to control roaches and rats. These chemicals, which have all too often been used in close proximity to humans, have, as their primary acting agent, toxic forms of arsenic (ASO_4^{3-}), boron (H_3BO_3), and S (SO_2).

The chemical structure of organic pesticides controls their waste solubility, mobility, environmental persistence, and toxicity. The first generation of organic pesticides had multiple chlorine groups inserted into their structures to give them a broad spectrum of biotoxic effects. However, the chlorine groups also made them very difficult to degrade, making them very persistent. The next step in pesticide development sought a compromise between persistence and toxicity, with chemical structures that are moderately soluble in water and with more targeted toxicity effects. The next generation of pesticides again sought to decrease the persistence of these chemicals in the environment by making them even more water soluble and continued to focus their toxic effects. This class of pesticides seldom bioaccumulate in humans or animals and have short life span (days) in the environment. However, when misused, these chemicals can be found in water sources. For example, today the members of the triazine family are the most commonly found pesticides in surface and groundwater resources. Conversely, chlorinated pesticides are seldom found in water but can still be found in soils and sediments.

Animals generate significant amount of residues that are benign to the environment in open environments with low concentrations of animals. However, in the last 100 years, large-scale animal production systems have created concentrated sources of animal-derived contaminants. Large-scale animal feeding operations include feedlots for beef, swine, and poultry production, dairies, and fish farms. Nitrate N, ammonium-N, and phosphate-P are the three most common contaminants derived from unregulated animal waste disposal practices. These three chemicals are usually found at concentrations ranging form 1,000 to 50,000 mg kg^{-1} (elemental form) in animal wastes. Nitrates are very mobile in the environment and can only be controlled by plant and microorganism uptake or by the process of denitrification. Large release of ammonium can have several detrimental effects in the environment. First the ammonium ion is unstable; it can volatilize in alkaline water or be oxidized to nitrate, increasing the pool of this anion. Second, the ammonium ion is very toxic to fish. Finally, the process of ammonium oxidation to nitrate (nitrification) release acidity into the environment.

Phosphates are much less mobile in the environment. However, small quantities (>1 mg L^{-1}) can be extremely deleterious to stagnant water bodies because phosphates can trigger excessive microbial growth that leads to eutrophication.

Industrial and Manufacturing Activities

There are numerous sources of industrial chemical contaminants, the result of controlled or uncontrolled waste disposal and releases into the environment. Industrial wastes may contain contaminants classified by the Federal government as hazardous and nonhazardous.

However, this classification primarily separates wastes containing high concentrations of pollutants versus wastes that contain low concentrations. For example, metal-plating industrial wastes contain high concentrations of toxic metals such as Cr, Ni, and Cd and are usually classified as hazardous. However, municipal wastes, classified as nonhazardous, also contain these metals and many others, but at much lower concentrations. Most industrial contaminants originate from a few general categories of industrial wastes. Industrial and manufacturing activities have produced many pollution problems for surface water and ground water resources.

MUNICIPAL WASTE

Municipal wastewater treatment plants produce wastes that contain many potential contaminants. Reclaimed wastewater is usually clean enough to be used for irrigation, but routinely contains higher (~ 1.5 times) concentrations of dissolved solids than the source water. Also, chlorine-disinfected reclaimed water can contain significant trace amounts of disinfection by-products such as trihalomethanes and haloacetic acids. In addition, an emerging issue for municipal wastewater treatment is pharmaceutical waste. There is growing concern that pharmaceuticals (including hormones from birth control pills and antibiotics) that are excreted in urine and disposed of in wastes may end up in water supply resources. Many of these compounds are not fully treated in current wastewater treatment systems. There is concern about the effects that these compounds may have on humans and wildlife.

The solid residues of wastewater treatment plants, called biosolids, typically contain common inorganic chemicals, and may also contain heavy metals, synthetic organic compounds found in household products, and microbial pathogens. Since biosolids usually contain macro- and micronutrients and organic carbon, they are routinely applied to agricultural lands as fertilizer and soil amendments. Regulations in many states allow for the annual application of up to 8 tons (dry weight) of biosolids on farmland, depending on the metal content of each biosolids source. Land disposal of biosolids completes the natural C and N cycle in the environment. However, repeated application of biosolids often increases the concentrations of metals P, and some salts in the soil environment. In addition, excessive, concentrated, or uneven plications of biosolids can result in surface and groundwater pollution.

Stormwater is a source of nonpoint-source pollution for both urban and rural communities. Stormwater runoff picks up pollutants as it flows over the ground surface. In urban areas, stormwater runoff will flow over a variety of impervious surfaces, including driveways, sidewalks, and streets, acquiring pollutants such as dirt, debris, and hazardous wastes such as insecticides, pesticides, paint, solvents, used motor oil, and other auto fluids. In agricultural areas, stormwater runoff may include dirt, debris, excess nutrients, pesticides, bacteria, and other pathogens. Stormwater will either flow into a sewer system or directly into a lake, stream, river, wetland, or coastal water. In some cities, stormwater runoff flows into a storm sewer system and the collected water is discharged untreated into water bodies. In many areas, stormwater and municipal wastewater enter the same sewer system. During large storm events, wastewater treatment facilities often receive more municipal and storm water than the facility can handle. When facilities are unable to handle incoming waste, untreated municipal wastewater and stormwater are discharged without treatment.

Septic systems are another respiratory for municipal waste. One-fourth of all homes in the United States use a septic system for household wastewater disposal, with more than 4 billion gallons of wastewater disposed below the ground surface daily. Septic systems utilize microbial communities to decompose and digest waste. Most bacteria recover quickly after small amounts of cleaning products have entered the system. However, excess chemical use can cause a septic system to tail. To prevent pollutants in household waste water from entering the groundwater, it is extremely important to maintain household septic systems and to make sure they are functioning properly. Typical household wastewater pollutants include nitrogen, phosphorous, and disease-causing bacteria and viruses. To ensure that a septic system is working properly, it should be inspected every three years and pumped every three to five years.

Municipal solid waste, more commonly known as trash or garbage, is another potential source of pollution. Municipal solid waste consists of items such as paper, food scraps, grass clippings, product packaging, bottles, clothes, and furniture. Many households also improperly discard hazardous household waste into their municipal waste receptacles. Hazardous household waste products can be dangerous to human health and the environment, and should be sent to a proper disposal facility. Examples of hazardous household waste include paint, cleaners, oils, pesticides, and batteries. Municipal solid waste is collected and disposed of by landfill or combustion/incineration. Burning municipal solid waste will reduce its volume by up to 90% and its weight by up to 75%. However, air emissions pose an environmental concern. Landfilling municipal solid waste also cause an environmental concern. Landfills produce carbon dioxide and methane, both of which are greenhouse gases. Many landfills capture methane to use as an energy source. Another source of landfill pollution is landfill leachate, which is formed when water percolates through the landfill, dissolving compounds along the way. Landfill leachate may contain heavy metals, ammonia, toxic organic compounds, and pathogens, and is of concern as a groundwater pollutant.

Service-related Activities

There are many service activities that produce waste materials that are potential sources of environmental pollution, especially for groundwater. The service industries that produce substantial amounts of waste include dry cleaners and laundry plants, automotive service and repair shops, and fuel stations. These facilities are subject to regulation under the Resource Conservation and Recovery Act (RCRA) if they generate waste that fall under RCRA's definition of a hazardous waste. Dry cleaning, a service industry involved in the cleaning of textiles, uses solvents in the cleaning process that are considered as hazardous waste. These solvents include tetrachlorethene, petroleum solvents, and 1,1,1-trichloroethane. Along with spent solvents, other waste produced are solvent containers, spent filter cartridges, residues from solvent distillation, and solvent-contaminated wastewater.

Underground storage tanks (USTs) are used to hold petroleum products and certain hazardous substances for several service-related activities. Until 1984, many USTs were not equipped with spill, overfill, and corrosion protection. As a result, these USTs have leaked and polluted soil and groundwater. Vapors and odors form leaking underground storage tanks (LUSTs) can collect in basements, utility vaults, and parking garages. Collected vapors can cause explosions, fires, asphyxiation, or other adverse health effects. Petroleum-based fuels, such as gasoline, diesel fuel, and aviation fuels, are ubiquitous sources of contamination at automotive, train, and aviation fuel stations. The lower molecular weight, more soluble constituents, such as benzene and toluene, are of special concern with respect to groundwater contamination potential. In addition, some fuel additives may also be concern. For example, *methyl-tertiary-butyl ether* (MTBE) is a hydrocarbon derivative that has been added to gasoline for the past several years to boost the oxygen content of the fuel. This was done in accordance with federal regulations formulated to improve air quality. However, MTBE is a very soluble compound that is also resistant to

biodegradation. It is a very mobile and persistent compound, and this nature has lead to widespread groundwater contamination. Low levels of MTBE can make water supplies undrinkable due to its offensive taste and odor. The use of MTBE is gasoline is now being phases out as a result of this situation. Automotive service and repaid shops can be a source of numerous contaminants. Various types of solvents are use to decrease and clean engine parts. Metal contaminants can originate form batteries, circuit boards, and other vehicle components. Fuel-based contaminants are also typically present.

Resource Extraction/Production

Mineral extraction (mining) and petroleum and gas production are major resource-extraction activities that provide the raw materials to support our economic infrastructure. An enormous amount of pollution is generated from the extraction and use of natural resources. The Environmental Protection Agency's Toxic Release Inventory report lists mining as the single largest source of toxic waste of all industries in the United states. Mineral extraction sites, which include strip mines, quarries, and underground mines, contribute to surface and groundwater pollution, erosion, and sedimentation. The mining process involves the excavation of large amounts of waste rock in order to remove the desired mineral ore. The ore is then crushed into finely ground tailings for chemical processing and separation to extract the target minerals. After the minerals are processed, the waste rock and mine tailing are stored in large above ground piles and contaminant areas. These waste piles, along with the bedrock walls exposed from mining, pose a huge environmental problem because of the metal pollution associated primarily with acid mine drainage. Acid mine drainage is caused when water draining through surface mines, deep mines, and waste piles comes in contact with exposed rocks containing pyrite, an iron sulfide, causing a chemical reaction. The resulting water is high in sulfuric acid and contains elevated levels of dissolved iron. This acid runoff also dissolves heavy metals such as lead, copper, and mercury, resulting in surface and groundwater contamination. Wind erosion of mine tailings is also a significant problem.

Petroleum and natural gas extraction pose environmental threats such as leaks and spills that occur during drilling and extraction from wells, and air pollution as natural gas is burned off at oil wells. The petroleum and natural gas extraction process generates production wastes including drilling cuttings and muds, produced water, and drilling fluids. Drilling fluids, which contain many different components can be oil based, consisting of crude oil or other mixtures of organic substances like diesel oil and paraffin oils, or water based, consisting of freshwater or seawater mixed with bentonite and barite. Each component of a drilling fluid has a different chemical function. For example, barite is used to regulate hydrostatic pressure in drilling wells. As a result of being exposed to these drilling fluids, drilling cuttings and muds contain hundreds of different substances. This waste is usually stored in waste pits, and if the pits are unlined, the toxic chemicals in the spent waste cuttings and muds, such as hydrocarbon based lubricating fluids, can pollute soil, surface, and groundwater systems. *Produced water* is the wastewater created when water is injected into oil and gas reservoirs to force the oil to the surface, mixing with formation water (the layer of water naturally residing under the hydrocarbons). At the surface, produced water is treated to remove as much oil as possible before it is reinjected, and eventually when the oil field is depleted, the well fills with the produced water. Even after treatment, produced water can still contain oil, low-molecular-weight hydrocarbons, inorganic salts, and chemicals used to increase hydrocarbon extraction.

Mined and extracted resources can also be potential pollutants once they are used for production. For example, fossil fuels are key resources for energy production. Coal-burning power plants produce nitrogen and sulfur oxides, which are known to be the primary causes of acid rain. In addition, fossil fuel combustion produces carbon dioxide, which is a primary culprit in global warming.

Radioactive Contaminants

Radioactive waste primarily originates from nuclear fuel production and reprocessing, nuclear power generation, military weapons development, and biomedical and industrial activities. The largest quantities of radioactive waste, in terms of both radioactivity and volume, are generated by commercial nuclear power and military nuclear weapons production industries, and by activities that support these industries, such as uranium mining and processing. However, radioactive material can also originate from natural sources. Groundwater contamination by radioactive waste is a major problem at several Department of Energy facilities in the U.S.

Naturally occurring sources of radioactive materials, including soil, rocks, and minerals that contain radionuclides, can be considered and exposed by human industrial activities such as uranium mining, oil and gas production, and phosphate fertilizer production. For example, when uranium is mined using in-situ leeching or surface methods, bulk waste material is generated from excavated topsoil, uranium waste rock, and subgrade ores, all of which can contain radionuclides or radium, thorium, and uranium. Other extraction and processing practices that can generate and accumulate radioactive wastes similar to that of uranium mining are aluminum and copper mining, titanium or extraction, and petroleum production. According to EPA reports, the total amounts of naturally occurring radioactive waste that are enhanced by industrial practices number in excess of 1 billion tons annually. Sometimes, the levels of radiation are relatively low in comparison to the large volume of material that contains the radioactive wastes. This causes a problem because of the high cost of disposing of radioactive waste in comparison with the relative waste is separated. Additionally, relatively few landfills or other licensed disposal locations can accept radioactive waste.

Radioactive wastes are classified for disposal according to their physical and chemical properties, along with the source form which the wastes originated. The half-life of the radionuclide and the chemical form in which it exists are the most influential of the physical properties that determine waste management. The United States divides its radioactive waste into the following categories: high-level waste, transuranic waste, and low-level water. High-level waste consists of spent irradiated nuclear fuel from commercial reactors, and the liquid waste from solvent extraction cycles along with the solids that liquid wastes have been converted into from reprocessing. Transuranic wastes are alpha-emitting residues that contain elements with atomic numbers greater than 92, which is the atomic number of uranium. Wastes are considered transuranic when the elements have half-lives greater than 20 years and concentrations exceeding 100 nCi g^{-1}. Wastes in this category originate primarily form military manufacturing, with plutonium and americium being the principal elements of concern. Low-level waste encompasses the radioactive waste that is not classified under the above categories. Low-level wastes are separated into subcategories: Classes A, B, C, and Greater-Than-Class-C (GTCC), with Class A being the least hazardous and GTCC being the most hazardous. Commercial low-level waste is generated by industry, medical facilities, research institutions and universities, and a few government facilities.

In some commercial and military activities, radioactive wastes are mixed with hazardous waste, creating a complex environmental problem. Mixed waste is dually regulated by the EPA and the United States Nuclear Regulatory Commission, and waste handlers must comply with both the Atomic energy Act and the Rescurce Conservation and Recovery Act statutes and regulations once a waste is deemed a mixed waste. Military sources are regulated by the Department of Energy and comply with the Atomic Energy Act in regard to radiation safety.

Radon, a naturally occurring radioactive gas that is produced by the radioactive decay of uranium in rock, soil, and water, is of great concern because of the potential for the gas to become concentrated in buildings and homes. The higher the uranium levels in the rocks, the greater the chances that a home or building may have radon gas contamination. Once the parent material decays into radon, it dissolves into the water contained in the pore spaces between soil grains. A fraction of the radon in the pore water volatilizes into the soil atmosphere gas, rendering it more mobile via gas-phase diffusion.

Exposure of humans to radon occurs in several ways. Decay products of radon are electrically charged when formed, so they tend to attach themselves to atmospheric dust particles that are normally present in the air. This dust can be inhaled, and while the inert gases are mostly exhaled immediately, a fraction of the dust particles deposit on the lungs, building up with every breath. Radon dissolved in groundwater is another source of human exposure, mainly because radon gas is released into the home atmosphere form water as it exits the tap. Another source of human exposure ni home and building settings is the tendency for radon gas to enter structures via diffusion through their foundations and from certain construction materials. Radon gas availability in structures is mainly associated with the concentration of radon in the rock fractures and soil pores surrounding the structure and the permeability of the ground to gases. Slight pressure differentials between structure and soil foundations, which can be caused by barometric changes, winds, and temperature differentials, creates a gradient for radon gas to move from soil gas, through the foundations, and into the structural atmosphere.

Natural Sources of Contaminants

The contaminant sources presented above are associated with human activities involving the production, use and disposal of chemicals and products. It is important to realize that there are also natural sources of contaminants. A major source of such contaminants is drinking water pumped from aquifers composed of sediments and rocks containing naturally occurring elements that dissolve into the groundwater. One example, that of radioactive contaminants such as radon, was discussed in the previous section. Another major example is arsenic, which has become of great concern in recent years.

4

MICROBIAL CONTAMINANTS

London's Dr. John Snow (1813–58) was one of the first to make a connection between certain infectious diseases and drinking water contaminated with sewage. In his famous study of London's Broad Street pump, published in 1854, he noted that people afflicted with cholera were clustered in a single area around the broad Street pump, which he identified as the source of the infection. When, at his insistence, city officials removed the handle of the pump, Broad Street residents were forced to obtain their water elsewhere. Subsequently, the cholera epidemic in that area subsided. However successful the effect, Snow's explanation of the cause was not generally accepted because disease-causing germs had not been discovered at the time.

In the United States, the concept of *waterborne disease* was equally poorly understood. During the Civil War (1861–1865), encamped soldiers often disposed of their waste up river, but drew drinking water form downriver. This practice resulted in widespread dysentery. In fact, dysentery, together with its sister disease typhoid, was the leading cause of death among the soldiers of all armies until the 20th century. It was not until the end of the 19th century that this state of affairs began to change. By that time, the germ theory was generally accepted, and steps were taken to properly treat wastes and protect drinking water supplies.

In 1890, more than 30 people out of every 100,000 in the United States died of typhoid. But by the 1907 water filtration was becoming common in the most U.S. Cities, and in 1914 chlorination was introduced. Because of these new practice, the national typhoid death rate in the United States between 1900 and 1928 dropped from 36 to 5 cases per 100,000 people. The lower death toll was largely the result of a reduced number of outbreaks of waterborne diseases. In Cincinnati, for instance, the yearly typhoid rate of 379 per 100,000 people in the years 1905–1907 decreased to 60 per 100,000 people between 1908 and 1910 after the inception of sedimentation and filtration treatment. The introduction of chlorination after 1910 decreased this rate even further.

Poor water quality and sanitation account for 1.7 million deaths a year worldwide, mainly through infections and diarrhea. Nine out of 10 are children and virtually all are from developing countries.

Although many diseases have been eliminated or controlled in the developed countries, microorganisms continue to be the major cause of waterborne illness today. Most outbreaks of such diseases are attributable to the use of untreated water, inadequate or faulty treatment (i.e., no filtration or disinfection), or contamination after treatment. In addition, some pathogens, such as *Cryptoporidium*, are very resistant to removal by conventional drinking water treatment and disinfection. Moreover, an increasing proportion of waterborne disease outbreaks are associated with nonbacterial microorganisms such as enteric viruses and protozoan parasites, because of their successful resistance to water treatment process.

The true incidence of waterborne disease in the United States is not known because neither investigation nor reporting of waterborne disease outbreaks is required. Investigations are difficult because waterborne disease is not easily recognized in large communities and epidemiological studies are costly to conduct. Nevertheless, between 12 and 20 waterborne disease outbreaks per year are documented in the United States, and the true incidence may be 10 to 100 times greater.

Classes of Disease and Types of Pathogens

Disease-causing organisms, or pathogens, that are related to water can be classified into four groups.

Waterborne Diseases

Waterborne diseases are those transmitted through the ingestion of contaminated water that serves as the passive carrier of the infectious or chemical agent. The classic waterborne diseases, cholera and typhoid fever, which frequently ravaged densely populated areas throughout human history, have been effectively controlled by the protection of water sources and by the treatment of contaminated water supplies. In fact, the control of these classic diseases gave water supply treatment its reputation and played an important role in the reduction of infectious diseases. Other diseases caused by bacteria or by viruses, protozoa, and helminths may also be transmitted by contaminated drinking water. However, it is important to remember that waterborne diseases are transmitted through the fecal-oral route, form human to human or animal to human, so that drinking water is only one of several possible sources of infection.

Water-washed Diseases

Water-washed diseases are those closely related to poor hygiene and improper sanitation. In this case, the availability of a sufficient quantity of water is generally considered more important than the quality of the water. The lack of water for washing and bathing contributes to diseases that affect the eye and skin, including infectious conjunctivitis and trachoma, as well as to diarrheal illness, which are a major cause of infant mortality and morbidity in the developing countries. The diarrheal diseases may be directly transmitted through person-to-person contact or indirectly transmitted through contact with contaminated foods and utensils used by persons whose hands are fecally contaminated. When enough water is available for hand washing, the incidence of diarrheal diseases has been shown to decrease, as the prevalence of enteric pathogens such as *Shigella*.

Water-based Disease

Water-based disease are caused by pathogens that either spend all (or essential parts) of their lives in water or depend upon aquatic organisms for the completion of their life cycles. Examples of such organisms are the parasitic helminth *Schistosoma* and the bacterium *Legionella*, which cause schistosomiasis and Legionnaries' disease, respectively.

The three major schistosome species that develope to maturity in humans are *Schistosoma japonicum*, *S. haematobium*, and *S. mansoni*. Each has a unique snail host and a different geographic distribution. It is estimated that more than 200 million people in Asia, Africa, South America, and the Caribbean are currently infected with one, or perhaps two, of these schistosome species. Although schistosomiasis is not indigenous to North America, schistosomiasis dermatitis has been documented in the United States, immigrants to the United States have been found to be infected with schistosomiasis, and some 300,000 persons in Puerto Rico are probably infected. The economic effects of schistosomiasis have been estimated at $642 million annually—a figure that includes only the resource loss attributable to reduced productivity, not the cost of public health programs, medical care, or compensation of illness.

Legionella pneumophila, the cause of *Legionnaires' disease*, was first described in 1976 in Philadelphia, Pennsylvania. This bacterium is ubiquitous in aquatic environments. Capable of growth at temperatures above 40°C, it can proliferate in cooling towers, hot water heaters, and water fountains. If growth occurs at high temperatures, these bacteria become capable of causing pneumonia in humans if they are inhaled as droplets or in an aerosol.

Water-related Diseases

Water-related diseases, such as yellow fever, dengue, filariasis, malaria, onchocerciasis, and sleeping sickness, are transmitted by insects that breed in water (like the mosquitoes that carry malaria) or live near water (like the flies that transmit the filarial infection onchocerciasis). Such insects are known as *vectors*.

Types of Pathogenic Organisms

Pathogenic organisms identified as capable of causing illness when present in water include such microorganisms as viruses, bacteria, protozoan, parasites, and blue-green algae, as well as some macroorganisms—the helminths, or worms—which can grow to considerable size.

1. *Viruses* are organisms that usually consist solely of nucleic acid (which contains the genetic information) surrounded by a protective protein coat or *capsid*. The nucleic acid may be either ribonucleic acid (RNA) or deoxyribonucleic acid (DNA). They are always obligate parasites; as such, they cannot grow outside of the host organisms (i.e., bacteria, plants, or animals), but they do not need food for survival. Thus, they are potentially capable of surviving for long periods of time in the environment. Viruses that infect bacteria are called *bacteriophages* and those bacteriophages that infect intestinal, or coliform, bacteria are known as *coliphages*.
2. *Bacteria* are prokaryotic single-celled organisms surrounded by a membrane and cell wall. Bacteria that grow in the human intestinal or gastrointestinal (GI) tract are referred to as *enteric bacteria*. Enteric bacterial pathogens usually cannot survive for prolonged periods of time in the environment.
3. *Protozoa* are single-celled animals. Protozoan parasites that live in the GI tract are capable of producing environmentally resistant

cysts or oocysts. These oocysts have very thick walls, which make them very resistant to disinfection.

3. *Helminths* (literally "worms") are multicellular animals that parasitize humans. They include roundworms, hookworms, tapeworms, and flukes. These organisms usually have both an intermediate and a final host. Once these parasites enter their final human host, they lay eggs that are excreted in the feces of infected persons and spread by wastewater, soil, or food. These eggs are very resistant to environmental stresses and to disinfection.
4. *Blue green algae*, or *cyanobacteria*, are prokaryotic organisms that do not contain an organized nucleus—unlike the green algae. Cyanobacteria, which may occur as unicellular, colonial, or filamentous organisms, are responsible for algal blooms in lakes and other aquatic environments. Some species produce toxins that may kill domestic animals or cause illness in humans.

Viruses

More than 140 different types of viruses are known to infect the human intestinal tract, form which they are subsequently excreted in feces. Viruses that infect and multiply in the intestines are referred to as *enteric viruses*. Some enteric viruses are capable of replication in other organs such as the liver and the heart, as well as in the eye, skin, and nerve tissue. For example, hepatitis A virus infects the liver, causing hepatitis. Enteric viruses are generally very host specific; therefore, human enteric viruses cause disease only in humans and sometimes in other primates. During infection, large numbers of virus particles, up to 10^8–10^{12} per gram, may be excreted in feces, whence they are borne to sewer systems.

Enteroviruses, which were the first enteric viruses ever isolated form sewage and water, have been the most extensively studied viruses. The common enteroviruses include the polioviruses (3 types), coxsackieviruses (30 types), and the echoviruses (34 (types). Although these pathogens are capable of causing a wide range of serious illness, most infections are mild. Usually only 50% of the people infected actually develop clinical illness. However, coxsackieviruses can cause a number of life-threatening illnesses, including heart disease, meningitis, and paralysis; they may also play a role in insulin-dependent diabetes.

Infectious viral hepatitis is caused by *hepatitis A* virus (HAV) and *hepatitis E* virus (HEV). These types of viral hepatitis are spread by fecally contaminated water and food, whereas other types of viral hepatitis, such as hepatitis B virus (HBV), are spread by exposure to contaminated blood. Hepatitis A and E virus infections are very common in the developing world, where as much as 98% of the population may exhibit antibodies against HAV. HAV is not only associated with waterborne outbreaks, but is also commonly associated with foodborne outbreaks, especially shellfish. HEV has been associated with large waterborne outbreaks in Asia and Africa, but no outbreaks have been documented in developed countries. HAV is one of the enteric viruses that is very resistant to inactivation by heat.

Rotaviruses (5 types) have been identified as the major cause of infantile gastroenteritis, that is, acute gastroenteritis in children under 2 years of age. This condition is the leading cause of mortality in children and is responsible for millions of childhood death per year in Africa, Asia, and Latin America. These viruses are also responsible for outbreaks of gastroenteritis among adult populations, particularly among the elderly, and can cause "traveler's diarrhea" as well. Several waterborne outbreaks have been associated with rotaviruses.

The *norovirus*, first discovered in 1968 after an outbreak of gastroenteritis in Norwalk, Ohio, causes an illness characterized by vomiting and diarrhea that lasts a few days. This virus is the agent most commonly identified during water and foodborne outbreaks of viral gastroenteritis in the United States. It has not yet been grown in the laboratory. Norovirus is a genus in the calicivirus family.

The ingestion of just a few viruses is enough to cause infection. But because enteric viruses usually occur in relatively low numbers in the environment, large volumes of environmental samples must usually be collected before the presence of these viruses can be detected. For example, from 10 to 1,000 L of water must be collected in order to assay these pathogens in surface and drinking water. This volume must first be reduced in order to concentrate the viruses. The water sample is thus passed through microporous filters to which the viruses adsorb; then the adsorbed viruses are eluted from the filter. This process is followed by further concentration, down to a few milliliters of sample, leaving a highly concentrated virus population. Next, the concentrate is assayed by using either cell culture or molecular techniques. Cell cultures techniques involving animal cells are effective, but they may require several weeks for results; thus, bacteriophages may sometimes be used as timely and cost-effective surrogates. For example, coliphages are commonly used as models to study virus fate during water and wastewater treatment and in natural waters.

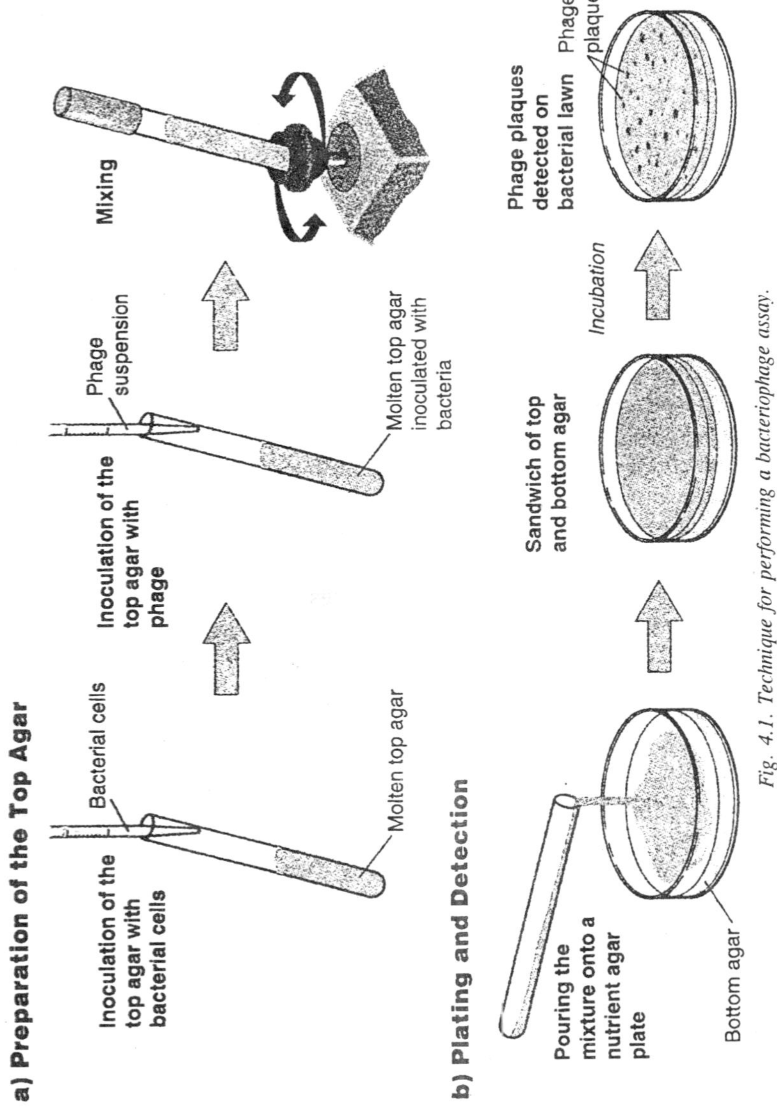

Fig. 4.1. Technique for performing a bacteriophage assay.

Bacteria

Enteric bacteria

The existence of some enteric bacterial pathogens has been known for more than a hundred years. At the beginning of the 20th century, modern conventional drinking water treatment involving filtration and disinfection was shown to be highly effective in the control of such enteric bacterial diseases as typhoid fever and cholera. Today, outbreaks of bacterial waterborne disease in the United States are relatively rare: they tend to occur only when the water is contaminated after treatment, or when nondisinfected drinking water is consumed. The major bacteria of concern are members of the genus *Salmonella*, *Shigella*, *Campylobacter*, *Yersinia*, *Escherichia*, and *Vibrio*.

Salmonella is a very large group of bacteria comprising more than 2,000 known serotypes. All these serotypes are pathogenic to humans and can cause a range of symptoms from mild gastroenteritis to severe illness or even death. *Salmonella* are capable of infecting a large variety of both cold-and warm-blooded animals. Typhoid fever, caused by *S. typhi*, is an enteric fever that occurs only in humans and primates. In the United States, salmonellosis is primarily due to foodborne transmission, because the bacteria infect beef and poultry and are capable of growing in foods. The pathogen produces a toxin that causes fever, nausea, and diarrhea, and may be fatal if not properly treated.

Shigella spp. infect only human beings, causing gastroenteritis and fever. They do not appear to survive long in the environment, but outbreaks from drinking and swimming in untreated water continue to occur in the United States. *Campylobacter* and *Yersinia* spp. occur in fecally contaminated water and food and are believed to originate primarily form animal feces. *Campylobacter*, which infects poultry is often implicated as a source of foodborne outbreaks; it is also associated with the consumption of untreated drinking water in the United States. *Escherichia coli* is found in the gastrointestinal tract of all warm-blooded animals and is usually considered harmless organisms. However, several strains are capable of causing gastroenteritis; these referred to as *enterotoxigenic* (ETEC), *enteropathogenic* (EPEC), or *enterohemorrhagic* (EHEC) strains of *E. coli*. Enterotoxigenic *E. coli* causes a gastroenteritis with profuse watery diarrhea accompanied by nausea, abdominal cramps, and vomiting. This bacterium is another common cause of traveler's diarrhea. EPEC strains are similar to ETEC isolate but contain toxins similar to those found in the shigellae. Enterohemorrhagic *E. coli* almost always belong to the single serological type 0157:H7. This strain generates a potent group of toxins that produce bloody diarrhea and damage the kidneys. It can be fatal in infants and the elderly. This organisms can contaminate both food and water. Cattle are a major source of this organism in the environment.

The genus *Vibrio* comprises a large number of species, but only a few of these species infect human beings. One such is *V. cholerae*, which causes cholera exclusively in humans. Cholera can result in profuse diarrhea with rapid loss of fluid and electrolytes. Fatalities exceed 60% for untreated cases, but death can be averted by replacement of fluids. Cholera outbreaks were unknown in the Western Hemisphere in this century until 1990, when an outbreak that began in Peru spread through South and Central America. The only cases that occur in the United States are either imported of result form consumption of improperly cooked crabs or shrimp harvested from Gulf of Mexico coastal waters. *Vibrio cholera* is a native marine microorganisms that occurs in low concentrations in warm coastal waters.

Usually, the survival rate of enteric bacterial pathogens in the environment is just a few days, which is less than the survival rates of enteric viruses and protozoan parasites. They are also easily inactivated by disinfectants commonly used in drinking water treatment. Analysis of environmental samples for enteric bacteria is not often performed because they are difficult to isolate. Instead, indicator bacteria are used to indicate their possible presence.

Legionella

The pathogen *Legionella pneumophila* was unknown until 1976, when 34 people died after an outbreak at the annual convention of the Pennsylvania Department of the American legion in Philadelphia. *Legionellosis*, the acute infection resulting from *L. pneumophila*, is currently associated with two different diseases: Pontiac fever and Legionnaires's disease. Since 1976, numerous deaths from Legionnaires' disease have been reported. Pontiac fever is a milder type of legionellosis. Both these diseases are *noncommunicable*, that is, not transmitted person-to-person. The Centers for Disease Control estimates that between 50,000 and 100,000 cases of legionellosis occur annually in the United States, an unknown number of which are due to contaminated drinking water.

Scientists, however, point out the error of referring to *L. pneumophila* as a classical contaminant. Although this organism occupies an ecological niche (just as do hundreds of other microorganisms in the water environment), no outbreak of legionellosis has yet been directly associated with a natural waterway such as a lake, stream, or pond. The only scientifically documented habitats for *Legionella pneumophila* are damp or moist environments. Evidently, it takes human activity—

and certain systems like cooling towers, plumbing components, or even dentist water lines—to harbor or grow the organisms. Therefore, while *L. pneumophila* may be common to natural water, they can proliferate only when taken into distribution systems where water is allowed to stagnate and temperatures are favorable.

Legionella pneumophila can grow to a level that can cause disease in areas that restrict water flow and cause buildup of organic matter. Moreover, the optimum temperature for the growth of *L. pneumophila* is 37°C. Thus, *L. pneumophila* has been discovered in the hot water tanks of hospitals, hotels, factories, and homes. Ironically, some hospitals and hotels keep their water-heater temperatures low to save money and to avert lawsuits from people burned by hot water, thereby rendering themselves vulnerable to *Legionella* growth. Once established, *Legionella* tends to be persistent. One survey of a hospital water system showed that *L. pneumophila* can exist for long periods under such conditions, collecting in shower heads and faucets in the system. It is believed that showerheads and faucets can emit aerosols composed of very small particles that harbor *L. pneumophila*. Such aerosols, owing simply to their smaller size, can reach the lower respiratory tract of humans.

A link between the presence of *L. pneumophila* in the water system and Legionnaires' disease in susceptible hospital patients has been established by the medical community. It is this abundance of susceptible people, together with the nature of the water system, that has resulted in outbreaks in hospitals. The great majority of people who have contracted Legionnaires' disease were immunosuppressed or compromised because of illness, old age, heavy alcohol consumption, or heavy smoking. Although some healthy people have come down the Legionnaries' disease, outbreaks that included healthy individuals have usually resulted in the milder Pontiac fever. But the fact that *L. pneumophila* exists in a water system does not necessarily mean disease is inevitable. *Legionella* bacteria have been detected in systems where no disease or only a few random cases were found. Therefore, the condition or susceptibility of the host or patient is considered to the single most important factor in whether the infection develops.

Legionella has the ability to survive conventional water treatment. It appears to be considerably more resistant to chlorination than coliform bacteria is, and can survive for extended periods in water with low chlorine levels. In addition, it can gain access to municipal water systems through broken or corroded piping, water-main work, and cross connections.

Opportunistic bacterial pathogens

Some bacteria common in water and soil are, at times, capable of causing illness. This are referred to as opportunistic pathogens. Segments of the population particularly susceptible to opportunistic pathogens are the newborn, the elderly, and the sick. This groups includes heterotrophic Gram-negative bacteria belonging to the following genera: *Pseudomonas*, *Aeromonas*, *Klebsiella*, *Flavobacterium*, *Enterobacter*, *Citrobacter*, *Serratia*, *Acinetobacter*, *Proteus*, and *Providencia*. These organisms have been reported in high numbers in hospital drinking water, where they may attach to water distribution pipes or grow in treated drinking water. However, their public health significance with regard to the population at large is not well understood. Other opportunistic pathogens are the nontubercular mycobacteria, which cause pulmonary and other diseases. The most frequently isolated nontubercular mycobacteria belong to the species *Mycobacterium avium intracellular*. Potable water, particularly that found in hospital water supplies, can support the growth of these bacteria, which may be linked to infections of hospital patients.

Indicator bacteria

The routine examination of water for the presence of intestinal pathogens is currently a tedious, difficult, and time-consuming task. Thus, scientists customarily tackle such examinations by looking first for certain indicator bacteria whose presence indicates the possibility that pathogenic bacteria may also be present. Developed at the turn of the 19th century, the indicator concept depends upon the fact that certain nonpathogenic bacteria occur in the feces of all warm-blooded animals. These bacteria can easily be isolated and quantified by simple bacteriological methods. Detecting these bacteria in water means that fecal contamination has occurred and suggests that enteric pathogens may also be present.

For example, *coliform bacteria*, which normally occur in the intestines of all warm-blooded animals, are excreted in great numbers in feces. In polluted water, coliform bacteria are found in densities roughly proportional to the degree of fecal pollution. Because coliform bacteria are generally hardier than disease-causing bacteria, their absence from water is an indication that the water is bacteriologically safe for human consumption. Conversely, the presence of the coliform group of bacteria is indicative that other kinds of microorganisms capable of causing disease also may be present, and that the water is unsafe to drink.

The coliform group, which includes *Escherichia*, *Citrobacter*, *Enterobacter*, ·and *Klebsiella* genus, is relatively easy to detect; specifically, this group includes all aerobic and facultatively anaerobic, Gram-negative, nonspore-forming, rod-shaped bacteria that produce gas upon lactose fermentation is prescribed culture media within 48 hours at 35°C. In short, they're hard to miss.

Scientists commonly use three methods to identify total coliforms in water. These are the *most probable number* (MPN), the *membrane filter* (MF), and the *presence-absence* (P-A) tests.

Most probable number (MPN) test

The MPN test allows scientists to detect the presence of coliforms in a sample and to estimate their numbers. This test consists of three steps: a presumptive test, a confirmation test, and a completed test. In the *presumptive test* lauryl sulfate tryptose lactose broth is added to a set of test tubes containing different dilutions of the water to be tested. Usually, three to five test tubes are prepared per dilution. These tests tubes are incubated at 35°C for 24 to 48 hours, then examined for the presence of coliforms, which is indicated by gas and acid production. Once the positive tubes have been identified and recorded, it is possible to estimate the total number of coliform in the original sample by using an MPN table that gives numbers of coliforms per 100 ML conformation.

In the *confirmation test*, the presence of coliforms is verified by inoculating such selective bacteriological agars as Levine's Eosin Methylene Blue (EMB) agar to Endo agar with a small amount of culture from the positive tubes. Lactose-fermenting bacteria re indicated on the media by the production of colonies with a green sheen or colonies with a dark center. In some cases, a *completed test* is performed in which colonies from the agar are inoculated back into lauryl sulfate tryptose lactose broth to demonstrate the production of acid and gas.

Membrane filter (MF) test

The membrane filter (MF) test also allows scientists to confirm the presence and estimate the number of coliforms in a sample, but it is easier to perform than the MPN test because it requires fewer test tubes and less handling. In this technique, a measured amount of water (usually 100 mL for drinking water) is passed through a membrane filter (pore size 0.45 μm) that traps bacteria on its surface. This membrane is then placed on a thin absorbent pad that has been saturated with a specific medium designed to permit growth and differentiation of the organisms are sought, a modified Endo medium is used. For

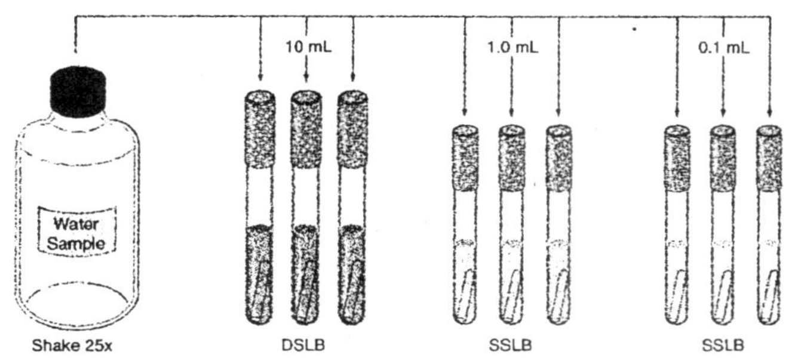

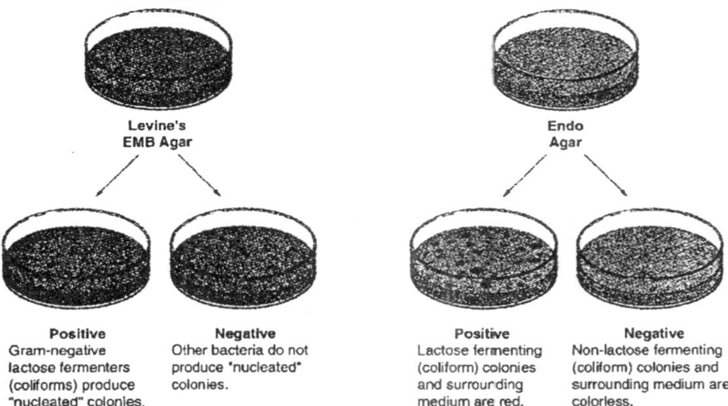

Fig. 4.2. Procedure for performing an MPN test for coliforms on water samples.

coliform bacteria, the filter is incubated at 35°C for 18 to 24 hours. The success of the method depends on using effective differential or selective media that can facilitate identification of the bacterial colonies growing on the membrane filter surface. To determine the number of coliform bacteria in a water sample, the colonies having a green sheen are enumerated.

Presence-absence (P-A) test

Presence-absence tests are not quantitative tests—rather they answer the simple question of whether the target organism is present in a

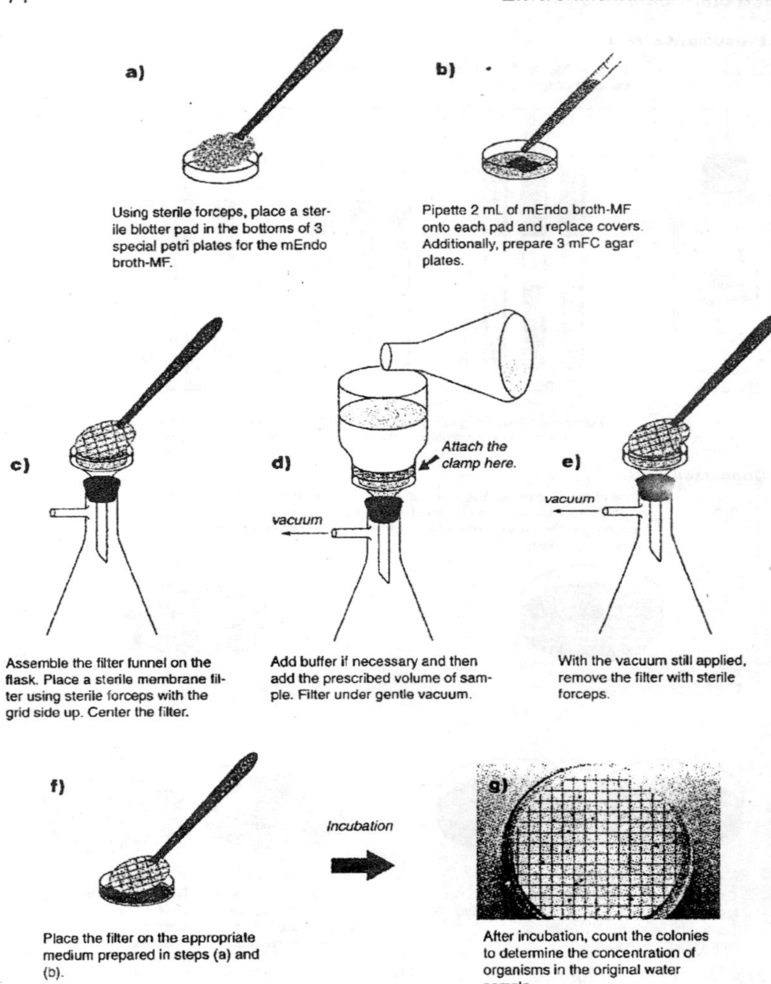

Fig. 4.3. The membrane filtration method for determining the coliform count in a water sample.

sample or not. The use of a single tube of lauryl sulfate tryptose lactose broth as used in the MPN test, but without dilutions, would be used as a P-A test. Enzymatic assays have been developed that allow for the detection of both total coliform bacteria and *E. coli* in water and wastewater at the same time. These assays can be a simple P-A test or an MPN assay. One commercial P-A test commonly used is the Colilert test, also called the ONPG-MUG (for *O*-nitrophenyl-β-Dgalactopyranoside 4-methylumbelliferyl-β-D-glucuronide) test. The test is performed by adding the sample to a single bottle (P-A·test) or MPN tubes that contain(s) powdered ingredients consisting of salts and specific enzyme substrates that serve as the only carbon source for the organisms. The enzyme substrate used for detecting total coliform is ONPG and that used for detecting of *E. coli* is MUG. After 24 hours of incubation, samples positive for total coliforms turn yellow, whereas *E. coli*-positive samples fluoresce under long-wave UV illumination.

Although the total coliform group has served as the main indicator of water pollution for many years, many of the organisms in this group are not limited to fecal sources. Thus methods have been developed to restrict the enumeration to those coliforms that are more clearly of fecal origin—that is, the *fecal coliforms*. These organisms, which include the genera *Escherichia* and *Klebsiella*, are differentiated in the laboratory by their ability to ferment lactose with the production of acid and gas at 44.5°C within 24 hours. In general, then, this test indicates fecal coliforms; it does not, however, distinguish between human and animal contamination.

Although coliform and fecal coliform bacteria have been successfully used to assess the sanitary quality of drinking water, they have not been shown to be useful indicators of the presence of enteric viruses and protozoa. While outbreaks of enteric bacterial waterborne disease are rare in the United States, outbreaks of waterborne disease have occurred in which coliform bacteria were not found. Enteric viral and protozoan pathogens are move resistant to inactivation by disinfectants than bacteria. Viruses are also more difficult to remove by filtration, due to their smaller size. For this reason, other potential indicators have been investigated. These include bacteriophages (i.e., bacterial viruses) of the coliform bacteria (known as coliphages), fecal streptococcus, enterococci, or *Clostridium perfringens*.

Fecal streptococci

The fecal streptococci are a group of Gram-positive Lance-field group D streptococci. The fecal streptococci belong to the genera *Enterococcus* and *Streptococcus*. The genus *Enterococcus* include all streptococci that share certain biochemical properties and have a wide range of tolerance of adverse growth conditions. They are differentiated from other streptococci by their ability to grow in 6.5% sodium chloride, pH 9.6, and 45°C and include *Ent. avium*, *Ent. faecium*, *Ent. durans*, *Ent. faecalis*, and *Ent. gallinarum*. In the water industry the genus is often given as *Streptococcus* for this group. Of the genus *Streptococcus*, only *S. bovis* and *S. equinus* are considered to be true fecal streptococci. These two species of *Streptococcus* are predominately found in animals; *Ent. faecalis* and *Ent. faecium* are more specific to the human gut. Fecal streptococci are considered to have certain advantages over the coliform and fecal coliform bacteria as indicators.

1. They rarely multiply in water
2. They are more resistant to environmental stress and chlorination than coliforms.
3. They generally persist longer in the environment.

A relationship between the number of enterococci in water and gastroenteritis in water and gastroenteritis in bathers has been observe in several studies and has been used in standards for recreational waters.

Heterotrophic plate count

An assessment of the numbers of aerobic and facultatively anaerobic bacteria in water that derive their carbon and energy from organic compounds is conducted via the *heterotrophic plate count* (HPC). This group includes Gram-negative bacteria belonging to the following genera: *Pseudomonas*, *Aeromonas*, *Klebsiella*, *Flavobacterium*, *Enterobacter*, *Citrobacter*, *Serratia*, *Acinetobacter*, *Proteus*, *Alcaligenes*, *Enterobacteter*, and *Moraxella*. In drinking water, the number of HPC bacteria may vary from less than 1 to more than 10^4 colony forming units (CFU)/mL, and their numbers are influenced mainly by temperature, presence of residual chlorine, and the level of organic matter.

In reality, these counts themselves have no or little health significance. However, there has been concern because the HPC can grow to large numbers in bottled water and charcoal filters on household taps. In response to this concern, studies have been performed to evaluate the impact of HPC on illness. These studies have not demonstrated a conclusive impact on illness in persons who consume water with high HPC. Although the HPC is not a direct indicator of fecal contamination, it does indicate variation in water quality and potential for pathogen survival and regrowth. These bacteria may also interfere with coliform and fecal coliform detection when present in high numbers. It has been recommended that the HPC should not exceed 500 per mL in tap water.

Heterotrophic plate counts are normally done by the spread plate method using yeast extract agar incubated at 35°C for 48 hours. A low-nutrient medium, R_2A, has seen widespread use and is recommended for disinfectant-damaged bacteria. This medium is recommended for use with an incubation period of 5-7 days at 28°C. HPC numbers can vary greatly depending on the incubation temperature, growth medium, and length of incubation.

Bacteriophage

Because of their constant presence in sewage and polluted waters, the use of bacteriophage (or bacterial viruses) as appropriate indicators of fecal pollution has been proposed. The organisms have also been suggested as indicators of viral pollution. This is because the structure, morphology, and size, as well as behavior in the aquatic environment of many bacteriophage closely resemble those of enteric viruses. For these reasons, they have also been used extensively to evaluate virus resistance to disinfectants, to evaluate virus fate during water and wastewater treatment, and as surface and groundwater tracers. The use of bacteriophage as indicators of fecal pollution is based on the assumption that their presence in water samples denotes the presence of bacteria capable of supporting the replication of the phage. Two groups of phage in particular have been studied: the *somatic coliphage*, which infect *E. coli* host strains through cell wall receptors, and the *F-specific RNA coliphage*, which infect strains of *E. coli* and related bacteria through the F^+ or sex pili. A significant advantage of using coliphage is that they can be detected by simple and inexpensive techniques that yield results in 8–18 hours. Both a plating method (the agar overlay method) and the MPN method can be used to detect coliphage in volumes ranging from 1 to 100 ml. The F-specific coliphage (male-specific phage) have received the greatest amount of attention because they are similar in size and shape to many of the pathogenic human enteric viruses. Because F–specific phage are infrequently detected in human fecal matter and show no direct relationship to the fecal pollution level, they cannot be considered indicators of fecal pollution. However, their presence in high numbers in wastewaters and their relatively high resistance to chlorination contribute to their consideration as an index of wastewater contamination as potential indicator of enteric viruses.

Protozoa

Giardia

Anton van Leeuwenhoek (1632-1723), the inventor of the microscope, was the first person to identify the protozoan *Giardia* in 1681. However, *Giardia lamblia*, the specific microorganisms responsible for giardiasis, was unknown in the United States until 1965, when the first case of giardiasis was reported in Aspen, Colorado. Giardiasis is a particularly nasty disease whose acute symptoms include gas, flatulence, explosive watery foul diarrhea, vomiting, and weight loss. In most people these symptoms last from one to four weeks, but have been known to last as little as three or four days or as long as several months. The incubation period ranges from one to three weeks. *Giardia lamblia* occurs in the environment—usually water–as a cyst, which can survive in cold water for months and is fairly resistant to chlorine disinfection.

Humans become infected with *G. lamblia* by ingesting the environmentally resistant stage. Once ingested, it passes through the stomach and into the upper intestine. The increase in acidity via passage through the stomach stimulates the cyst to excyst, which releases two trophozoites into the upper intestine. The trophozoites attach to the epithelial cells of the small intestines. It is believed that the trophozoites use their sucking disks to adhere to epithelial cells. It can cause both acute and chronic diarrhea within 1–4 weeks of ingestion of cysts, resulting in foul-smelling, loose, and greasy stools.

Outbreaks of giardiasis have occurred throughout the United States, but commonly in mountainous areas in the New England, Rocky Mountain, and Pacific Northwestern states, where high-quality water is often expected. That is, most of these areas are mistakenly thought to be void of sewage or microbial contamination, and communities there tend to use smaller, less comprehensive treatment plants. The majority of these outbreaks are the result of consumption or contact with surface water that is either untreated or treated solely with chlorine. In fact, outbreaks in swimming pools used by small children have also been identified.

Researchers have identified three factors contributing to the greatest risk of *Giardia* infection: drinking untreated water; contact with contaminated surface water; and having children in a day-care center.

Giardia cysts may be constantly present at low concentrations, even in isolated and pristine watersheds. Moreover, wild animals have been implicated as the cause of giardiasis outbreaks. For example, beavers have been blamed as the source that originally transferred the disease to humans. Another study showed that although giardiasis outbreaks occur most often in surface water systems, *Giardia* cysts may also be present in groundwater supplies, such as springs.

Giardia outbreaks occur most often in the summer months, especially among visitors of recreational areas.

Cryptosporidium

Cryptosporidium, an enteric protozoan first described in 1907, has been recognized as a cause of waterborne enteric disease in humans since 1980. Within five years of its recognition as human pathogen, the first disease outbreak associated with *Cryptosporidium* was described in the United States. Since then, many outbreaks have been reported, and several studies have documented that *Cryptosporidium parvum* is widespread in U.S. surface waters. Moreover, this species is responsible for infection in both human beings and domesticated animals. For example, this species infects cattle, which, in turn, serve as a major source of the organism in surface waters.

The prevalence of *Cryptosporidium* infection is largely attributable to its life cycle. The organism produces an environmentally stable oocyst that is released into the environment in the feces of infected individuals. The spherical oocysts of *Cryptosporidium parvum* range in size from 3 to 6 μm in diameter. After ingestion, the oocysts undergoes excystation, releasing sporozoite, which then initiate the intracellular infection within the epithelial cells of the gastrointestinal tract. Once in the GI tract, *Cryptosporidium* in humans cause *cryptosporidiosis*, characterized by profuse watery diarrhea, which can result in fluid losses averaging 3 or more liters a day. Other symptoms of cryptosporidiosis may include abdominal pain, nausea, vomiting, and fever. These symptoms, which usually set in about three to six days after exposure, can be severe enough to cause death.

Studies have indicated that *Cryptosporidium* oocysts occur in 55 to 87% of the world's surface waters. Thus, *Cryptosporidium* oocysts are generally more common in surface water than are the cysts of *Giardia*. But like *Giardia* cysts, *Cryptosporidium* oocysts are very stable in the environment, especially at low temperatures, and may survive for many weeks. Levels are lowest in pristine waters and protected watersheds, where human activity is minimal and domestic animals are scarce.

Occurrence of *Cryptosporidium* outbreaks associated with conventionally treated drinking water suggests that the organism is unusually resistant to removal by this process. So far, the oocysts of *Cryptosporidium* have proved to be the most resistant of any known enteric pathogens to inactivation by common water disinfectants. Concentrations of chlorine commonly used in drinking water treatment (1-2 mg L^{-1}) are not enough to kill the organism. Water filtration is the primary technique used to protect water supplies from contamination by this organism. However, the oocysts are easily inactivated by ultraviolet light disinfection. Several large outbreaks of waterborne disease in the United States and Europe attest to the fact that conventional drinking water treatments involving filtration and disinfection may not be sufficient to prevent disease outbreaks when large concentrations of this organism occur in surface waters. For example, one U.S. outbreak in Carrollton, Georgia, involved illness in 13,000 people—fully one-fifth of the county's total population. In this case, oocysts were identified in the drinking water and in the stream from which the conventional drinking water plant drew its water. Another outbreak of *Cryptosporidium*, which occurred in Milwaukee, Wisconsin, was the largest outbreaks of waterborne disease ever documented in the United States. In other cases, *Cryptosporidium* infection has been transmitted by contact with, or swimming in, contaminated water.

As in the case with other enteric organisms, only low number of *Giardia* cysts and *Cryptosporidium* oocysts need to be ingested to cause infection. Thus, large volumes of water are sampled (from 100 to 1,000 L) for analysis. The organisms are entrapped on filters with a pore size smaller than the diameter of the cysts and oocysts. After extraction from the filter, they can be further concentrated and detected by observation with the use of a microscope. Antibodies tagged with a fluorescent compound are used to aid in the identification of the organisms.

Helminths

In addition to the unicellular protozoa, some multicellular animals—the helminths—are capable of parasitizing humans. These include the Nematoda (roundworms) and the Platyhelminthes, which are divided into two subgroups: the Cestoda, or tapeworms and the Trematoda, or flukes. In these parasitic helminths, the microscopic ova, or eggs, constitute the infectious stage. Excreted in the feces of infected persons and spread by wastewater, soil, or food, these ova are very resistant to environmental stresses and to disinfection.

Ascaris, a large intestinal roundworm, is a major cause of nematode infections in humans. This disease can be acquired through ingestion of just a few infective eggs. Since one female Ascaris can produce approximately 200,000 eggs per day and each infected person can excrete a large quantity of eggs, this nematode is very common. Worldwide estimates indicate that between 800 million and 1 billion people are infected, with most infections being in the tropics or subtropics. In the

United States, infections tend to occur in the Gulf Coast. The life cycle of this parasite includes a phase in which the larvae migrate through the lungs and cause pneumonitis (known as Loeffler's syndrome). Although the eggs are dense, and hence readily removed by sedimentation in wastewater treatment plants, they are quite resistant to the action of chlorine. Moreover, they can survive for long periods of time in sewage sludge after land application, unless they were previously removed by sludge treatment.

Although *Taenia saginata* (beef tapeworm) and *Taenia solium* (pig tapeworm) are now relatively rare in the United States, they can still be found in developing countries around the world. These parasites develop in an intermediate animal host, where they reach a larval stage called *cysticercus*. Then these larvae are passed, via meat products, to humans, who serve as final hosts. For instance, cattle that ingest the infective ova while grazing serve as intermediate hosts for *Taenia saginata*, while pigs are the intermediate hosts for *Taenia solium*. The cysticerci invade the muscle, eye, and brain tissue of the intermediate host and can cause severe enteric disturbances, such as abdominal pains and weight loss in their final hosts.

Blue-green Algae

Blue-green algae, or *cyanobacteria*, occur commonly in all natural waters, where they play an important role in the natural cycling of nutrients in the environment and the food chain. However, a few species of blue-green algae, such as *Microcystis*, *Aphanizomenon*, and Anabaena, produce toxins capable of causing illness in humans and animals. These toxins can cause gastroenteritis, neurological disorders, and possibly cancer. In this case, illness is caused by the ingestion of the toxin produced by the organisms, rather than ingestion of the organism itself, as is the case with helminths. Numerous cases of livestock, pet, and wildlife poisonings by the ingestion of water blooms of cyanobacteria have been reported, and evidence has been mounting that humans are also affected. Heavy blooms of cyanobacteria can occur in surface waters when sufficient nutrients are available, resulting in sewage contaminated water supplies.

Sources of Pathogens in the Environment

Waterborne enteric pathogens are excreted, often in large numbers, in the feces of infected animals and humans, whether or not the infected individual exhibits the symptoms of clinical illness. In some cases, infected individuals may excrete pathogens without ever developing symptoms; in other cases, infected individuals may excrete pathogens for many months—long after clinical signs of the illness have passed. Such *asymptomatic* infected individuals are known s carriers, and they may constitute a potential source of infection for the community. Owing to such sources, pathogens are almost always present in sewage of any community. However, the actual concentration of pathogens in community sewage depends on many factors: the incidence of enteric disease (i.e., the number of individuals with the disease in a population), the number of carriers in the community, the time of year, sanitary conditions, and per capital water consumption.

The peak incidence of many enteric infections is seasonal in temperate climates. Thus, the highest incidence of enterovirus infection is during the late summer and early fall, which rotavirus infections tend to peak in the early fall, while rotavirus infections tend to peak in the early winter, and *Cryptosporidium* infections peak in the early spring and fall. The reason for the seasonality of enteric infections is not completely understood, but several factors may play a role. It may be associated with the survival of different agents in the environment during the different seasons: *Giardia*, for example, can survive winter temperatures very well. Alternatively, excretion differences among animal reservoirs may be involved, as is the case with *Cryptosporidium*. It may well be that greater exposure to contaminated water, as in swimming, is the explanation for increased incidence in the summer months.

Certain populations and subpopulations are also more susceptible to infection. For example, enteric infection is more common in children, because they usually lack previous protective immunity. Thus, the incidence of enteric virus and protozoa infections in day-care centers, where young children are in close proximity, is usually much higher than that in the general community. A greater incidence of enteric infections is also evident in lower socioeconomic groups, particularly where lower standards of sanitary conditions prevail. Concentrations of enteric pathogens are much greater in sewage in the developing world than in the industrialized world. For example, the average concentration of enteric viruses in sewage in the United States has been estimated at 10^3 L^{-1}, while concentration as high as 10^5 L^{-1} have been observed in Africa and Asia.

Sludge

During municipal sewage treatment, *biosolids*—(or sludges)—are produced. Biosolids are a by-product of physical (primary treatment), biological (activated sludge), and physicochemical precipitation of suspended solids (by chemicals) treatment processes. Although treatment by anaerobic or aerobic digestion and/or dewatering reduces the numerical population of disease agents in these biosolids, significant numbers of the pathogen present in raw sewage often remain in biosolids. On a volume basis, the concentration of pathogens in biosolids can be fairly high because of settling (of the large organisms, especially helminths) and adsorption (especially viruses). Moreover, most microbial species found in raw sewage are concentrated in sludge during primary sedimentation. And although enteric viruses are too low in mass to settle alone, they are also concentrated in sludge because of their strong binding affinity to particulates.

The densities of pathogenic and indicator organisms in *primary sludge* represent typical, average values detected by various investigators. Note that the indicator organisms are normally present in fairly constant amounts. But bear in mind that different sludges may contain significantly greater or fewer number of any organisms, depending upon the kind of sewage from which the sludge was derived. Similarly, the quantities of pathogenic species are especially variable because these figures depend on which kind are present in a specific community at a particular time. Finally, note that concentrations determined in any study are dependent on assays for each microbial species; thus, these concentrations are only as accurate as the assays themselves, which may be compromised by such factors as inefficient recovery of pathogens from environmental samples.

Secondary sludge are produced following the biological treatment of wastewater. Microbial populations in sludges following these treatments depend on the initial concentrations in the wastewater, die-off or growth during treatments, and the association of these organisms with sludge. Some treatment processes, such as the activated sludge process, may limit or destroy certain enteric microbial species. Viral and bacterial pathogens, for example, are reduced in concentration by activated sludge treatment. Even so, the ranges of pathogen concentration in secondary sludges obtained form this and most other secondary treatments are usually not significantly different from those of primary sludges.

Solid Waste

Municipal solid waste may contain a variety of pathogens, a source of which is often disposable diapers—it has been found that as many as 10% of the fecally soiled disposable diapers entering landfills contain enteroviruses. Another primary source of pathogens is sewage biosolids, where co-disposal is practiced. Pathogens may also be present in domestic pet waste (e.g., cat litter) and food wastes. Municipal solid wastes from households have been found to average 7.7 × 10^8 coliforms and 4.7 × 10^8 fecal coliforms per gram. *Salmonella* have also been detected in domestic solid waste. In unlined landfills, such pathogen may be present in the leachate beneath landfills.

Fate and Transport of Pathogens in the Environment

There are many potential routes for the transmission of excreted enteric pathogens. The ability of an enteric pathogen to be transmitted by any of these routes depends largely on its resistance to environmental factors, which control its survival, and its capacity to be carried by water as it moves through the environment. Some routes can be considered "natural" routes for the transmission of waterborne disease, but others—such as the use of domestic wastewater for groundwater recharge, large-scale aquaculture projects, or land disposal of disposable diapers—are actually new routes created by modern human activities.

Human and animal excreta are sources of pathogens. Humans become infected by pathogens through consumption of contaminated foods, such as shellfish from contaminated waters or crops irrigated with wastewater; from contaminated waters or crops irrigated with wastewater; from drinking contaminated water; and through exposure to contaminated surface waters as may occur during bathing or at recreational sites. Furthermore, those individuals infected by the above processes become sources of infection through their excrement, thereby completing the cycle.

In general, viral and protozoan pathogens survive longer in the environment than enteric bacterial pathogens. How long pathogen survives in a particular environment depends on a number of complex factors. Of all the factors, temperature is probably the most important. Temperature is a well-defined factor with a consistently predictable effect on enteric pathogen survival in the environment. Usually, the lower the temperature, the longer the survival time. But freezing temperatures generally result in the death of enteric bacteria and protozoan parasites. Viruses, however, can remain infectious for months or years at freezing temperatures. Moisture—or lack thereof—can cause decreased survival of bacteria. The UV light form the sun is a major factor in the inactivation of indicator bacteria in surface waters; thus, die-off in marine waters can be predicted by amount of exposure to daylight. Viruses are much more resistant to inactivation by UV light.

Many laboratory studies have shown that the microflorae of natural waters and sewage are antagonistic to the survival of enteric pathogens. It has been shown, for example, that enteric pathogens survive longer in sterile water than in water from lakes, rivers, and oceans. Bacteria in natural waters can feed upon indicator bacteria. Suspended matter (clays, organic debris, and the like) and fresh or marine sediments has been shown to prolong their survival time.

Standards and Criteria for Indicators

Bacterial indicators such as coliforms have been used for the development of *water quality standards*. For example, the U.S. Environmental Protection Agency (U.S. EPA) has set a standard of no detectable coliforms per 100 ml of drinking water. A drinking water standard is legally enforceable in the United States. If these standards are violated by water suppliers, they are required to take corrective action or they may be fined by the state or federal government. Authority for setting drinking water standards was given to the U.S. EPA in 1974, when Congress passes the Safe Drinking Water Act. Similarly, authority for setting standards for domestic wastewater discharges is given under the Clean Water Act. In contrast, standards for recreational waters and wastewater use are determined by the individual states.

Criteria and guidelines are terms used to describe recommendations for acceptable levels of indicator microorganisms. They are not legally enforceable but serve as guidance indicating that a potential water quality problem exist. Ideally, all standards would indicate that an unacceptable public health threat exists or that some relationship exists between the amount of illness and the level of indicator organisms. Such information is difficult to acquire because of the involvement of costly epidemiological studies that are often difficult to interpret because of confounding factors. An area where epidemiology has been used to develop criteria is that of recreational swimming. Epidemiological studies in the United States have demonstrated a relationship between swimming-associated gastroenteritis and the densities of enterococci and fecal coliforms. No relationship was found for coliform bacteria. It was suggested that a standard geometric average of 35 enterococci per 100 ml be used for marine bathing waters. This would mean accepting a risk of 1.9% of the bathers developing gastroenteritis. Numerous other epidemiological studies of bathing-acquired illness have been conducted. These studies have shown slightly different relationship to illness and that other bacterial indicators were more predictive of illness rates. These differences probably arise because of the different sources of contamination (raw versus disinfected wastewaters), types of recreational water (marine versus fresh), types of illness (gastroenteritis, eye infections, and skin complaints), immune status of the population, length of observation, and so on. Various guidelines for acceptable numbers of indicator organisms have been in use, but there is no general agreement on standards.

The use of microbial standards also requires the development of standard methods and quality assurance or quality control plans for the laboratories that will do the monitoring. Knowledge of how to sample and how often to sample is also important. All of this information is usually defined in the regulations when a standard is set. For example, frequency of sampling may be determined by the size (number of customers) of the utility providing the water. Sampling must proceed in some random fashion so that the entire system is characterized. For drinking water, no detectable coliforms are allowed in the United States. However, in other countries some level of coliform bacteria is allowed. Because of the wide variability in numbers of indicators in water, some positive samples may be allowed or tolerance levels or averages may be allowed. Usually, *geometric averages* are used in standard setting because of the often skewed distribution of bacterial numbers. This prevents one or two high values from giving overestimates of high levels of contamination, which would appear to be the case with *arithmetic averages*.

Geometric averages are determined as follows

$$\log \overline{x} = \frac{\Sigma(\log x)}{N} \qquad \text{...(1)}$$

$$\overline{x} = \text{antilog} (\log \overline{x}) \qquad \text{...(2)}$$

where N is the number of samples $\overline{x}$ is and the geometric average, and x is the number of organisms per sample volume.

As can be seen, standard setting and the development of criteria is a difficult process and there is no ideal standard. A great deal of judgment by scientists, public health officials, and the regulating agency is required.

5

ATMOSPHERIC POLLUTION

In this chapter we discuss air, pollutants, including their sources and effects on human activity, as well as their transport to, and fate in, atmosphere. We also describe the role of air pollution in such major environmental issues as global warming and stratospheric ozone depletion.

An *air pollutant* is any gas or particulate that, at thigh enough concentration, may be harmful to life, the environment, and/or property. A pollutant may originate from natural an anthropogenic source, or both. Pollutants occur throughout much of the troposphere however, pollution close the earth's surface within the boundary layer is of most concern because of the relatively high concentrations resulting form sources at the surface.

Atmospheric pollutant concentrations depend mainly on the total mass of pollution emitted into the atmosphere, together with the atmospheric conditions that affect its fate and transport. Obviously, air pollution has many and varied sources, including cars, smokestacks, and other industrial inputs into the atmosphere as well as wind erosion of soil. Large emissions form both anthropogenic and natural sources over long periods enhance concentrations, as do the chemical and physical properties of these pollutants. For example, when nitrogen oxides and hydrocarbons in car exhaust are emitted into warm, sunlit air, they readily form ozone molecules (O_3). Similarly the solubility of a pollutant affects how efficiently it is removed by rainfall.

Atmospheric conditions have a major effect upon pollutants once these pollutants are emitted into (e.g., nitrogen oxides from car exhaust) or formed within (e.g., O_3) the atmosphere. Pollution dispersal is controlled by atmospheric motion, which is affected by wind, stability, and the vertical temperature· variation within the boundary layer. Stability, in turn, influences both air and the depth at which mixing of polluted air takes place.

Wind determines the horizontal movement of pollution in the atmosphere. Pollution emitted from a point source such as a smokestack, is generally dispersed downwind in the form of a *plume*. Wind speed establishes the rate at which the plume contents are transported. Strong winds flowing over rough land surfaces enhance mixing of air by producing shear stress (mechanical mixing) much like that created when an electric an circulates air in a room. Also, wind direction establishes the path followed by the pollution.

Once present in the atmospheric boundary layer, a pollutant may undergo a series of complex transformations leading to new pollutants, such as O_3. Also, the removal of pollutants from air by rain and snow, by gravity, or by surface deposition is influenced by boundary-layer conditions. These removal processes, in turn, are also affected by the type and roughness of the underlying ground surface.

Even when emissions are relatively constant, pollutant concentrations can quickly change, owing to variations in atmospheric conditions. When atmospheric conditions, are stable, relatively low emissions can cause a buildup of pollution to hazardous levels. This situation can occur during radiation inversion at night. In contrast, unstable conditions may effectively dilute pollution to relatively "safe" concentrations despite a fairly high rate of emissions.

Air pollution, which is of major public concern, is currently the object of extensive scientific research. Its effects on life, including human health, productivity, and property, are not yet fully understood, even though exposure to high levels of pollution is a daily experience for many people. The cost of such pollution, whether expressed in terms of direct biological consequences or in terms of economic impact, is enormous. Worldwide, urban air pollution affects nearly a billion people, exposing them to possible health hazards. In the United States, billions of dollars are spend annually to prevent, control, and clean up air pollution; other developed nations are incurring similar costs. The United Nations considers air pollution to be a major global problem.

Most commonly, air pollution poses a health risk that can and does harm life. It harms the human respiratory and pulmonary system. Emphysema, asthma, and other respiratory illnesses may result from or be aggravated by chronic exposure to certain pollutants, such as O_3

or particulates. Research conducted in Southern California indicates that breading polluted air slows lung development in children as much as having a parent who smokes tobacco. Teenagers who are chronically exposed to polluted air are five times as likely to have reduced lung function as are teens who breathe clean air. Children and adults with chronic exposure to elevated ozone levels are more likely to develop asthma than individuals in cleaner air. Breathing polluted air can also thicken human artery walls, which is an important risk factor for hearth failure and strokes. In 1991, researchers at the U.S. Environmental Protection Agency (EPA) concluded that about 60,000 U.S. residents die each year due to heart attacks and respiratory illness caused by breathing particulates (dust) at concentrations within the federal PM_{10}. air quality standard.

Air pollution also poses an ecological risk. Vegetation can also be harmed by uptake of pollutants through the leaf stomata or by deposition of pollutants on the idea of ozone, for example, may cause leaf lesions in susceptible plants. Chronic exposure to relatively low levels of pollution can harm plants by reducing their resistance to disease and insect predators. Crop yields can be lowered by air pollution. The presence of certain air pollutants, such as ozone (formed form nitrogen oxides and hydrocarbons), enhances the earth's natural greenhouse effect within the troposphere. This enhancement warms the earth and may change rainfall patterns, which could markedly alter the distribution of life on earth.

Air pollution can also damage property. It can erode the exterior surfaces of buildings, particularly those constructed of limestone materials that react with acids in precipitation. Further evidence of the deleterious effect of air pollution on property can be seen in damaged paint finishes on cars regularly parked downwind form one smelters.

Sources, Types, and Effects of Air Pollution

Air pollution is not a new problem. Lead in Swedish lake sediments indicates that air pollution produced form lead lining and silver production in ancient Greece and Rome affected air quality throughout Europe. Early written accounts, of air pollution refer mainly to smoke form burning wood and coal. For example, in the 13th century, King Edward I of England prohibited the use of sea coal, the burning of which produced large amounts of soot and sulfur dioxide (SO_2) in the atmosphere over London. The industrial Revolution increased pollution so markedly that air quality deteriorated significantly in Europe and North America. By the mid-19th century, many cities in the U.S. and

Europe were experiencing the consequences of air pollution. By the early 20th century, the term "smog" was coined to describe the adverse combination of smoke and fog in London. IN Los Angeles, photochemical smog alerts became common by the mid-1940s. The first major air pollution disaster in the United States occurred in 1948, when approximately 20 lives were lost as a result of industrial pollutants trapped in very stable air over Donora, Pennsylvania, in the Monogahela River Valley. During one week in December 1952, stagnant air and coal burning caused severe smog conditions in London that ultimately took the lives of nearly 12,000 people over a three-month period.

Virtually all metropolitan areas are affected by air pollution, especially those situated in valleys surrounded by mountains or along coastal mountain ranges. But even unpopulated areas far form cities may be affected by long-range transport of pollution, either form urban areas or from such rural sources as ore smelters or coal-burning power plants. For example, pollution from a coal-burning power plant in northern Arizona may be reducing visibility in Grand Canyon National Park, located 400 kilometers west of the plant.

Most of the air we breathe is elemental oxygen (O_2) and nitrogen (N_2). About 1% is composed of naturally occurring trace constituents such as carbon dioxide (CO_2) and water vapor. A small part of this 1% may, however, be air pollutants, including gases and *particulate matter* suspended as aerosols. Anthropogenic air pollution enters the atmosphere from both fixed and mobile sources. Fixed sources, include factories, electrical power plants, ore smelters, and farms, while mobile sources include all forms of transportation that burn fossil fuels. Mobile sources account for 56% of the Air pollutants emitted to the atmosphere in the United States. Fuel combustion from stationary sources accounts for nearly 15%, and industrial processes account for about 7% of emissions in the United States. Natural sources of air pollution include winds eroding dust from cultivated farm fields, smoke form forest fires, and volcanic ash that is emitted into the troposphere and stratosphere.

There are many types of air pollutants. Some gases, such as CO_2, although produced by burning fossil fuels, are generally not considered pollutants because they are essential to plant life. Many pollutants, such as dust particles, exist naturally in the atmosphere and become hazardous only when their concentrations exceed air-quality standards set by such regulatory agencies as the U.S. EPA. The EPA classifies air pollutants according to two broad categories primary and secondary air pollutants.

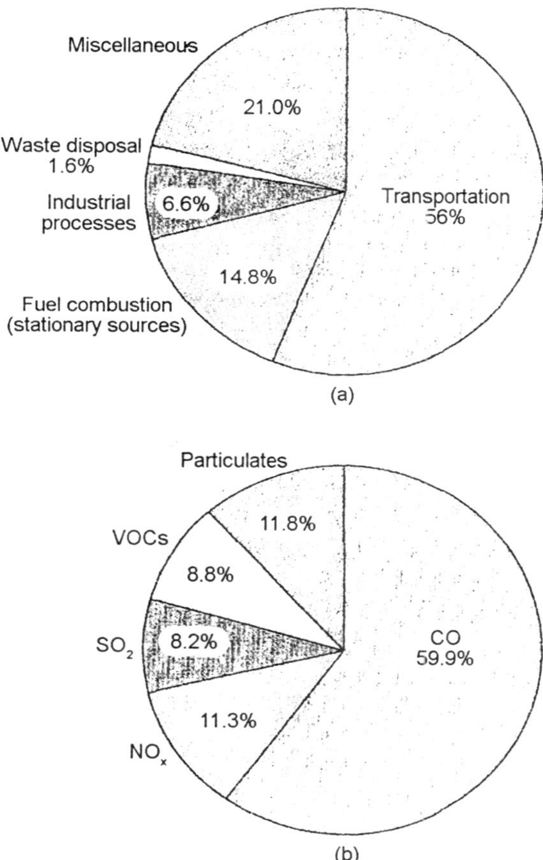

Fig. 5.1. (a) Source contributions of primary air pollutants and (b) the percentage of total primary air pollutants by type.

Primary Pollutants

Primary air pollutants enter the atmosphere directly from various sources. The EPA designates six types of primary air pollutants for regulatory purposes:

1. Carbon monoxide
2. Hydrocarbons
3. Particulate matter
4. Sulfur dioxide
5. Nitrogen oxides
6. Lead

Carbon monoxide

Carbon monoxide (CO_2) which is the major pollutant in urban air, is a product of incomplete combustion of fossil fuels. Carbon monoxide has relatively few natural sources. It is a part of cigarette smoke, but the internal combustion engine is the major source, with about 50% of all CO emission in the United States originating form cars and trucks. Emissions, therefore, are highest along heavily traveled highways and streets. Of the EP-designated primary pollutants in the United States, CO emissions currently contribute about 60% of the total emissions. Fortunately, CO concentrations are decreasing in the United States, because newer cars have higher fuel efficiencies.

Carbon monoxide is highly poisonous to most animals. The EPA standards currently limit human exposure to a 24-hour average of 9 nL L^{-1} or a 1-hour average of 35 nL L^{-1}. When inhaled, CO reduces the ability of blood hemoglobin to attach oxygen. Although relatively stable, it is short-lived in the atmosphere because it is quickly oxidized to CO_2 by reaction with hydroxide radicals. Some atmospheric CO may be removed by soil microbes. In order to increase the oxidation of CO to CO_2 during fuel combustion, some cities require the use of oxygenated gasoline containing ethanol or other additives during winter months.

Hydrocarbons

Hydrocarbons (HCs), or *volatile organic carbons* (VOCs), are compounds composed of hydrogen and carbon. *Methane* (CH_4) the most abundant hydrocarbon in the atmosphere, is an active greenhouse gas. Volatile organics include the *nonmethane hydrocarbons* (NMHCs), such as benzene, and their derivative, such as formaldehyde. Some of these compounds (e.g., benzene) are carcinogenic and some relatively reactive HCs contribute to ozone production in photochemical smog.

Hydrocarbons are produced naturally from decomposition of organic matter and by certain types of plants (e.g., pine trees, creosote bushes). In fact, HCs emitted from vegetation may be a major factor in smog formation in some cities, particularly those near forested areas of the south-eastern United States. A large proportion of HCs and NHMCs are generated by human activity. Some NHMCs, including formaldehyde, are readily emitted from indoor sources, such as newly manufactured carpeting. Hydrocarbons are also emitted into the atmosphere by fossil fuel combustion and by evaporation of gasoline during fueling of cars. To mitigate this latter source, some municipalities require that service-station gasoline pumps be fitted with a special trap to collect HC vapors emitted during fueling of vehicles. Because transportation is the primary source of HCs, concentrations tend to be highest near heavily traveled roadways.

Particulate matter

The category of particulate matter comprises solid particles or liquid droplets (aerosols) small enough to remain suspended in air. Such particles have no general chemical composition and may, in fact, be very complex. Examples include soot, smoke, dust, asbestos fibers, and pesticides, as well as some metals (including Hg, Fe, Cu, and Pb). We can characterize particulate matter by size. Particles whose diameters are 10 μm or larger generally settle out of the atmosphere in less than a day, whereas particles whose diameters are 1 μm or less can remain suspended in air for weeks. Smaller particulate matter, whose particles are 10 μm or less, have come to be known as PM_{10}. They very small particles with diameters 2.5 μm or less are known as $PM_{2.5}$.

The effects of particulates in the air are various. Some particulates, especially those containing sulfur compounds, are emitted by volcanoes. These particulates can reach the stratosphere, where they may significantly alter the radiation and thermal budgets of the atmosphere and thus produce cooler temperatures at the earth's surface. Tropospheric particulates may cause or exacerbate human respiratory illnesses. Especially harmful to the human respiratory system is the fraction of mid-sized particles, PM_{10} and $PM_{2.5}$. In large cities, particulates also reduce visibility. In the United States in 2002, about 62% of particulates came from roads and transportation, with another 26% contributed by agriculture, forestry, and fires. Construction is now considered to make a large contribution to PM_{10} levels, but percentages form the EPA aren't available yet.

Sulfur dioxide

About 90% of *sulfur dioxide* (SO_2) emissions come from burning sulfur-containing fossil fuels, such as coal, which may contain up to 6% sulfur. Ore smelters and oil refineries also emit significant amounts of SO_2. At relatively high concentrations, SO_2 causes severe respiratory problems. Sulfur dioxide is also a source of acid rain, which is produced when SO_2 combines with water droplets to form sulfuric acid (H_2SO_4). At sufficiently high concentrations, SO_2 exposure is harmful to susceptible plant tissue. Sulfur dioxide and other tropospheric aerosols containing sulfur are believed to affect the radiation balance of the atmosphere, which may cause cooling in certain regions.

Nitrogen oxides (NO_x)

Nitrogen oxides (NO_x stands for an indeterminate mixture of NO and NO_2) are formed mainly form N_2 and O_2 during high-temperature combustion of fuel in cars. Catalytic converters are used to reduce emissions. Nevertheless, NO causes a reddish-brown haze in city air that contribute to heart and lung problems and may be carcinogenic. Nitrogen oxides also contribute to acid rain because they combine with water to produce nitric acid (HNO_3) and other acids. Natural sources of nitrogen oxides include those produced during the metabolism of certain soil bacteria.

Lead

Lead is highly toxic, and its effects on humans have been recognized since the Roman Empire era. Lead can produce chronic impairment of the formation of blood and it affects infant neurological development. Concentrations of lead in the environment in the United State are no longer as high as they were prior to the introduction of nonleaded gasoline in the 1970s, but it is still a concern in many localities. Lead from human sources may be present in soil and it is often found in particulate matter in older urban environments. Lead based paints continue to be a source of concern in situations where children are exposed to paints that have peeled from building surface. Lead-based paint was banned in the U.S. in 1978. Homes built before 1978 may have lead-based paint that can be a health hazard when sanded, chipped, or removed.

Secondary Pollutants

Secondary air pollutants are formed during chemical reactions between primary air pollutants and other atmospheric constituents, such as water vapor. Generally, these reactions must occur in sunlight; thus, they ultimately produce *photochemical smog*. Photochemical smog is most common in the urban areas where solar radiation is very intense.

A simplified set of some of the reaction involved in photochemical smog formation is given below

$$N_2 + O_2 \rightarrow 2NO$$
$$2NO + O_2 \rightarrow 2NO_2$$
$$NO_2 + h\nu \rightarrow NO + O$$
$$O + O_2 \rightarrow O_3$$
$$NO + O_3 \rightarrow NO_2 + O_2$$
$$HC + NO + O_2 \rightarrow NO_2 + PAN$$

As indicated by the reaction above, photochemical smog is composed mainly of O_3, *peroxyacetyl nitrate* (PAN), and other oxidants. Ozone formation is closely tied to weather conditions. Favorable conditions for O_3 formation include:

(i) air temperatures exceeding 32°C

(ii) low winds

(iii) intense radiation

(iv) low precipitation

Unfortunately many major U.S. cities exceed the federal air quality standard for O_3 (an average O_3 concentration > 80 nl L^{-1} for 1 hour 1 day per year averaged over a 3-year period). As the reactions indicate, HCs are necessary for ozone buildup in the atmosphere. In the absence of HCs, solar UV breaks down the NO_2 into NO and O. Next, the O atom combines with O_2 from O_3, which then combines with the NO reform NO_2 and O_2. Ozone would not accumulate in the atmosphere if it was not for the fact that HCs disrupt the reaction cycle by reacting with NO and form PAN+ NO_2. Hydrocarbons from car emissions and other sources, therefore, play an important part in O_3 in the lower atmosphere results from human activities; natural sources include lighting and the diffusion of some O_3 downward from the stratosphere.

In most wester U.S. cities, photochemical smog is often referred to as *brown cloud* (O_3 + PAN + NO_x). Industrial eastern and mid-western U.S. cities also have photochemical smog, but they generally receive less intense sunlight than western cities; thus, smog in those cities is sometimes referred to as *gray air* because of particles (especially $PM_{2.5}$) and SO_2 emanating from burning fossil fuel.

Ozone may be either hazardous or beneficial, depending largely on where it is. For example, it is hazardous as an oxidant in smog (smog ozone), but in the O_3 layer, it is beneficial because it absorbs UV radiation. Smog ozone reduces the normal functioning of lungs because it inflames the cells that line the respiratory tract. Other health effects include increased incidence of asthma attacks, increased risk of infection and reduced heart and circulatory functions.

Smog O_3 can also damage plant life. In vegetation the main damage occurs in foliage, with smaller effects on growth and yield. In the United States, it has been implicated in the loss of conifer trees near Los Angeles and is suspected of doing similar damage to trees in the Appalachian Mountains. Some plant species are also very susceptible to PAN in smog, and this is known to affect plants in the Los Angeles area.

Ozone and NO_x pollution in the troposphere is not limited to urban areas. In the mid-1990s, the EPA reported that O_3, and NO_X concentrations were increasing in rural areas in the southeastern and midwestern United States. Most of this increase is probably attributable to upwind urban sources; however, in some rural areas, soil bacteria may be a greater NO_X source than is fossil fuel combustion. In fact, some estimates indicate that soil bacteria may emit as much as 40% of the total amount of NO_X emitted into the atmosphere. This percentage is very uncertain, since data on measurement of NO_X fluxes from soils are scanty. Soil NO_X fluxes may also be highly spatially and temporally variable.

Tropospheric NO_X strongly controls the concentrations of oxidants such as OH and O_3, which may affect the health of about one-quarter of the U.S. population. As in urban areas, O_3 in the rural atmosphere is controlled by reactions involving NO_X, HCs, OH, and other tropospheric species. The study of the production and destruction processes of O_3 in the rural troposphere is currently an area of active research by the EPA and other government agencies. Many questions remain unanswered concerning the reasons why O_3 concentrations continue to be high in both urban and rural areas despite recent efforts to curb emissions of the O_3 precursors NO_X and HCs.

Toxic and Hazardous Air Pollutants

In addition to primary and secondary pollutants, the EPA has identified 188 chemicals (or classes of chemicals) that are considered to be *hazardous air pollutants* (HAPs) or *urban air toxic* (UATs). Many of these are volatile organic chemicals, such as benzene found in gasoline and used as solvent, and trichlorethylene, which is used as a solvent/degreaser. Mercury is an example of a hazardous inorganic compound.

Pollutants with Radioactive Effects

Some air pollutants greatly influence the interactions between radiation of various wavelengths and the atmosphere. Some radioactively active pollutants contribute strongly to the natural greenhouse effect, while others impact the amount of ozone present within the atmosphere. This section described these pollutants and their radiative effects.

Greenhouse gases

Carbon dioxide is sometimes not considered to be an air pollutant because it is not hazardous to human health at ambient atmospheric concentrations; moreover, it is essential for carbon fixation by plants. It is, however, an important greenhouse gas and a major by product of fossil-fuel burning, which steadily increases the atmospheric concentration of carbon dioxide.

Carbon dioxide is by far the most abundant and important atmospheric trace gas contributing to the natural *green-house effect*. It is released to the atmosphere by various processes including deforestation and land clearing, fossil-fuel combustion, and respiration form living organisms. Carbon dioxide is readily absorbed by water, with warm water absorbing more than cold water, so it is removed from the atmosphere by the oceans and other bodies of water. Photosynthesis by land and water plants (phytoplankton) also removes significant amount of CO_2 from the atmosphere. Removal by plants is particularly apparent during the summer, when average CO_2 concentrations decrease. In addition, large amounts of CO_2 may eventually be fixed as limestone by deposition of the skeletons of some marine invertebrates. The atmosphere currently contains about 750 billion metric tons (BMT) of carbon in the form of CO_2, and 3-MT excess enters the atmosphere each year. Research indicates that this excess gives rise to a mean annual increase of about 1.5 μL L–1 in the global concentration of CO_2.

In addition of CO_2 the other main greenhouse gases are CH_4, N_2O, *chlorofluorocarbons* (CFCs), and O_3. Water vapors is also an important, but variable, greenhouse gas. All of these gases are, as the term "greenhouse: implies, efficient absorbers of long-wave radiation. This absorption helps maintain relatively warm climate on earth. However, because greenhouse gas concentrations continue to increase, it is conceivable that the earth's climate may be altered and become much warmer. Therefore, much scientific research is currently being directed toward improving our understanding of the atmospheric budgets of these trace gases and their role in the greenhouse effect.

Atmospheric CH_4 concentrations have also steadily increased at a rate of about 1% per year in recent decades. This rapid increase is commonly attributed to increased worldwide rice and livestock production. Increased mining of natural gas resources for energy production may also be an important factor.

Synthetic CFCs are also significant contributors to the greenhouse effect. Chlorofluorocarbons are used in refrigerators, air conditioners, foam insulation, and industrial processes. In addition to being very efficient long-wave absorbers, CFCs are also involved in depleting stratospheric O_3. Fortunately, because of concerted international effort resulting in the 1987 Montreal Protocol on Substances that Deplete the Ozone Layer, CFC emissions to the atmosphere have decreased substantially in recent years.

Nitrous Oxide (N_2O) is an especially good absorber of long-wave radiation; 1 molecule of N_2O is equivalent to about 200 CO_2 molecules in terms of its ability to absorb longwave radiation. Currently, atmospheric N_2O accounts for only about 5% of the greenhouse effect, but this percentage is expected to increase in coming years. A 25% N_2O increase in atmospheric concentrations may, according to numerical model predictions, increase global mean temperature by about 0.1 K. Worse N_2O has a very long atmospheric lifetime, estimated to be about 150 years, which is far longer than the atmospheric lifetime of any other nitrogen oxide. Thus, the current buildup of N_2O could affect the earth's climate well beyond the 21st century.

Stratospheric pollution

Stratospheric O_3 depletion is another global environmental concern related to pollution. Concern about O_3 first emerged in the early 1970s, when modeling studies indicated that a proposed fleet of supersonic transport (SST) aircraft could emit enough NO_x to damage the O_3 layer. The results from the modeling studies helped put an end to plants to build the fleet, but such considerations remain major factor in plans for aircraft development.

In the mid-1970, concern shifted to the possible O_3-depleting effects of manufactured CFCs used as refrigerants, propellants, cleaning compounds, and foam insulation. Intensive study of the effects of CVDs on stratospheric O_3 led to a 1979 U.S. ban on the use of CFC propellants in aerosol spray cans. Growing worldwide use of CFCs, together with evidence of CFC-induced decline of stratospheric O_3 concentrations over Antarctica, convinced 24 industrialized nations to sing the Montreal Protocol (1987 and 1990), which called for a complete phase out of the production of CFCs by the year 2000.

Stratospheric O_3 absorbs UV light, decreasing the amount of UV striking living organisms on the earth's surface. Satellite and ground-based measurements have shown that there is a temporary decrease in O_3 concentration (50 to 75% of total) over Antarctica each year. This has come to be known as the ozone hole, which is defined as the geographic area above the Antarctic where the total ozone is less than 220 Dobson units between 1 October and 30 November. In humans, increased UV would probably increase the incidence of skin cancer,

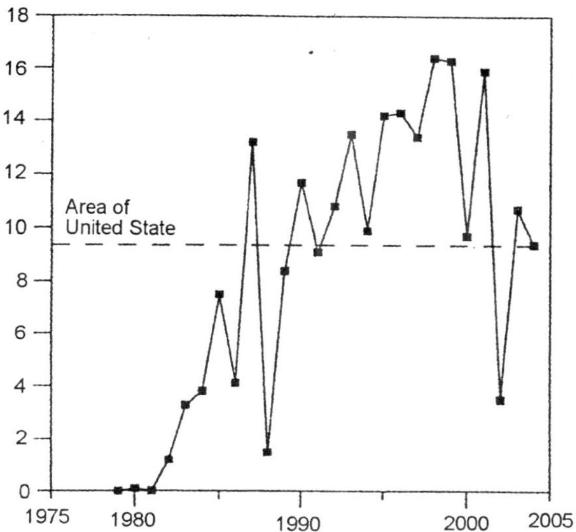

Fig. 5.2. Year-to-year variations in the average size of the Antarctic ozone hole between 1 October and 30 November.

including melanoma. Other organisms are also vulnerable to UV; phytoplankton, for example, has declined by 6-12% in areas near Antarctica. The decline in this one-organism is thought to be due to increased amounts of UV that are reaching surface waters.

The chemical pathways leading to the formation of Stratospheric O_3 start with the photodissociation of molecular oxygen (O_2) by solar UV radiation (photons of energy hv, where h is Planck's constant and v is the frequency). The UV photon splits O_2 into two oxygen atoms (O), each of which recombines with undissociated O_2 (in presence of another chemical species, M) to form two O_3 molecules. These two reactions, which result in a net formation of O_3 are given here:

$$O_2 + h\nu \rightarrow O + O$$
$$2O_2 + 2O + M \rightarrow 2O_3 + M$$
$$\text{Net Reaction:} \quad 3O_2 + h\nu \rightarrow 2O_3$$

The two O_3 molecules quickly convert back to molecular oxygen via

$$O_3 + h\nu \rightarrow O + O_2$$
$$O_3 + O \rightarrow 2O$$
$$\text{Net Reaction:} \quad 2O_3 + h\nu \rightarrow 3O_2$$

The process of production and loss of the O_3 molecules by photodissociation is very important because, overall, it helps prevent harmful UV from roaching the earth's surface. These production/destruction schemes indicate that the chemistry of stratospheric O_3 would be straight forward if there were no other reactive chemical species in the stratosphere. However, other chemicals, such as CFCs and NO_x, are present and play an important destructive role. This is indicated by the following general catalytic cycle:

$$X + O_3 \rightarrow XO + O_2$$
$$O_3 + h\nu \rightarrow O + O_2$$
$$XO + O \rightarrow X + O_2$$
$$\text{Net Reaction: } 2O_3 + h\nu \rightarrow 3O_2$$

where X and XO represent the compounds or free radicals that catalyze the destruction of O_3 molecules. Mainly NOx, water vapor, and CFCs, these are summarized in table 5.1

Table 5.1. Chemical species that are believed to catalyze the destruction of O_3 molecules in the atmosphere

Cycle	*X*	*XO*
NO_X	NO	NO_2
Water	HO•	HO_2•
CFD	Cl•	ClO•

Of these catalysts, CFCs are entirely anthropogenic, whereas nitrogen oxides come from both natural and synthetic sources. Stratospheric water vapor comes mainly form natural processes. In addition to the three main catalysts, other chemicals may play a role in controlling stratospheric O_3 levels. For example, recent evidence indicates that methyl bromide, which is used as a soil fumigant, may reach the stratosphere, where it can undergo a catalytic reaction sequence with O_3, similar to those of the three main chemical species.

The catalytic reactions do not destroy all the O_3 present in the stratosphere. The reason they don't is that reactions also occur between the catalysts, and these reactions result in chemicals that do not deplete O_3. Some of the chemicals eventually return to the earth's surface (e.g., HNO_3 in rain).

NO_x/O_3 destruction cycle

The nitrogen oxides in the stratosphere come mainly form photodissociation of nitrous oxide, which originates mostly form microbial processes at the earth's surface. Nitrous oxide is also a major greenhouse gas. It is produced mainly within moist soils by microbial denitrification of nitrate fertilizer, but it can also be biologically produced in oceans. Since the 1970s there has been concern that increased agricultural use of nitrogen fertilizers could increase the amount of nitrous oxide reaching the stratosphere, ultimately depleting O_3. Measurements of atmospheric N_2O indicate that its concentration is increasing by about 0.25% per year. A 25% increase in N_2O by the last 21st century could reduce total stratospheric O_3 by 3-4% which could increase the incidence of skin cancer by 2-10%.

Nitrous oxide is not known to be lost within the troposphere; however, it is converted to NO in the stratosphere mainly by the following reactions:

$$N_2O + h\nu \rightarrow N_2O\ (^1D)$$

$$N_2O + O \rightarrow 2NO$$

The two NO molecules formed initiate the O_3 destruction reactions described previously. Note that $O(^1D)$ in equation (given above) denotes atomic oxygen in an electronically excited state.

H_2O/O_3 destruction cycle

The stratosphere is generally very dry. However, enough water vapor is present to react with electronically excited atomic oxygen to produce the free radical HO• via

$$H_2O + O\ (^1D) \rightarrow 2HO\bullet$$

The catalytic water cycle has less influence upon O3 concentrations, than do other reaction cycles, but it can be significant when sufficient water vapor is present

CFC/O_3 destruction cycle

Chloroflurocarbons (e.g., $CFCl_3$ and CF_2Cl_2) are relatively stable in the troposphere, but once in the stratosphere, they are photodissociated by UV. This photodissociation produces the catalysts Cl and ClO, both of which deplete O_3. There is evidence that links the O_3 depletion in the Antarctic region to CFCs and other pollutants that carry chlorine and bromine into the stratosphere. Chlorine monoxide (ClO) has been identified as the chief cause of O_3 depletion in polar regions.

Chloroflurocarbons are also implicated in possible global warming. Because many are extremely efficient absorbers of longwave radiation, they contribute to the earth's greenhouse effect.

Weather and Pollutants

What happen to pollutants in the atmosphere? The answer depends on several factors. Pollutants are transported by wind and turbulence, and they may undergo chemical transformation before being deposited on the earth's surface. Thus, weather conditions strongly affect the fate of air pollutants.

Stability and Inversions

The stability of boundary-layer air largely determines how quickly pollutants are moved upward from their ground sources. Stability primarily a function of the vertical air temperature gradient relative to the adiabatic lapse rate. Strong instability associated with buoyancy causes efficient air mixing and pollution dispersal over a large mixing depth of the boundary layer (From 100 to 1,000 m). Good mixing often occurs on warm days when the ground is heated by sunlight. In contrast, pollution is poorly dispersed on days or nights when the atmosphere is stable. At those times, turbulent movement of pollution upward is slow or nearly nonexistent.

We know that temperature inversions influence atmospheric stability; thus, they play an important role in determining the concentrations of air pollutants. The effects of inversions are intensified by limited air drainage out of enclosed valleys, as is the case in Los Angeles and Mexico City. Various processes may generate inversions, including surface cooling caused by loss of infrared radiation or by evaporation, atmospheric subsidence, and topographic effects.

Ground-surface cooling is caused mainly by infrared radiation emission from the surface to the sky. It generally occurs during clear, calm nights, with inversion heights extending about 100 m above the ground. Such inversions commonly occur throughout the western united states during fall, winter, and spring, when the air is relatively dry and skies are clear. Such conditions readily permit cooling by longwave loss of energy from the ground. Tucson, Arizona, for example, often experiences radiation inversions in the cooler months, so that wintertime pollution problems are exacerbated in the area. Cooling of the ground by evaporation of water form soil and plants may also establish inversions. Evaporative cooling can occur during the day or night, particularly over irrigated fields. This type of inversion may be important in relation to certain agricultural activities, such as the aerial application of pesticides over large irrigated fields. The depth of an evaporatively cooled inversion layer is usually just a few meters.

Warming of the atmosphere by subsidence causes inversions over regions that have semi-permanent high pressure (anti-cyclonic flow), such as the southwester United States. As air subsides (sinks), it encounters higher pressure and thus is warmed. Within regions of high pressure, an inversion height may be several hundred meters above ground; thus, the air may be very stable over a large depth of the atmosphere. Because subsidence inversion may last from several days to weeks, the result is highly polluted conditions at ground level. For example, subsidence inversions are a major factor in reducing air quality in the Los Angeles basin.

Inversions associated with topography result from adiabatic warming of air as it flows downslope over mountainous terrain. These inversions may exacerbate air pollution problems in populated, mountainous areas, such as Denver, Colorado, or Salt Lake City, Utah.

Wing and Turbulence in Relation to Air Pollution

Wind affects turbulence near the ground, thus affecting the dispersion of pollutants released into other air. Turbulence (largely fine scale vertical and horizontal motion of air) is generated in part by air flow over rough ground. The greater the wind speed, the greater the turbulence, and hence the greater the dispersion of pollutants that are near the ground.

We can visualize the dispersion of pollutants in air by looking at the familiar cloud or "plume" of pollution emitted continuously by a smokestack. As the plume contents are carried away form the stack by the wind, the size of the plume increases owing to dispersion. Because of dispersion, the pollutant concentration within the plume decrease with increasing distance from the source.

Dispersion of pollution downwind from a smokestack is affected by the roughness of the ground surface. Because of friction between the atmosphere and the ground, wind speed is slowed markedly near the ground. If the surface is relatively rough, as it is when trees and buildings are present, the air flow tends to the turbulent and the increase of wind speed with increasing height is relatively small. Greater surface roughness increases turbulence, which helps disperse pollutants. Air flow over a smooth surface, such as a large mowed lawn, tends to be less turbulent and the decrease in wind speed near the ground is relatively small.

Several factors affect the plume, including the effective high (*H*) of emission, which is a measure of how high the pollutants are emitted into the atmosphere directly above the source. The height is dependent upon source characteristics and atmospheric conditions. Generally, a tall smokestack produces relatively low ground-level pollutant concentrations, because turbulence tends to dilute the pollution before reaching the ground. Driven by buoyancy, fast-moving pollutants are initially transported high up into the atmospheric boundary layer because they are warmer than the surrounding air. But as the pollutants cool and merge with the ambient air; the plume begins to move sideways with the wind. Then turbulence caused by the air flow over the surface and by possible instability governs the diffusion of the plume contents.

Usually, turbulence helps mix plume contents uniformly in such a way that the concentration follows a Gaussian distribution about the plume's central axis. Mathematically, pollutant concentration $\chi_{(x,y,zH)}$ (kg m^{-3}) at any point in the plume is described by

$$\chi_{(x,y,z,H)} = \frac{Q}{2\pi\sigma_y\sigma_z\bar{u}}$$

$$\cdot\exp\left(\frac{y^2}{2\sigma_y^2}\right)$$

$$\cdot\left[\exp\left(-\frac{(z-H)^2}{2\sigma_z^2}\right)+\exp\left(-\frac{(z+H)^2}{2\sigma_z^2}\right)\right]$$

where:

Q is the rate of emission of pollution from the source (kg s^{-1})

σ_y and σ_z are the horizontal and vertical standard deviations of the pollutant concentration distributions in the y and z direction

$\bar{u}$ is the mean horizontal wind speed within the plume (m s^{-1}).

This model, which is applicable to continuous sources of gases and particulates less than about 10 μm in diameter (larger particles quickly settle to the ground), can be used to model plume concentrations over horizontal distance of 10^2 to 10^4 m. With this Gaussian plume model, it is assumed that no deposition of plume contents to the ground surface takes place. In fact, it is assumed that plume contents are "reflected" from the ground back to the air. The value of σ in the equation are estimated form any one of several empirical formulas that relate σ to downwind distance (x) and stability condition. These formulas include the following equations, which were developed by the *Brookhaven National Laboratory* (BNL).

$$\sigma_y = ax^b \text{ and } \sigma_z = cx^d$$

where a, b, c, and d are parameters dependent upon stability. At ground level, $z = 0$, and along the plume centerline, $y = 0$. Thus, the concentrations can be calculated by

$$\chi_{(x,H)} = \frac{Q}{\pi\sigma_y\sigma_z\bar{u}}\exp\left(-\frac{H^2}{2\sigma_z^2}\right)$$

$$= \frac{Q}{\pi a x^b c x^d \bar{u}} \exp\left(-\frac{H^2}{2(cx^d)^2}\right)$$

One type of plume typically occurs under windy conditions with stability conditions at or near neutral. Within such a plume, mixing occurs mainly by frictionally generated turbulence and pollutant diffusion is nearly equal in all directions (i.e., the σ values are nearly equal and the plume spreads out in the familiar cone pattern, known as *coning*). Coning can occur day or night, and is often seen during cloudy and windy conditions. Depending upon effective source height and atmospheric conditions, the plume may reach the ground close to the source. Using Equations, we can estimate the ground level (z = 0) concentration of the plume composed of a pollutant, say, SO_2, emitted into the atmosphere at a known effective height. Suppose we have the following: Q = 0.5 kg s^{-1}, H = 25 m; $\bar{u}$ = 2 m s^{-1}, near neutral stability, and BNL parameters a = 0.32, b = 0.78, c = 0.22, and d = 0.78. Then the ground level SO_2 concentration along the plume centerline at an arbitrary distance of x = 500 m form the source will be 4.7×10^{-5} kg m^{-3} (or 47 mg m^{-3}).

Plumes may change because of changes in the wind velocity and boundary layer stability. When the atmospheric boundary layer is strongly stable, such as during radiation inversions at night or during subsidence inversions, a *fanning* pattern may be evident in the plume. Under these conditions, there is almost no vertical motion and the BNL parameters are a = 0.31, b = 0.71, c = 0.06, and d = 0.71. Lack of vertical motion thus effectively forces the plume into a relatively narrow layer, while changes in wind direction may spread the plume out laterally, resulting in a V- or fan pattern; hence, the term. A constant wind direction, however, force the plume into tightly closed fan pattern, which follows a relatively straight and narrow path. Over flat terrain the plume may be unchanged for very long distances. If there is no vertical air movement, ground level concentrations downwind of a tall smokestack can be nearly zero. However, if the source is close to the ground (i.e., H is small) or if changes in topography cause the plume to intercept the ground, the ground level concentrations can be very large.

By midmorning, surface heating by solar radiation typically beings to break down the inversion developed during the previous night. Unstable conditions develop near the ground, resulting in vertical mixing the air. With moderately unstable conditions, a = 0.36, b = 0.86, c

= 0.22, and d = 0.86. In this situation, pollution is transported downward toward ground level. Stable conditions above, however, limit dispersion of pollutants upward. Thus the remaining inversion effectively puts a "lid" over the ground level pollution. This situation is known as *fumigation* and generally lasts for periods of an hour or less. Fumigation is highly conducive to enhanced ground level pollutant concentrations.

By early afternoon, lapse conditions (i.e. negative vertical temperature gradient) generally become fully established within the boundary layer due to strong surface heating by the sun. During much of the afternoon, air motion mainly exhibits the large turbulent eddies associated with buoyancy. These eddies are generally larger than the plume diameter and thus transport the plume upward and downward in a sinusoidal path or *looping* pattern. The loops are carried with the overall wind pattern and generally increase in size with increasing distance downwind from the source. The motion may bring the plume contents to ground level quite close to the source. Because of turbulence, however, the plume eventually becomes dispersed at relatively large distances.

By early evening, a radiation inversion often rebuilds form ground level upward. Stable conditions near the ground inhibit transport of plume contents downward, but unstable air aloft (above the inversion height) allows dispersal upward. This upward transport, known as *lofting*, is highly favorable for dispersing pollutants. Lofting is only effective when the source is above the inversion height. Plume contents emitted below the inversion height are essentially trapped in a fan-type plume configuration.

Topography downwind form pollution sources affects air quality, especially in mountainous areas. For example, air drainage into relatively enclosed valleys during winter and/or inversion conditions can cause accumulation of pollutants within the valleys. Thus urban areas in valleys with restricted air flow are particularly prone to high pollution levels. In addition, in coastal areas, air flow from the ocean can be blocked or channeled by mountain ranges. This situation is common in Los Angeles basin, which is surrounded by mountains that restrict air flow from the pacific Ocean. Thus, dispersal of pollutants form sources in the basin is inhibited.

Pollutant Transformation and Removal

As pollutants move with the wind, chemical reactions often occur between the pollutants and other atmospheric chemical species.

Although the pathways and rates of many of these chemical reactions are poorly understood, they are an important factor affecting the fates of many air pollutants.

Most pollutants, such as CO, remain the atmosphere for relatively brief periods, lasting only a few days or weeks. Thus, if emissions were completely curtailed, the lower atmosphere would quickly lose nearly all of its pollutants. However, some pollutants—volcanic ash and sulfur-containing aerosols, for example–emitted high into the stratosphere can remain there for months before settling back to the surface. These long-lasting upper-atmospheric pollutants can alter the earth's climate, as evidenced by lower air temperatures resulting from volcanic eruptions. In addition, synthetic *chlorofluorocarbon* (CFC) compounds can remain in the atmosphere for many years before they break down.

Pollution can be removed from the atmosphere by gravitational setting, dry deposition, condensation, and wet deposition.

Gravitational settling

Gravitational setting removes most particles whose diameters are greater than about 10 μm. Particles less than 10 μm in diameter are often small enough to stay in the atmosphere for long periods. Particles greater than about 10 μm in diameter quickly settle out.

Dry deposition

Dry deposition is a mass-transfer process that results in adsorption of gaseous pollutants by plants and soil. Dry deposition to plants is dependent upon uptake of the pollution through stomatal openings in plant leaves and upon turbulent transport in the air. Dry deposition to bare soil involves not only turbulent transport of pollutants in air above the soil, but also soil microorganisms that take up such pollutants such as CO.

Condensation

Volatile organic compounds can condense on cold surfaces during winter in temperate and polar regions. The process of evaporation, transport, and condensation of toxic compounds, such as dioxins and the pesticide, dichlorodiphenyltrichloroethane (DDT), may be responsible for causing high levels of toxic organic pollutants in the Arctic.

Wet deposition

Rain is very effective at removing gases and small particulates. Raindrops increase in size as they fall toward the ground, and thus they increasingly capture more pollutants. Raindrops, in effect, "sweep up" pollution as it falls through the air. The ability of the rain to remove pollutants depends upon the rainfall intensity, the size and electrical properties of the drops, and the solubility of the polluting species.

POLLUTION TRENDS

Emissions of nearly all types of primary air pollutants have generally declined or held steady in the United States since about 1970. This decline is mostly attributable to general compliance with the federal air quality regulations set forth in response to the U.S. Clean Air Act of 1970. Although air quality is improving overall, many specific urban areas fail to meet the air quality standards set for some pollutants. Poor air quality is estimated to affect the lives of about 100 million people in the United States alone.

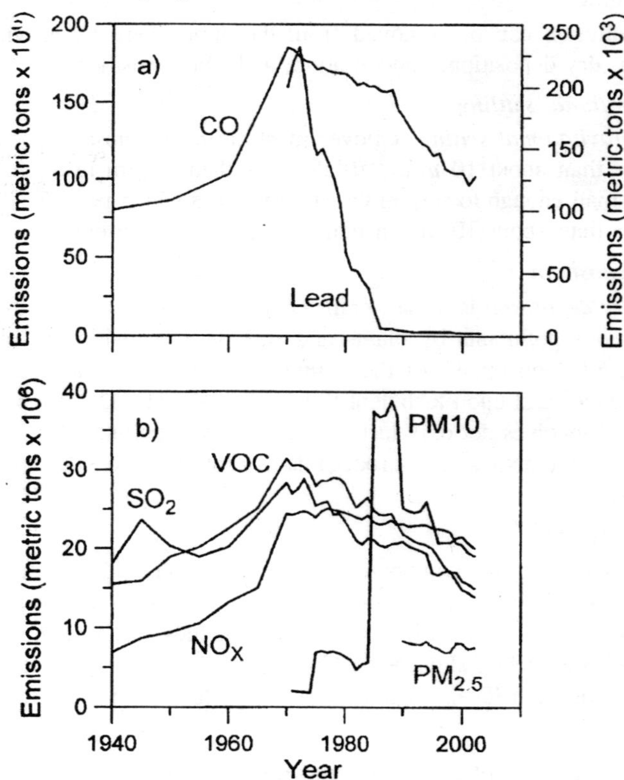

Fig. 5.3. Air pollution emissions have generally decreased since the 1970s with the exception of PM_{10}.

Despite the fact that transportation continues to be a major source of pollution in the United States, the proportion of its contribution is diminishing. While the number of cars is increasing in most urban areas, fuel efficiencies have increased and pollutant emissions per vehicle are declining owing to improvements in technology such as catalytic converters and other pollution control devices. Evidence of improved air quality is shown by the marked decline of atmospheric lead (Pb) concentrations since 1970. Atmospheric lead comes mainly form the burning of lead-containing gasoline in cars and trucks. Thus, the introduction of unleaded gasoline was a significant factor in this decline. Now required for cars in the United States because of environmental health concerns, unleaded gasoline is also used because leaded fuels deactivate catalytic converters.

It is generally recognized that reducing air pollution through control of emissions at the source is the best approach, which is the goal of the EPA and other regulatory agencies. Total control of pollutant emissions is certainly not feasible for various economic and technological reasons, but efforts at reducing emissions are helping to improve air quality in most locations. There are various physical and chemical precipitators/concentrators/burners that can be used to control emissions.

6

AIR POLLUTION AND ITS CONTROL

This chapter addresses inorganic and organic air pollutants of various kinds. It discusses their origins, the processes that they undergo in the atmosphere, there effects, and their treatment. Some air pollutants are potentially so damaging that they may affect the global atmosphere, and even life on Earth.

One of the biggest concerns regrading air pollution is its effect upon plants. In many areas of the world exposure to air pollutants has significantly reduced yields of crops grown for food and other purposes. Some forests have been seriously damaged by air pollution. An example is the killing of trees in Germany's Black Forest by exposure to acidic precipitation.

The first of several kinds of inorganic air pollutants addressed here are particles, often formed from reactions of gaseous pollutants that enter the atmosphere as the result of human activities. Gaseous air pollutants include CO, SO_2, NO, and NO_2, as well as less abundant NH_3, N_2O, N_2O_5, H_2S, Cl_2, HCl, and HF. (Their quantities are relatively small compared to the amount of CO_2 in the atmosphere).

There is a strong connection between inorganic and organic substances in the atmosphere. For example, inorganic NO_2 photo-dissociates to start the processes by which organic vapors form aldehydes, oxidants, and other substances in photochemical smog. As another example, smog-generated oxidants convert inorganic SO_2 to much more acidic sulfuric acid, the major contributor to acid precipitation.

Organic pollutants may strongly affect atmospheric quality. Such pollutants may come from both natural and artificial sources. In some cases contaminants from both kinds of sources interact to produce a pollution effect, such as occurs when terpene hydrocarbons from trees interact with NO_x from autos to make photochemical smog.

The effects of atmospheric pollutants may be divided between *direct effects*, from *primary pollutants*, such as cancer caused by exposure to vinyl chloride, and effects resulting from *secondary pollutants* produced by atmospheric reactions of primary pollutants, such as photochemical smog or acid rain. Generally, secondary pollutants are more important. In some localized situations, particularly the workplace, direct effects of organic air pollutants may be equally important.

Natural Sources of Air Pollution

It is difficult to give a simple, comprehensive definition of pollution. The word comes from the Latin *pollutus*, which means made foul, unclean, or dirty. Some authors limit the use of the term to damaging materials that are released into the environment by human activities. There are, however, many natural sources of air quality degradation. Volcanoes spew out ash, acid mists, hydrogen sulfide, and other toxic gases. Sea spray and decaying vegetation are major sources of reactive sulfur compounds in the air. Forest fires create clouds of smoke that blanket whole continents. Trees and bushes emit millions of tons of volatile organic compounds (terpenes and isoprenes), creating, for example, the blue haze that gave the Blue Ridge Mountains their name. Pollen, spores, viruses, bacteria, and other small bits of organic material in the air cause widespread suffering from allergies and airborne infections. Storms in arid regions raise dust clouds that transport millions of tons of soil and can be detected half a world away. Bacterial metabolism of decaying vegetation in swamps and of cellulose in the guts of termites and ruminant animals is responsible for as much as two-thirds of the methane (natural gas) in the air.

In many cases, the chemical compositions of pollutants from natural and human-related sources are identical, and their effects are inseparable. Sometimes, however, materials in the atmosphere are considered innocuous at naturally occurring levels, but when humans add to these levels, overloading of natural cycles or disruption of essential processes can occur. While the natural sources of suspended particulate material in the air outweigh human sources at least tenfold worldwide, in many cities more than 90 percent of the airborne particulate matter is anthropogenic (human-caused).

Human-Caused Air Pollution

What are the major types of air pollutants and where do they come from? In this section, we will define some general categories and sources of air pollution and survey the characteristics and emission levels of the seven conventional pollutants regulated by the Clean Air Act.

Primary and Secondary Pollutants

Primary pollutants are those released directly from the source into the air in a harmful form. *Secondary pollutants*, by contrast, are modified to a hazardous form after they enter the air or are formed by chemical reactions as components of the air mix and interact. Solar radiation often provides the energy for these reactions. Photochemical oxidants and atmospheric acids formed by these mechanisms are probably the most important secondary pollutants in terms of human health and ecosystem damage. We will discuss several important examples of such pollutants in this chapter.

Fugitive emissions are those that do not go through a smokestack. By far the most massive example of this category is dust from soil erosion, strip mining, rock crushing, and building construction (and destruction). In the United States, natural and anthropogenic sources of fugitive dust add up to some 100 million metric tons per year. The amount of CO_2 released by burning fossil fuels and biomass is nearly equal in mass to fugitive dust. Fugitive industrial emissions are also an important source of air pollution. Leaks around valves and pipe joints contribute as much as 90 percent of the hydrocarbons and volatile organic chemicals emitted from oil refineries and chemical plants.

Conventional or "Criteria" Pollutants

The U.S. Clean Air Act of 1970 designated seven major pollutants (sulfur dioxide, carbon monoxide, particulates, hydrocarbons, nitrogen oxides, photochemical oxidants, and lead) for which maximum *ambient air* (air all around us) levels are mandated. These seven *conventional* or *criteria pollutants* contribute the largest volume of air-quality degradation and also are considered the most serious threat of all air pollutants to human health and welfare. Now let's look more closely at the sources and characteristics of each of these major pollutants.

Sulfur compounds

Natural sources of sulfur in the atmosphere include evaporation of sea spray, erosion of sulfate-containing dust from arid soils, fumes from volcanoes and fumaroles, and biogenic emissions of hydrogen sulfide (H_2S) and organic sulfur-containing compounds, such as dimethylsulfide, methyl mercaptan, carbon disulfide, and carbonyl sulfide. Total yearly emissions of sulfur from all sources amounts to some 114 million metric tons. Worldwide, anthropogenic sources represent about two-thirds of the total sulfur flux, but in most urban areas they contribute as much as 90 percent of the sulfur in the air. The predominant form of anthropogenic sulfur is sulfur dioxide (SO_2) from combustion of sulfur-containing fuel (coal and oil), purification of sour (sulfur-containing) natural gas or oil, and industrial processes, such as smelting of sulfide ores. China and the United States are the largest sources of anthropogenic sulfur, primarily from coal burning.

Sulfur dioxide is a colorless corrosive gas that is directly damaging to both plants and animals. Once in the atmosphere, it can be further oxidized to sulfur trioxide (SO_3), which reacts with water vapor or dissolves in water droplets to form sulfuric acid (H_2SO_4), a major component of acid rain. Very small solid particles or liquid droplets can transport the acidic sulfate ion (SO_4^{-2}) long distances through the air or deep into the lungs where it is very damaging. Sulfur dioxide and sulfate ions are probably second only to smoking as causes of air pollution-related health damage. Sulfate particles and droplets reduce visibility in the United States as much as 80 percent.

Nitrogen compounds

Nitrogen oxides are highly reactive gases formed when nitrogen in fuel or combustion air is heated to temperatures above 650°C (1200°F) in the presence of oxygen, or when bacteria in soil or water oxidize nitrogen-containing compounds. The initial product, nitric oxide (NO), oxidizes further in the atmosphere to nitrogen dioxide (NO_2), a reddish brown gas that gives photochemical smog its distinctive color. Because of their interconvertibility, the general term NO_x is used to describe these gases. Nitrogen oxides combine with water to make nitric acid (HNO_3), which is also a major component of atmospheric acidification.

The total annual emissions of reactive nitrogen compounds into the air are about 230 million metric tons worldwide. Anthropogenic sources account for 60 percent of these emissions. About 95 percent of all human-caused NO_x in the United States is produced by fuel combustion in transportation and electric power generation. Nitrous oxide (N_2O) is an intermediate in soil denitrification that absorbs ultraviolet light and plays an important role in climate modification.

Excess nitrogen is causing fertilization and eutrophication of inland waters and coastal seas. It also may be adversely affecting terrestrial plants both by excess fertilization and by encouraging growth of weedy species that crowd out native varieties.

Carbon oxides

The predominant form of carbon in the air is carbon dioxide (CO_2). It is usually considered nontoxic and innocuous, but increasing atmospheric levels (about 0.4 percent per year) due to human activities appear to be causing a global climate warming that may have disastrous effects on both human and natural communities. More than 90 percent of the CO_2 emitted each year is from respiration (oxidation of organic compounds by plant and animal cells). These releases are usually balanced by an equal uptake by photosynthesis in green plants.

Burning of fossil fuels and biomass contribute about 7.3 billion metric tons per year to the air. Where all the anthropogenic carbon goes is somewhat mysterious. Two billion metric tons is taken up by the oceans, while 3.4 billion metric tons accumulate in the atmosphere. The other 1.9 billion metric tons of carbon are unaccounted for. It may be taken up by plants and stored in roots or soil or perhaps some other, yet unrecognized process sequesters large amounts of carbon.

Carbon monoxide (CO) is a colorless, odorless, nonirritating but highly toxic gas produced by incomplete combustion of fuel (coal, oil, charcoal, or gas), incineration of biomass or solid waste, or partially anaerobic decomposition of organic material. CO inhibits respiration in animals by binding irreversibly to hemoglobin. About 1 billion metric tons of CO are released to the atmosphere each year, half of that from human activities. In the United States, two-thirds of the CO emissions are created by internal combustion engines in transportation. Land-clearing fires and cooking fires also are major sources. About 90 percent of the CO in the air is consumed in photochemical reactions that produce ozone.

Metals and Halogens

Many toxic metals are mined and used in manufacturing processes or occur as trace elements in fuels, especially coal. These metals are released to the air in the form of metal fumes or suspended particulates by fuel combustion, ore smelting, and disposal of wastes. Worldwide lead emissions amount to about 2 million metric tons per year, or two-thirds of all metallic air pollution. Most of this lead is from

Table 6.1. Estimated fluxes of pollutants and trace gases to the atmosphere.

Species	*Sources*	*Approximate Annual Flux*	
		Natural	*Anthropogenic*
		(millions of metric tons/yr)	
CO_2 (carbon dioxide)	Respiration, fossil fuel burning, Land clearing, industrial processes	100,000*	7,300
CH_4 (methane)	Rice paddies & wetlands, gas drilling, landfills, animals, termites	155	350
CO (carbon monoxide)	Incomplete combustion, CH_4 oxidation, biomass burning, plant metabolism	1,580	930
NMHC hydrocarbons)	Fossil fuels, industrial uses, plant isoprenes & other biogenics	86092 (nonmethane	
NO_x (nitrogen oxides)	Fossil fuel burning, lightning, biomass burning, soil microbes	90	140
SO_x (sulfur oxides)	Fossil fuel burning, industry, biomass burning, volcanoes, oceans	35	79
SPM (suspended particulate materials)	Biomass burning, dust, sea salt, biogenic aerosols, gas to particle conversion	583	362

leaded gasoline. Lead is a metabolic poison and a neurotoxin that binds to essential enzymes and cellular components and inactivates them. An estimated 20 percent of all inner-city children suffer some degree of mental retardation from high environmental lead levels.

Table 6.2 Source of fate of anthropogenic atmospheric carbon.

CO_2 production	*Millions of metric tons/Yr*
Fossil fuel burning	5,700
Biomass burning	1,600
CO_2 Uptake	
Oceans	2,000
Accumulate' in Atmosphere	3,400
Unaccounted for	1,900

Mercury is another dangerous neurotoxin that is widespread in the environment. The two largest sources of atmospheric mercury appear to be coal-burning power plants and waste incinerators. Mercuric fungicides in house paint were once a major source of this deadly pollutant but now are restricted. Long-range transport of lead and mercury through the air is causing bioaccumulation in aquatic ecosystems far from the emission sources. It is now dangerous to eat fish from some once-pristine lakes and rivers because of toxic metal contamination.

Other toxic metals of concern are nickel, beryllium, cadmium, thallium, uranium, cesium, and plutonium. Some 780,000 tons of arsenic, a highly toxic metalloid, are released from metal smelters, coal combustion, and pesticide use each year. Halogens (fluorine, chlorine, bromine, and iodine) are highly reactive and generally toxic in their elemental form. About 600 million tons of highly persistent chlorofluorocarbons (CFCs) are used annually worldwide in spray propellants, refrigeration compressors, and for foam blowing. They diffuse into the stratosphere where they release chlorine and fluorine atoms that destroy the ozone shield that protects the earth from ultraviolet radiation. We'll return to this topic later.

Particulate material

An *aerosol* is any system of solid particles or liquid droplets suspended in a gaseous medium. For convenience, we generally describe all atmospheric aerosols, whether solid or liquid, as *particulate material.* This includes dust, ash, soot, lint, smoke, pollen, spores, algal cells, and many other suspended materials. Anthropogenic particulate emissions amount to about 362 million metric tons per year worldwide. Wind-blown dust, volcanic ash, and other natural materials may contribute considerably more suspended particulate material.

Particulates often are the most apparent form of air pollution since they reduce visibility and leave dirty deposits on windows, painted surfaces, and textiles. Respirable particles smaller than 2.5 micrometers are among the most dangerous of this group because they can be drawn into the lungs, where they damage respiratory tissues. Asbestos fibers and cigarette smoke are among the most dangerous respirable particles in urban and indoor air because they are carcinogenic.

Volatile organic compounds

Volatile organic compounds (VOCs) are organic chemicals that exist as gases in the air. Plants are the largest source of VOCs, releasing an estimated 350 million tons of isoprene (C_5H_8) and 450 million tons of terpenes ($C_{10}H_{15}$) each year (fig. 18.5). About 400 million tons of methane (CH_4) are produced by natural wetlands and rice paddies and by bacteria in the guts of termites and ruminant animals. These volatile hydrocarbons are generally oxidized to CO and CO_2 in the atmosphere.

In addition to these natural VOCs, a large number of other synthetic organic chemicals, such as benzene, toluene, formaldehyde, vinyl chloride, phenols, chloroform, and trichloroethylene, are released into the air by human activities. About 28 million tons of these compounds are emitted each year in the United States, mainly unburned or partially burned hydrocarbons from transportation, power plants, chemical plants, and petroleum refineries. These chemicals play an important role in the formation of photochemical oxidants.

The EPA requires industries to report releases of some 332 toxic organic chemicals into the air. In the mid-1990s, emissions totaled *2 million* metric tons or 5 billion pounds. The largest carcinogen emission was 52,000 tons (115 million lbs) of dichloromethane, which is used as an industrial solvent and paint stripper.

Photochemical Oxidants

Photochemical oxidants are products of secondary atmospheric reactions driven by solar energy. One of the most important of these reactions involves formation of singlet (atomic) oxygen by splitting nitrogen dioxide (NO_2). This atomic oxygen then reacts with another molecule of O_2 to make *ozone* (O_3). Ozone formed in the stratosphere provides a valuable shield for the biosphere by absorbing incoming ultraviolet radiation. In ambient air, however, O_3 is a strong oxidizing reagent and damages vegetation, building materials (such as paint, rubber, and plastics), and sensitive tissues (such as eyes and lungs). Ozone has an acrid, biting odor that is a distinctive characteristic of photochemical smog. Hydrocarbons in the air contribute to accumulation of ozone by removing NO in the formation of compounds, such as peroxyacetyl nitrate (PAN), which is another damaging photochemical oxidant.

Unconventional Pollutants

The EPA has authority under the Clean Air Act to set *emission standards* (regulating the amount released) for certain *unconventional* or *noncriteria pollutants* that are considered especially toxic or hazardous. Among the materials regulated by emission standards are asbestos, benzene, beryllium, mercury, polychlorinated biphenyls (PCBs), and vinyl chloride. Most of these materials have no natural source in the environment (to any great extent) and are, therefore, only anthropogenic in origin.

In addition to these toxic air pollutants, some other unconventional forms of air pollution deserve mention. *Aesthetic degradation* includes any undesirable changes in the physical characteristics or chemistry of the atmosphere. Noise, odors, and light pollution are examples of atmospheric degradation that may not be life-threatening but reduce the quality of our lives. This is a very subjective category. Odors and noise (such as loud music) that are offensive to some may be attractive to others. Often the most sensitive device for odor detection is the human nose. We can smell styrene, for example, at 44 parts per billion (ppb). Trained panels of odor testers often are used to evaluate air samples. Factories that emit noxious chemicals sometimes spray "odor maskants" or perfumes into smokestacks to cover up objectionable odors.

In most urban areas, it is difficult or impossible to see stars in the sky at night because of dust in the air and stray light from buildings, outdoor advertising, and streetlights. This light pollution has become a serious problem for astronomers.

Indoor Air Pollution

We have spent a considerable amount of effort and money to control the major outdoor air pollutants, but we have only recently become aware of the dangers of indoor air pollutants. The EPA has found that indoor concentrations of toxic air pollutants are often higher than outdoors-up to twenty times higher for some toxins. Furthermore, people generally spend more time inside than out and therefore are exposed to higher doses of these pollutants.

Smoking is without doubt the most important air pollutant in the United States in terms of human health. The Surgeon General estimates that 450,000 people die each year in the United States from emphysema, heart attacks, strokes, lung cancer, or other diseases caused by smoking. Eliminating smoking probably would save more lives than any other pollution-control measure.

Atmospheric oxidant production:

1. NO + VOC → 10 NO_2 (nitrogen dioxide)
2. NO_2 + UV → 10 NO + 0 (nitric oxide + atomic oxygen)
3. O + O_2 → O_3 (ozone)
4. NO_2 + VOC → PAN, etc. (peroxyacetyl nitrate)

Net results:

NO + VOC + O_2 + UV → O_3, PAN, and other oxidants

Other major indoor air pollution health hazards include asbestos, formaldehyde, vinyl chloride, radon, and combustion gases. Asbestos was widely used in the past in floor and ceiling tiles, plaster, cement, insulation, and soundproofing. It is a serious concern in indoor air because of its carcinogenicity. Formaldehyde still is used in more than three thousand products, including such building materials as particle board, waferboard, and urea-formaldehyde foam insulation. Vinyl chloride is used in plastic plumbing pipe, floor and wall coverings, and countertops. New carpets and drapes typically contain two dozen chemicals designed to kill bacteria and molds, resist stains, bind fibers, and retain colors.

In some cases, indoor air in homes has concentrations of chemicals that would be illegal outside or in the workplace. The EPA has found that concentrations of such compounds as chloroform, benzene, carbon tetrachloride, formaldehyde, and styrene can be seventy times higher in indoor air than in outdoor air. Many people are highly sensitive to these chemicals, and it is not uncommon to trace illness to a "sick building syndrome" caused by polluted indoor air. Next to smoking, radon gas leaking into homes from surrounding soil and rock is considered by the EPA to be the most serious indoor air pollutant in the United States.

In the less-developed countries of Africa, Asia, and Latin America where such organic fuels as firewood, charcoal, dried dung, and agricultural wastes make up the majority of household energy, smoky, poorly ventilated heating and cooking fires represent the greatest source of indoor air pollution. The World Health Organization (WHO) estimates that 2.5 billion people-nearly half the world's population-are adversely affected by pollution from this source. Women especially spend long hours each day cooking over open fires or unventilated stoves in enclosed spaces. The levels of carbon monoxide, particulates, aldehydes, and other toxic chemicals can be one hundred times higher than would be legal for outdoor ambient concentrations in the United States. Designing and building cheap, efficient, nonpolluting energy sources for the developing countries would not only save shrinking forests but would make a major impact on health as well.

Climate, Topography, and Atmospheric Processes

Topography, climate, and physical processes in the atmosphere play an important role in transport, concentration, dispersal, and removal of many air pollutants. Wind speed, mixing between air layers, precipitation, and atmospheric chemistry all determine whether pollutants will remain in the locality where they are produced or go elsewhere. In this next section, we will survey some environmental factors that affect air pollution levels.

Inversions

Temperature inversions occur when a stable layer of warmer air overlays cooler air, reversing the normal temperature decline with increasing height and preventing convection currents from dispersing pollutants. Several mechanisms create inversions. When a cold front slides under an adjacent warmer air mass or when cool air subsides down a mountain slope to displace warmer air in the valley below, an inverted temperature gradient is established. These inversions are usually not stable, however, because winds accompanying these air exchanges tend to break up the temperature gradient fairly quickly and mix air layers.

The most stable inversion conditions are usually created by rapid nighttime cooling in a valley or basin where air movement is restricted. Los Angeles is a classic example of the conditions that create temperature inversions and photochemical smog. The city is surrounded by mountains on three sides and the climate is dry and sunny. Extensive automobile use creates high pollution levels. Skies are generally clear at night, allowing rapid radiant heat loss, and the ground cools quickly. Surface air layers are cooled by conduction, while upper layers remain relatively warm. Density differences retard vertical mixing. During the night, cool, humid, onshore breezes slide in under the contaminated air, squeezing it up against the cap of warmer air above and concentrating the pollutants accumulated during the day.

Morning sunlight is absorbed by the concentrated aerosols and gaseous chemicals of the inversion layer. This complex mixture quickly cooks up a toxic brew of hazardous compounds. As the ground warms later in the day, convection currents break up the temperature gradient and pollutants are carried back down to the surface where more contaminants are added. Nitric oxide (NO) from automobile exhaust is oxidized to nitrogen dioxide. As nitrogen oxides are used up in reactions with unburned hydrocarbons, the ozone levels begin to rise. By early afternoon, an acrid brown haze fills the air, making eyes water and throats burn. On summer days, ozone concentrations in the Los Angeles basin can reach 0.34 ppm or more by late afternoon and the pollution index can be 300, the stage considered a health hazard.

Dust Domes and Heat Islands

Even without mountains to block winds and stabilize air layers, many large cities create an atmospheric environment quite different from the surrounding conditions. Sparse vegetation and high levels of concrete and glass in urban areas allow rainfall to run off quickly and create high rates of heat absorption during the day and radiation at night. Tall buildings create convective updrafts that sweep pollutants into the air. Temperatures in the center of large cities are frequently 3° to 5°C (5° to 9°F) higher than the surrounding countryside. Stable air masses created by this "heat island" over the city concentrate pollutants in a "dust dome." Rural areas downwind from major industrial areas often have significantly decreased visibility and increased rainfall (due to increased condensation nuclei in the dust plume) compared to neighboring areas with cleaner air. In the late 1960s, for instance, areas downwind from Chicago and St. Louis reported up to 30 percent more rainfall than upwind regions.

Long-Range Transport

Fine aerosols can be carried great distances by the wind. Florida researchers recently showed that as much as half of the fine reddish dust visible in Miami's air during summer months is blown across the Atlantic from the Sahara Desert.

Industrial pollutants are also transported great distances by wind currents. Some of the most toxic and corrosive materials delivered by long-range transport are secondary pollutants (such as sulfuric and nitric acids or ozone), produced by the mixing and interaction of atmospheric contaminants as they travel through the air. Tracing the sources of these chemically altered pollutants can be difficult. Lakes and forests in Sweden were showing evidence of sulfuric acid contamination years before the source of the acidity was traced to Germany, England, and other distant parts of Europe.

Controlling long-range pollutants is a highly political process. Germany and England were not very sympathetic about acid precipitation until their own forests began to die. In another case, 90 percent of the pollution falling into Lake Superior originates thousands of kilometers away in the United States, Canada, and even Mexico. Farms and industries in these distant regions resist spending money, however, to reduce emissions to protect someone else's environment.

Increasingly sensitive monitoring equipment has begun to reveal industrial contaminants in places usually considered among the cleanest in the world. Samoa, Greenland, and even Antarctica and the North Pole, all have heavy metals, pesticides, and radioactive elements in their air. Since the 1950s, pilots flying in the high Arctic have reported dense layers of reddish-brown haze clouding the arctic atmosphere. Aerosols of sulfates, soot, dust, and toxic heavy metals such as vanadium, manganese, and lead travel to the Pole from the industrialized parts of Europe and Russia. These contaminants, trapped by winds that circle the pole, concentrate at high latitudes and eventually, falling out in snow and ice, enter the food chain. The Inuit people of Broughton Island, well above the Arctic Circle, have higher levels of polychlorinated biphenyls (PCBs) in their blood than any other known population, except victims of industrial accidents. Far from any source of this industrial by-product, these people accumulate PCBs from the flesh of fish, caribou, and other animals they eat.

Stratospheric Ozone

In 1985, the British Antarctic Atmospheric Survey announced a startling and disturbing discovery: ozone levels in the stratosphere over the South Pole were dropping precipitously during September and October every year as the sun reappears at the end of the long polar winter. This ozone depletion has been occurring at least since the 1960s but was not recognized because earlier researchers programmed their instruments to ignore changes in ozone levels that were presumed to be erroneous.

The 1997 ozone "hole" over Antarctia was the largest ever recorded, covering 22 million km^2 (8.5 million mi^1) in which all the ozone between 14 and 20 kilometers altitude was destroyed. Ominously, this phenomenon is now spreading to other parts of the world as well.

About 10 percent of all stratospheric ozone worldwide was destroyed during the spring of 1997 and levels over the Arctic averaged 40 percent below normal.

Why are we worried about stratospheric ozone? At ground level, ozone is a harmful pollutant, damaging plants, building materials, and human health; in the the upper atmosphere, however, where it screens out dangerous ultraviolet (UV) rays from the sun, ozone is an irreplaceable resource. Without this shield, organisms on the earth's surface would be subjected to life-threatening radiation burns and genetic damage. A 1 percent loss of ozone results in a 2 percent increase in UV reaching the earth's surface and could result in about a million extra human skin cancers per year worldwide if no protective measures are taken. Thus it is urgent that we learn what is attacking the ozone layer and find ways to reverse these trends if possible.

The exceptionally cold temperatures (-85 to -90°C) in Antarctica play a role in ozone losses. During the long, dark winter months, the strong circumpolar vortex isolates Antarctic air and allows stratospheric temperatures to drop low enough to create ice crystals at high altitudes-something that rarely happens elsewhere over the world. Ozone and chlorine-containing molecules are absorbed on the surfaces of these ice particles. When the sun returns in the spring and provides energy to liberate chlorine ions, destructive chemical reactions proceed quickly.

Humans release a variety of chlorine-containing molecules into the atmosphere. The ones suspected of being most important in ozone losses are *chlorofluorocarbons* (CFCs) and halon gases. CFCs were invented in 1928 by scientists at General Motors who were searching for a less toxic refrigerant than ammonia. Commonly known by the trade name Freon, CFCs were regarded as wonderful compounds. They are nontoxic, nonflammable, chemically inert, cheaply produced, and useful in a wide variety of applications.

Because these molecules are so stable, however, they persist for decades or even centuries once released. When they diffuse out into the stratosphere, the intense UV irradiation releases chlorine atoms that destroy ozone. Since the chlorine atoms are not themselves consumed in these reactions, they continue to destroy ozone for years until they finally precipitate or are washed out of the air.

Until 1978, aerosol spray cans used more CFCs than any other product. Although we didn't know about the special conditions in the Antarctic at that time, it was suspected that CFCs might threaten stratospheric ozone, so laws were passed in the United States, Canada, and some European countries to ban nonessential uses. Still, some 320,000 metric tons of CFCs were used worldwide every year until 1988 as refrigerants, solvents, spray propellants, and foam-blowing agents.

The discovery of stratospheric ozone losses has brought about a remarkably quick international response. At a 1989 conference in Helsinki, eighty-one nations agreed to phase out CFC production by the end of the century. As evidence accumulated showing that losses were larger and more widespread than previously thought, the deadline for the elimination of all CFCs (halons, carbon tetrachloride, and methyl chloroform) was moved up to 1996 and a $500 million fund was established to assist poorer countries to switch to nonCFC technologies. Fortunately, alternatives to CFCs for most uses already exist. The first substitutes will be hydrochlorofluorocarbons (HCFCs), which release much less chlorine per molecule. Eventually, we hope to develop halogen-free molecules that work just as well and are no more expensive than CFCs.

There is some evidence that the CFC ban is already having an effect. The buildup of CFCs in the atmosphere is declining more rapidly than expected. In seventy years or so, stratospheric ozone levels are expected to be back to normal. Unfortunately, there may be a downside to stopping ozone destruction. Ozone is a potent greenhouse gas. Some models suggest that lower ozone levels have been offsetting the effects of increased CO_2. When ozone is restored, global warming may be accelerated. As so often is the case, when we disturb one environmental factor, we affect others as well.

In 1995, chemists Sherwood Rowland, Mario Molina, and Paul Crutzen shared the Nobel Prize for their work on atmospheric chemistry and stratospheric ozone. This was the first Nobel Prize for an environmental issue.

Effects of Air Pottution

So far we have looked at the major types and sources of air pollutants. Now we will turn our attention to the effects of those pollutants on human health, physical materials, ecosystems, and global climate.

Human Health

The EPA estimates that people in the most polluted cities in the United States are 15 to 17 percent more likely to die prematurely than those in cities with the cleanest air. Heart attacks, respiratory diseases, and lung cancer all are significantly higher in people who breathe dirty air, compared to matching groups in cleaner environments. This can mean as much as a 5- to 10-year decrease in life expectancy if you live in the worst parts of Los Angeles or Baltimore, compared to a place with clean air. Of course your likelihood of suffering ill health from air pollutants depends on the intensity and duration of exposure as well as your age and prior health status. You are much more likely to be at risk if you are very young, very old, or already suffering from some respiratory or cardiovascular disease. Some people are super-sensitive because of genetics or prior exposure. And those doing vigorous physical work or exercise are more likely to succumb than more sedentary folks.

Conditions are often much worse in other countries than Canada or the United States. The United Nations estimates that at least 1.3 billion people around the world live in areas where the air is dangerously polluted. In the "black triangle" region of Poland, Hungary, the Czech Republic, and Slovakia, for example, respiratory ailments, cardiovascular diseases, lung cancer, infant mortality, and miscarriages are as much as 50 percent higher than in cleaner parts of those countries. And in China, city dwellers are 4 to 6 times more likely than country folk to die of lung cancer. As mentioned earlier, the greatest air quality problem is often in poorly ventilated homes in poorer countries where smoky fires are used for cooking and heating. Billions of women and children spend hours each day in these unhealthy conditions. The World Health Organization estimates that 4 million children under 5 die each year from acute respiratory diseases exacerbated by air pollution.

How does air pollution cause these health effects? The most common route of exposure to air pollutants is by inhalation, but direct absorption through the skin or contamination of food and water also are important pathways. Because they are strong oxidizing agents, sulfates, SO_2, NO_x, and O_3 act as irritants that damage delicate tissues in the eyes and respiratory passages. Fine suspended particulate materials (less than 10 gm) penetrate deep into the lungs and are both irritants and fibrotic agents. Inflammatory responses set in motion by these irritants impair lung function and trigger cardiovascular problems as the heart tries to compensate for lack of oxygen by pumping faster and harder. If the irritation is really severe-see the example of Bhopal, so much fluid seeps into lungs through damaged tissues that the victim actually drowns.

Carbon monoxide binds to hemoglobin and decreases the ability of red blood cells to carry oxygen. Asphyxiants such as this cause headaches, dizziness, heart stress, and can even be lethal if concentra-tions are high enough. Lead also binds to hemoglobin and reduces oxygen-carrying capacity at high levels. At lower levels, lead causes long-term damage to critical neurons in the brain that results in mental and physical impairment and developmental retardation.

Some important chronic health effects of air pollutants include bronchitis and emphysema.

Bronchitis is a persistent inflammation of bronchi and bronchioles (large and small airways in the lung) that causes a painful cough and involuntary muscle spasms that constrict airways. Severe bronchitis can lead to *emphysema*, an irreversible obstructive lung disease in which airways become permanently constricted and alveoli are damaged or even destroyed. Stagnant air trapped in blocked airways swells the tiny air sacs in the lung (alveoli), blocking blood circulation. As cells die from lack of oxygen and nutrients, the walls of the alveoli break down, creating large empty spaces incapable of gas exchange. Thickened walls of the bronchioles lose elasticity and breathing becomes more difficult. Victims of emphysema make a characteristic whistling sound when they breathe. Often they need supplementary oxygen to make up for reduced respiratory capacity.

Irritants in the air are so widespread that about half of all lungs examined at autopsy in the United States have some degree of alveolar deterioration. The Office of Technology Assessment (OTA) estimates that 250,000 people suffer from pollution-related bronchitis and emphysema in the United States, and some 50,000 excess deaths each year are attributable to complications of these diseases, which are probably second only to heart attack as a cause of death.

Smoking is undoubtedly the largest cause of obstructive lung disease and preventable death in the world. The World Health Organization says that tobacco kills some 3 million people each year. This makes it rank with diarrhea and malaria as one of the world's leading killers. Because of cardiovascular stress caused by carbon monoxide in smoke and chronic bronchitis and emphysema, about twice as many people die of heart failure as die from lung cancer associated with smoking.

Plant Pathology

In the early days of industrialization, fumes from furnaces, smelters, refineries, and chemical plants often destroyed vegetation and created desolate, barren landscapes around mining and manufacturing centers. The copper-nickel smelter at Sudbury, Ontario, is a spectacular and notorious example of air pollution effects on vegetation and ecosystems. In 1886, the corporate ancestors of the International Nickel Company

(INCO) began open-bed roasting of sulfide ores at Sudbury. Sulfur dioxide and sulfuric acid released by this process caused massive destruction of the plant community within about 30 km (18.6 mi) of the smelter. Rains washed away the exposed soil, leaving a barren moonscape of blackened bedrock. Super-tall, 400 m smokestacks were installed in the 1950s and sulfur scrubbers were added twenty years later. Emissions were reduced by 90 percent and the surrounding ecosystem is beginning to recover. The area near the factory is still a grim, empty wasteland, however. Similar destruction occurred at many other sites during the nineteenth century. *Copperhill*, Tennessee; Butte, Montana; and the Ruhr Valley in Germany are some well-known examples, but these areas also are showing signs of recovery since corrective measures were taken.

There are two probable ways that air pollutants damage plants. They can be directly toxic, damaging sensitive cell membranes much as irritants do in human lungs. Within a few days of exposure to toxic levels of oxidants, mottling (discoloration) occurs in leaves due to chlorosis (bleaching of chlorophyll), and then necrotic (dead) spots develop. If injury is severe, the whole plant may be killed. Sometimes these symptoms are so distinctive that positive identification of the source of damage is possible. Often, however, the symptoms are vague and difficult to separate from diseases or insect damage.

Another mechanism of action is exhibited by chemicals, such as ethylene, that act as metabolic regulators or plant hormones and disrupt normal patterns of growth and development. Ethylene is a component of automobile exhaust and is released from petroleum refineries and chemical plants. The concentration of ethylene around highways and industrial areas is often high enough to cause injury to sensitive plants. Some scientists believe that the devastating forest destruction in Europe and North America may be partly due to volatile organic compounds.

Certain combinations of environmental factors have *synergistic effects* in which the injury caused by exposure to two factors together is more than the sum of exposure to each factor individually. For instance, when white pine seedlings are exposed to subthreshold concentrations of ozone and sulfur dioxide individually, no visible injury occurs. If the same concentrations of pollutants are given together, however, visible damage occurs. In alfalfa, however, SO_2 and O_3 together cause less damage than either one alone. These complex interactions point out the unpredictability of future effects of pollutants. Outcomes might be either more or less severe than previous experience indicates.

Pollutant levels too low to produce visible symptoms of damage may still have important effects. Field studies using open top chambers and charcoal-filtered air show that yields in some sensitive crops, such as soybeans, may be reduced as much as 50 percent by currently existing levels of oxidants in ambient air. Some plant pathologists suggest that ozone and photochemical oxidants are responsible for as much as 90 percent of agricultural, or namental, and forest losses from air pollution. The total costs of this damage may be as much as $10 billion per year in North America alone.

Acid Deposition

Most people in the United States became aware of problems associated with *acid precipitation* (the deposition of wet acidic solutions or dry acidic particles from the air) within the last decade or so, but English scientist Robert Angus Smith coined the term "acid rain" in his studies of air chemistry in Manchester, England, in the 1850s. By the 1940s, it was known that pollutants, including atmospheric acids, could be transported long distances by wind currents. This was thought to be only an academic curiosity until it was shown that precipitation of these acids can have far-reaching ecological effects.

pH and atmospheric acidity

We describe acidity in terms of pH (the negative logarithm of the hydrogen ion concentration in a solution). The pH scale ranges from 0 to 14, with 7, the midpoint, being neutral. Values below 7 indicate progressively greater acidity, while those above 7 are progressively more alkaline. Since the scale is logarithmic, there is a tenfold difference in hydrogen ion concentration for each pH unit. For instance, pH 6 is ten times more acidic than pH 7; likewise, pH 5 is one hundred times more acidic, and pH 4 is one thousand times more acidic than pH 7.

Normal, unpolluted rain generally has a pH of about 5.6 due to carbonic acid created by CO_2 in air. Volcanic emissions, biological decomposition, and chlorine and sulfates from ocean spray can drop the pH of rain well below 5.6, while alkaline dust can raise it above 7. In industrialized areas, anthropogenic acids in the air usually far outweigh those from natural sources. Acid rain is only one form in which acid deposition occurs. Fog, snow, mist, and dew also trap and deposit atmospheric contaminants. Furthermore, fallout of dry sulfate, nitrate, and chloride particles can account for as much as half of the acidic deposition in some areas.

Aquatic effects

It has been known for about thirty years that acids-principally H_2SO_4 and HNO_3-generated by industrial and automobile emissions in northwestern Europe are carried by prevailing winds to Scandinavia where they are deposited in rain, snow, and dry precipitation. The thin, acidic soils and oligotrophic lakes and streams in the mountains of southern Norway and Sweden have been severely affected by this acid deposition. Some 18,000 lakes in Sweden are now so acidic that they will no longer support game fish or other sensitive aquatic organisms.

Generally, reproduction is the most sensitive stage in fish life cycles. Eggs and fry of many species are killed when the pH drops to about 5.0. This level of acidification also can disrupt the food chain by killing aquatic plants, insects, and invertebrates on which fish depend for food. At pH levels below 5.0, adult fish die as well. Trout, salmon, and other game fish are usually the most sensitive. Carp, gar, suckers, and other less desirable fish are more resistant. There are several ways acids kill fish. Acidity alters body chemistry, destroys gills and prevents oxygen uptake, causes bone decalcification, and disrupts muscle contraction. Another dangerous effect (for us as well as fish) is that acid water leaches toxic metals, such as mercury and aluminum, out of soil and rocks.

In the early 1970s, evidence began to accumulate suggesting that air pollutants are acidifying many lakes in North America. Studies in the Adirondack Mountains of New York revealed that about half of the high altitude lakes (above 1,000 m or 3,300 ft) are acidified and have no fish. Areas showing lake damage correlate closely with average pH levels in precipitation. Some 48,000 lakes in Ontario are endangered and nearly all of Quebec's surface waters, including about 1 million lakes, are believed to be highly sensitive to acid deposition.

Much of the western United States has relatively alkaline bedrock and carbonate-rich soil, which counterbalance acids from the atmosphere. Recent surveys of the Rocky Mountains, the Sierra Nevadas in California, and the Cascades in Washington, however, have shown that many high mountain lakes and streams have very low buffering capacity (ability to resist pH change) and are susceptible to acidification.

Sulfates account for about two-thirds of the acid deposition in eastern North America and most of Europe, while nitrates contribute most of the remaining one-third. In urban areas, where transportation is the major source of pollution, nitric acid is equal to or slightly greater than sulfuric acids in the air. A vigorous program of pollution control has been undertaken by both Canada and the United States. Although SO_2 and NO_x emissions have decreased dramatically over the past three decades over much of Europe and eastern North America as a result of pollution control measures, rain falling in these areas remains acidic. Damage to natural ecosystems also continues to be greater than scientists expected. Apparently, alkaline dust that would once have neutralized acids in air has been depleted by years of acid rain and is now no longer effective. This may also lead to a loss of cations such as calcium, magnesium, sodium, and potassium essential to plant growth.

Forest damage

In the early 1980s, disturbing reports appeared of rapid forest declines in both Europe and North America. One of the earliest was a detailed ecosystem inventory on Camel's Hump Mountain in Vermont. A 1980 survey showed that seedling production, tree density, and viability of spruce-fir forests at high elevations had declined about 50 percent in fifteen years. By 1990, almost all the red spruce, once the dominant species on the upper part of the mountain, were dead or dying. A similar situation was found on Mount Mitchell in North Carolina where almost all red spruce and Fraser fir above 2,000 meters are in a severe decline. Nearly all the trees are losing needles and about half of them are dead.

European forests also are dying at an alarming rate. West German foresters estimated in 1982 only 8 percent of their forests showed air pollution damage. By 1983, some 34 percent of the forest was affected, and in 1985, more than 4 million hectares (about half the total forest) were reported to be in a state of decline. The loss to the forest industry is estimated to be about one billion DM (Deutsche marks) per year.

Similar damage is reported in Czechoslovakia, Poland, Austria, and Switzerland. Again, high elevation forests are most severely affected. This is a disaster for mountain villages in the Alps that depend on forests to prevent avalanches in the winter. Sweden, Norway, the Netherlands, Romania, China, and the former Soviet Union also have evidence of growth reduction, defoliation, root necrosis, lack of seedling growth, and premature tree death. The species afflicted vary from place to place, but the overall picture is of widespread forest destruction.

This complex phenomenon probably has many contributing factors, but air pollution and deposition of atmospheric acids are thought to be leading causes of forest destruction in many areas. Considerable research has shown that acids are directly toxic to tender shoots and roots. High-altitude forests are subjected to especially intense doses of these acids because clouds saturated with pollutants tend to hang on mountaintops, bathing forests in a toxic soup for days or even weeks at a time.

Scientists have suggested that other mechanisms may play a role in forest decline. Overfertilization by nitrogen compounds may make trees sensitive to early frost. Toxic metals, such as aluminum, may be solubilized by acidic groundwater. Plant pathogens and insect pests may damage trees or attack trees debilitated by air pollution. Fungi that form essential mutualistic associations (called mycorrhizae) with tree roots may be damaged by acid rain. Other air pollutants, such as sulfur dioxide, ozone, or toxic organic compounds may damage trees. Repeated harvesting cycles in commercial forests may remove nutrients and damage ecological relationships essential for healthy tree growth. Perhaps the most likely scenario is that all these environmental factors act cumulatively but in different combinations in the deteriorating health of individual trees and entire forests.

Buildings and monuments

In cities throughout the world, some of the oldest and most glorious buildings and works of art are being destroyed by air pollution. Smoke and soot coat buildings, paintings, and textiles. Limestone and marble are destroyed by atmospheric acids at an alarming rate. The Parthenon in Athens, the Taj Mahal in Agra, the Colosseum in Rome, frescoes and statues in Florence, medieval cathedrals in Europe, and the Lincoln Memorial and Washington Monument in Washington, DC, are slowly dissolving and flaking away because of acidic fumes in the air. Medieval stained glass windows in Cologne's gothic cathedral are so porous from etching by atmospheric acids that pigments disappear and the glass literally crumbles away. Restoration costs for this one building alone are estimated at three to four billion German marks ($1.5 to $2 billion).

On a more mundane level, air pollution also damages ordinary buildings and structures. Corroding steel in reinforced concrete weakens buildings, roads, and bridges. Paint and rubber deteriorate due to oxidization. Limestone, marble, and some kinds of sandstone flake and crumble. The Council on Environmental Quality estimates that U.S. economic losses from architectural damage caused by air pollution amount to about $4.8 billion in direct costs and $5.2 billion in property value losses each year.

Visibility reduction

Foul air obscuring the skies above industrialized cities has long been recognized as a problem, but we have realized only recently that pollution affects rural areas as well. Even supposedly pristine places like our national parks are suffering from air pollution. Grand Canyon National Park, where maximum visibility used to be 300 km (185 mi), is now so smoggy on some winter days that visitors can't see the opposite rim only 20 km (12.5 mi) across the canyon. Mining operations, smelters, and power plants (some of which were moved to the desert to improve air quality in cities like Los Angeles) are the main culprits. Similarly, the vistas from Shenandoah National Park just outside Washington, DC, are so hazy that summer visibility is often less than 1.6 km (1 mi) because of smog drifting in from nearby urban areas.

Historical records show that over the past four or five decades human-caused air pollution has spread over much of the United States. John Trijonis of the Santa Fe Corporation reports that a gigantic "haze blob" as much as 3,000 km (about 2,000 mi) across covers much of the eastern United States in the summer, cutting visibility as much as 80 percent. Smog and haze are so prevalent, Trijonis says, that it's hard for people to believe that the air once was clear. Studies indicate, however, that if all humanmade sources of air pollution were shut down, the air would clear up in a few days and there would be about 150 km (90 mi) visibility nearly everywhere rather than the 15 km to which we have become accustomed.

Air Pollution Control

What can we do about air pollution? In this section we will look at some of the techniques that can be used to avoid creating pollutants or to clean up effluents before they are released. We also will look at some legislation that regulates pollutant emissions and ambient air quality.

Moving Pollution to Remote Areas

Among the earliest techniques for improving local air quality was moving pollution sources to remote locations and/or dispersing emissions with smokestacks. These approaches exemplify the attitude that "dilution is the solution to pollution." One electric utility, for example, ran newspaper and magazine ads in the early 1970s, claiming to be a "pioneer" in the use of tall smokestacks on its power plants to "disperse gaseous emissions widely in the atmosphere so that ground level concentrations would not be harmful to human health or property." The company claimed that their smoke would be "dissipated over a wide area and come down finally in harmless traces." Far from being harmless, however, those "traces" are the main source of many of our current problems. We are finding that there is no "away" to which we can throw our unwanted products. A far better solution to pollution is to prevent its release. We will now turn our attention to emission-control technology.

Particulate Removal

Filters remove particles physically by trapping them in a porols mesh of cotton cloth, spun glass fibers, or asbestos-cellulose, which allows air to pass through but holds back solids. Collection efficiency is relatively insensitive to fuel type, fly ash composition, particle size, or electrical properties. Filters are generally shaped into giant bags 10 to 15 meters long and 2 or 3 meters wide.

Effluent gas is blown into the bottom of the bag and escapes through the sides much like the bag on a vacuum cleaner. Every few days or weeks, the bags are opened to remove the dust cake. Thousands of these bags may be lined up in a "baghouse." These filters are usually much cheaper to install and operate than electrostatic filters.

Electrostatic precipitators are the most common particulate controls in power plants. Fly ash particles pick up an electrostatic surface charge as they pass between large electrodes in the effluent stream. This causes the particle to migrate to and accumulate on a collecting plate (the oppositely charged electrode). These precipitators consume a large amount of electricity, but maintenance is relatively simple and collection efficiency can be as high as 99 percent. Performance depends on particle size and chemistry, strength of the electric field, and flue gas velocity. The ash collected by all of these techniques is a solid waste (often hazardous due to the heavy metals and other trace components of coal or other ash source) and must be buried in landfills or other solid waste disposal sites.

Sulfur Removal

As we have seen earlier in this chapter, sulfur oxides are among the most damaging of all air pollutants in terms of human health and ecosystem damage. It is important to reduce sulfur loading. This can be done either by using low-sulfur fuel or by removing sulfur from effluents.

Fuel switching and fuel cleaning

Switching from soft coal with a high sulfur content to low-sulfur coal can greatly reduce sulfur emissions. This may eliminate jobs, however, in such areas as Appalachia that are already economically depressed. Changing to another fuel, such as natural gas or nuclear energy, can eliminate all sulfur emissions as well as those of particulates and heavy metals. Natural gas is more expensive and more difficult to ship and store than coal, however, and many people prefer the sure dangers of coal pollution to the uncertain dangers of nuclear power. Alternative energy sources, such as wind and solar power, are preferable to either fossil fuel or nuclear power, and are becoming economically competitive in many areas. In the interim, coal can be crushed, washed, and gassified to remove sulfur and metals before combustion. This improves heat content and firing properties but may replace air pollution with solid waste and water pollution problems.

Limestone injection and fluidized bed combustion

Sulfur emissions can be reduced as much as 90 percent by mixing crushed limestone with coal before it is fed into a boiler. Calcium in the limestone reacts with sulfur to make calcium sulfite ($CaSO_3$), calcium sulfate ($CaSO_4$), or gypsum ($CaSO_4.2H_2O$). In ordinary furnaces, this procedure creates slag, which fouls burner grates and reduces combustion efficiency.

A relatively new technique for burning, called fluidized bed combustion, offers several advantages in pollution control. In this procedure, a mixture of crushed coal and limestone particles about a meter (3 ft) deep is spread on a perforated distribution grid in the combustion chamber. When high-pressure air is forced through the bed, the surface of the fuel rises as much as one meter and resembles a boiling fluid as particles hop up and down. Oil is sprayed into the suspended mass to start the fire. During operation, fresh coal and limestone are fed continuously into the top of the bed, while ash and slag are drawn off from below. The rich air supply and constant motion in the bed make burning efficient and prevent buildup of large slag clinkers. Steam generator pipes are submerged directly into the fluidized bed, and heat exchange is more efficient than in the water walls of a conventional boiler.

More than 90 percent of SO_2 is captured by the limestone particles, and NO_x formation is reduced by holding temperatures around 800°C (1500°F) instead of twice that figure in other boilers. These low temperatures also preclude slag formation, which aids in maintenance. The efficient burning of this process makes it possible to use cheaper fuel, such as lignite or unwashed subbituminous coal, rather than higher priced hard coal.

Flue gas desulfurization

Crushed limestone, lime slurry, or alkali (sodium carbonate or bicarbonate) can be injected into a stack gas stream to remove sulfur after combustion. These processes are often called flue gas scrubbing. Spraying wet alkali solutions or limestone slurry is relatively inexpensive and effective, but maintenance can be difficult. Rock-hard plaster and ash layers coat the spray chamber and have to be chipped off regularly. Corrosive solutions of sulfates, chlorides, and fluorides erode metal surfaces. Electrostatic precipitators don't work well because of fouling and shorting of electrodes after wet scrubbing.

Dry alkali injection (spraying dry sodium bicarbonate into the flue gas) avoids many of the problems of wet scrubbing, but the expense of appropriate reagents is prohibitive in most areas. A hybrid procedure called spray drying has been tested successfully in pilot plant experiments. In this process, a slurry of pulverized limestone or slaked lime is atomized in the stack gas stream. The spray rate and droplet size are carefully controlled so that the water flash evaporates and a dry granular precipitate is produced. Passage through a baghouse filter removes both ash and sulfur very effectively.

As with coal washing, scrubbing often results in a trade-off of an air pollution problem for a solid waste disposal problem. Sulfur slag, gypsum, and other products of these processes can amount to three or four times as much volume as fly ash. A large power plant can produce millions of tons of waste per year.

Sulfur recovery processes

Instead of making a throwaway product that becomes a waste disposal problem, sulfur can be removed from effluent gases by processes that yield a usable product, such as elemental sulfur, sulfuric acid, or ammonium sulfate. Catalytic converters are used in these recovery processes to oxidize or reduce sulfur and to create chemical compounds that can be collected and sold. Markets have to be reasonably close for economic feasibility, and fly ash contamination must be reduced as much as possible.

Nitrogen Oxide Control

Undoubtedly the best way to prevent nitrogen oxide pollution is to avoid creating it. A substantial portion of the emissions associated with mining, manufacturing, and energy production could be eliminated through conservation. Staged burners, in which the flow of air and fuel are carefully controlled, can reduce nitrogen oxide formation by as much as 50 percent. This is true for both internal combustion engines and industrial boilers. Fuel is first burned at high temperatures in an oxygenpoor environment where NO_x cannot form. The residual gases then pass into an afterburner where more air is added and final combustion takes place in an air-rich, fuel-poor, low-temperature environment that also reduces NO_x formation. Stratified-charge engines and new orbital automobile engines use this principle to meet emission standards without catalytic converters.

The approach adopted by U.S. automakers for NO_x, reductions has been to use selective catalysts to change pollutants to harmless substances. Three-way catalytic converters use platinumpalladium and rhodium catalysts to remove up to 90 percent of NO_x, hydrocarbons, and carbon monoxide at the same time. Unfortunately, this approach doesn't work on diesel engines, power plants, smelters, and other pollution sources because of problems with back pressure, catalyst life, corrosion, and production of unwanted by-products, such as ammonium sulfate (NH_4SO_4), that foul the system.

Raprenox (rapid removal of nitrogen oxides) is a new technique for removing nitrogen oxides that was developed by the U.S. Department of Energy Sandia Laboratory in Livermore, California. Exhaust gases are passed through a container of common, nonpoisonous cyanuric acid. When heated to 350°C (662°F), cyanuric acid releases isocyanic acid gas, which reacts with NO_x to produce CO_2, CO, H_2O, and N_2. In small-scale diesel engine tests, this system eliminated 99 percent of the NO_x. Whether it will work in full-scale applications, especially in flue gases contaminated with fly ash, remains to be seen.

Hydrocarbon Controls

Hydrocarbons and volatile organic compounds are produced by incomplete combustion of fuels or solvent evaporation from chemical factories, painting, dry cleaning, plastic manufacturing, printing, and other industrial processes that use a variety of volatile organic chemicals. Closed systems that prevent escape of fugitive gases can reduce many of these emissions. In automobiles, for instance, positive crankcase ventilation (PCV) systems collect oil that escapes from around the pistons and unburned fuel and channels it back to the engine for combustion. Modification of carburetor and fuel systems prevents evaporation of gasoline. In the same way, controls on fugitive losses from valves, pipes, and storage tanks in industry can have a significant impact on air quality. Afterburners are often the best method for destroying volatile organic chemicals in industrial exhaust stacks. High air-fuel ratios in automobile engines and other burners minimize hydrocarbon and carbon monoxide emissions, but also cause excess nitrogen oxide production. Careful monitoring of air-fuel inputs and oxygen levels in exhaust gases can minimize all these pollutants.

Clean Air Legislation

Throughout history, there have been countless ordinances prohibiting emission of objectionable smoke, odors, and noise. Air pollution traditionally has been treated as a local problem, however, to be regulated by local authorities. The Clean Air Act of 1963 was the first national legislation in the United States aimed at air pollution control. Federal grants were provided to states to combat pollution, but the act was careful to preserve states' rights to set and enforce air quality regulations. It soon became obvious that some pollution problems cannot be solved on a local basis.

In 1970, an extensive set of amendments essentially rewrote the Clean Air Act. These amendments identified the "criteria pollutants" discussed earlier in this chapter, and established national ambient air quality standards. These standards are divided into two categories. *Primary standards* are intended to protect human health, while *secondary standards* are set to protect materials, crops, climate, visibility, and personal comfort. Primary and secondary standards are generally the same for most pollutants.

Ambient standards assume that pollutants have no adverse effects beyond certain thresholds. They also assume that pollutants arising from numerous diverse sources are more reasonably and effectively regulated by setting maximum total levels in the atmosphere than by regulating individual emissions. Some environmentalists disagree with both of these assumptions. These standards are the basis of a warning system called the Air Pollutant Standards Index.

In 1990, after many years of acrimonious debate and political maneuvering, the Clean Air Act was extensively rewritten and updated. Important provisions included the following:

1. *Acid rain.* Sulfur dioxide releases will be cut from 24 million tons in 1990 to 10 million tons in 2000 by requiring the 111 largest sulfur emitters to meet strict standards. Nitrogen oxide emissions were reduced from 6 million tons in 1990 to 4 million tons per year.
2. *Urban smog.* Motor vehicle tailpipe emissions of hydrocarbons and nitrogen oxides were reduced 35 percent and 60 percent,

respectively, in all new cars. Oil companies are required to offer alternative fuels, such as methanol or ethanol (sometimes called oxygenated fuels), hydrogen, or compressed natural gas (methane) in cities with the worst pollution problems. Cities not meeting air quality standards for ozone and smog are divided into five categories (marginal, moderate, serious, severe, and extreme); deadlines for attaining standards are set for three, six, nine, fifteen, and twenty years, respectively.

3. *Toxic air pollutants.* Although the EPA has had authority to set emission standards for air toxics since 1970, only seven (beryllium, mercury, asbestos, lead, vinyl chloride, benzene, and PCBs) were regulated. Now 189 chemicals are listed in about 250 source categories (chemical factories, dry cleaners, coke furnaces, printing plants, etc.). The largest polluters will be required to install the best available technology to reduce emissions 90 percent by 2003. The EPA estimates that toxic emissions will be reduced by about 500,000 tons per year if full compliance is achieved.
4. *Ozone protection.* Chlorofluorocarbons and carbon tetrachl-oride will be phased out by the year 2000. Recovery and recycling programs for existing CFCs have been instituted. Methyl chloroform will be outlawed by 2002. Hydrochloro-fluorocarbons in aerosol cans and insulation will be phased out by 2030. Although these regulations already have reduced chlorine emissions, CFC smuggling from developing countries such as Mexico-where they are still cheap and legal-has become a serious problem.
5. *Marketing pollution rights.* Corporations are allowed to offset emissions by buying, selling, and "banking" pollution rights from other factories at an expected savings of $2 billion to $3 billion per year. This is a controversial freemarket approach that may make economic sense for industry and environmental sense on average but may be disastrous for some localities.
6. *Toxic organic compounds.* Rather than specify a single number for maximum admissible emissions or ambient air concentrations of volatile organic chemicals, these compounds now are regulated by hundreds of pages of detailed standards specifying designs of manufacturing or storage facilities, operating conditions, sampling methods, control or mitigation techniques, recordkeeping, and maintenance. These rules stipulate minute details such as specific types of valves and pumps to be used or the color of paint for storage tank tops.

In 1997, yet another set of changes to the U.S. Clean Air Act was approved by Congress and signed into law. Ambient ozone standards will be lowered from 0.12 ppm to 0.08 ppm. Soot and dust emission standards will apply to particles 2.5 microns or more in diameter rather than the previous 10 micron limit. To meet these new requirements, factories and power plants will have to clean up their smokestacks; auto pollution will have to be reduced either by getting cars off the road or by switching to new technologies such as electric vehicles. Under the worst conditions, homeowners might be forbidden from using fireplaces, two-cycle gasoline engines, highly volatile paints, solvents, and other sources of hydrocarbons.

The EPA estimates that costs of these measures could be as high as $8.5 billion per year, but that they should save 15,000 lives, cut hospital admissions for respiratory illnesses by 9,000, and reduce chronic bronchitis cases by 60,000 each year. Industry groups complain that costs will be up to ten times as high and that evidence for health benefits is shaky. Many cities and counties that had finally reached accord with earlier, less stringent standards, will now find themselves once more out of compliance.

The EPA won't fully implement these latest standards for ozone and fine soot until 2008 to give states a chance to set up monitoring systems and to find ways to eliminate pollution in the most cost-effective manner. During this time, controversy and political maneuvering over air regulations undoubtedly will continue. As you can see from this history of air pollution control, environmental protection tends to be a long, convoluted process. Regulations often are applied in an incremental and somewhat erratic manner.

California has gone further than the federal government in making specific plans for air pollution control. The South Coast Air Quality Management District has adopted 160 rules to clean the air in the Los Angeles Basin. If these measures are successful, smog-causing emissions could be reduced by 70 percent. By the year 2000, visibility would increase from a 10-mi current average to 60 mi. The number of days when the air is considered hazardous to breathe would decrease from 150 per year to 0 per year.

Reaching these goals will require substantial lifestyle changes for most Californians. Aerosol hair sprays, deodorants, charcoal lighter fluid, gasoline-powered lawnmowers, and drivethrough burger stands could be banned. More than 3,000 consumer products including automotive polishes, spot removers, herbicides, lubricants, and floor wax strippers must meet new pollution limits. Paints and cleaning solutions would have to contain fewer volatile solvents. Radial tires and more stringent emission controls would be mandated for automobiles. Clean-burning oxygenated fuels or electric motors would be required for all vehicles. Car pooling would be encouraged, parking lots would be restricted, and limits would be placed on the number of cars a family could have.

California's land-use zones and housing codes might have to be changed to accommodate new commuting patterns. Substantial relocations could result. The cost is estimated to be about 60 cents per person per day. Opponents argue that the price tag could be as high as $15 billion a year and 30,000 lost jobs. Whether Californians, or any of us, care enough about health and the environment to make these changes and pay these costs remains to be seen.

Current Conditions and Future Prospects

Although we have not yet achieved the Clean Air Act goals in many parts of the United States, air quality has improved dramatically in the last decade in terms of the major large-volume pollutants. For twenty-three of the largest U.S. cities, the number of days in which air quality reached the hazardous level (PSI greater than 300) is down 93 percent from an average of 1.8 days/year a decade ago to 0.13 days/year now. Of 97 metropolitan areas that failed to meet clean air standards in the 1980s, 41 were in compliance in 1991-92. For many cities, this was the first time they met air quality goals in twenty years. Still, the EPA estimates that some 86 million Americans breathe unhealthy air at least part of the time.

The EPA estimates that emissions of particulate materials are down 78 percent, lead is down 98 percent, $S0_2$ is down 32 percent, and CO is down 23 percent over the past 25 years. Industrial cities, such as Chicago, Pittsburgh, and Philadelphia, that suffered "smokestack" pollution have had 90 percent reductions in number of days exceeding NAAQS maxima. Filters, scrubbers, and precipitators on power plants and other large stationary sources are responsible for most of the particulate and SO_2 reductions. Catalytic converters on automobiles are responsible for most of the CO and O_3 reductions. The only conventional "criteria" pollutant that has not dropped significantly is NO_x, which had risen 300 percent since 1940, and is up 14 percent since 1970.

Because automobiles are the main source of NO_x, cities where pollution is largely from traffic still have serious air quality problems.

Los Angeles, Anaheim, and Riverside, California, are the only cities in the country in the extreme urban smog category. Industrial cities such as Baltimore, New York City, Chicago, Gary, Houston, Milwaukee, Muskegon, Philadelphia, and San Diego also have continuing problems. Eighty-five other urban areas are still considered nonattainment regions. In spite of these local failures, however, 80 percent of the United States now meets the NAAQS goals. This improvement in air quality is perhaps the greatest environmental success story in our history.

The outlook is not so encouraging in other parts of the world, however. The major metropolitan areas of many developing countries are growing at explosive rates to incredible sizes, and environmental quality is abysmal in many of them. The composite average annual levels of SO_2 in Tehran, Iran, for instance, are more than 150 tg/m^3, and peak levels can be up to ten times higher. Mexico City remains notorious for bad air. Pollution levels exceed WHO health standards 350 days per year and more than half of all city children have lead levels in their blood sufficient to lower intelligence and retard development. Its 131,000 industries and 2.5 million vehicles spew out more than 5,500 tons of air pollutants daily. Santiago, Chile, averages 299 days per year on which suspended particulates exceed WHO standards of 90 $\mu g/m^3$.

While there are few statistics on China's pollution situation, it is known that many of China's 400,000 factories have no air pollution controls. Experts estimate that home coal burners and factories emit 10 million tons of soot and 15 million tons of sulfur dioxide annually and that emissions have increased rapidly over the past twenty years. Sheyang, an industrial city in northern China, is thought to have the world's worst particulate problem with peak winter concentrations over 700 tg/m^3 (nine times U.S. maximum standards). Airborne particulates in Sheyang exceed WHO standards on 347 days per year. Beijing, Xian, and Guangzhou are nearly as bad. The high incidence of cancer in Shanghai is thought to be linked to air pollution.

As political walls came down across Eastern Europe and the Soviet Union at the end of the 1980s, horrifying environmental conditions in these centrally planned economies were revealed. Inept industrial managers, a rigid bureaucracy, and lack of democracy have created ecological disasters. Where governments own, operate, and regulate industry, there are few checks and balances or incentives to clean up pollution. Much of the Eastern bloc depends heavily on soft brown coal for its energy and pollution controls are absent or highly inadequate.

Southern Poland, northern Czech Republic, and Slovakia are covered most of the time by a permanent cloud of smog from factories and power plants. Acid rain is eating away historic buildings and damaging already inadequate infrastructures. The haze is so dark that drivers must turn on their headlights during the day. Residents complain that washed clothes turn dirty before they can dry. Zabrze, near Katowice in southern Poland, has particulate emissions of 3,600 metric tons per square kilometer. This is more than seven times the emissions in Baltimore, Maryland, or Birmingham, Alabama, the dirtiest cities (for particulates) in the United States. Home gardening in Katowice has been banned because vegetables raised there have unsafe levels of lead and cadmium.

For miles around the infamous Romanian "black town" of Copsa Mica, the countryside is so stained by soot that it looks as if someone had poured black ink over everything. Birth defects afflict 10 percent of infants in northern Bohemia. Workers in factories there get extra hazard pay-burial money, they call it. Life expectancy in these industrial towns is as much as ten years less than the national average. Espenhain, in the industrial belt of the former East Germany, has one of the world's highest rates of sulfur dioxide pollution. One of every two children has lung problems, and one of every three has heart problems. Brass doorknobs and name plates have been eaten away by the acidic air in just a few months.

Not all is pessimistic, however. There have been some spectacular successes in air pollution control. Sweden and West Germany (countries affected by forest losses due to acid precipitation) cut their sulfur emissions by two-thirds between 1970 and 1985. Austria and Switzerland have gone even further. They even regulate motorcycle emissions. The Global Environmental Monitoring System (GEMS) reports declines in particulate levels in 26 of 37 cities worldwide. Sulfur dioxide and sulfate particles, which cause acid rain and respiratory disease, have declined in 20 of these cities.

Ten years ago, Cubatao, Brazil, was described as the "Valley of Death," one of the most dangerously polluted places in the world. A steel plant, a huge oil refinery, and fertilizer and chemical factories churned out thousands of tons of air pollutants every year. Trees died on the surrounding hills. Birth defects and respiratory diseases were alarmingly high. Since then, however, the citizens of Cubatao have made remarkable progress in cleaning up their environment. The end of military rule and restoration of democracy allowed residents to publicize their complaints. The environment became an important political issue. The state of Sao Paulo invested about \$100 million, and the private sector spent twice as much to clean up most pollution sources in the valley. Particulate pollution was reduced 75 percent. Ammonia emissions were reduced 97 percent, hydrocarbons that cause ozone and smog were cut 86 percent, and sulfur dioxide production fell 84 percent. Fish are returning to the rivers, and forests are regrowing on the mountains. Progress is possible! We hope that similar success stories will be obtainable elsewhere.

Air pollution is not a new problem; it has been around for centuries. Over three centuries ago, the noted scientist and diarist John Evelyn described with great accuracy many of the effects of the air pollution arising from the combustion of coal : reduction in sunshine, morbidity and mortality from respiratory ailments, dust fall, corrosion of materials. Only in the 20th century, and especially the last few decades, have extensive experimental and epidemiological studies been carried out to verify these effects scientifically.

According to WHO, air pollution may be defined as follows

"Substances but into air by the activity of mankind into concen tration suffcient to cause harmful effect to his health, vegetable., property or to interfere with the enjoyment of his property"

Air pollution is considered to be one of the most dangerous and common kind. of environmental pollution that has been reported in most industrial towns and metropolitans of India and abroad such as Delhi, Bombay, Kolkatta, Kanpur, Chennai, Hyderabad, Jaipur, Ahmedabad, Nagpur, Firozabad and also in London, New York Tokyo, Pittsburg, etc. The first case of severe air pollution in modern times ocurred in the Meuse valley of Belgium in 1930; a killing smog in Donora, Pennsylvania along the Monongahela River in 1948, in which hundreds people died ; deadlier smog in London in 1952 in which 4,000 to 5,000 people died from respiratory failure ; "Episode 104" which blanketed all or part of 22 states east of the Mississipi, with air pollution haze in August, 1969 ; a massive hood of stagnant air stretched from Chicago and Milwaukee South to New Orleans and east to Philadelphia, creating dangerous air pollution level in rural as well urban areas. According to Newell (1971) 164 million metric tons of artificial pollutants enter the United Stated air every year.

BHOPAL GAS TRAGEDY (1984)

The MIC gas leak in Bhopal in 1984 has been regarded the worst industrial accident which is related to air pollution. Around 2,00,000

Bhopal residents were affected by the leak of poisonous MIC gas from the Union Carbide Pesticide plant there. Atleast 5000 people were killed and doctors estimated that some 50,000 people have been seriously affected and many go blind.

MIC i.e., Methyl-iso-cyanate is a toxic gas used in the manufacture of pesticides. It reacts quickly with water and causes the lungs to swell and eyes to develop cataract. Many died in Bhopal because their lungs had filled with fluid.

Bhopal's victims continue to die. Out of every 3 children born to women who were pregnant on the night of the disaster, only one survived. Out of 1,350 new born babies, 16 were physically deformed and 60 premature births. Deformities include children suffering from Coginital hearts, holes in arms and impaired eye sight. High levels of thiocyanates were detected in water in Bhopal and continued exposure to this may cause adverse functioning of organs like thyroid, which in turn may effect pregnancy.

The vegetation in an areas of 3.5 sq. km. around the Union Carbide factory at Bhopal was severally affected. Leaves bore the burnt of the damages. Consumption of fruit from trees in affected localities-especially ber, mango, papaya and tamarind was avoided for that season. Cultivated plants were more damaged than the wild plants. Plants submerged in water were less affected than the plants exposed to the gas.

Sources and Emission of Air Pollutants

A major source of air pollution has been the particulate and gaseous matter which gets released by the burning of fossil fuels such as coal, petroleum. etc. Out of this comes a variety of emissions :

1. Fine particles (less than 100μ in diameter), which include carbon particles, metallic dusts, tars, resins, aerosols, solid oxides, nitrates, and sulphates;
2. Coarser particles (over 200μm), largely carbon particles and heavy dust that is quickly removed by gravity from the air;
3. Sulphur compounds;
4. Nitrogen compounds;
5. Oxygen compounds;
6. Halogens; and
7. Radioactive substances.

These pollutants have been artificial pollutants and they are poured in air mainly by at least five major fuel-burning sources. *Automobiles* (cars, scooters, motorcycles) have been regarded the greatest sources of air pollution. They produce nearly two-thirds of the carbon monoxide and one-half of the hydrocarbons and nitrous oxides. The automobile exhaust has also leaded gas and particulate lead. *Electrical power plants* burning fossil fuels, particularly coal and sometimes petrol or diesel, produce two-thirds of the sulphur dioxides. *Industrial processors* like metallurgical plants and smelters, chemical plants, petroleum refineries, pulp and paper mills, sugar mills cotton mills, and synthetic rubber manufacturing plants have been responsible for about one-fifth of the air pollution. *Heating plants* for homes, apartments, schools, and industrial buildings are the fourth largest source of air pollution. The *transportation industry* exclusive of automobiles and including railroads, ships, aircrafts, trucks, buses, tractors etc., have been contributing the same type of pollutants as cars.

Other sources of air pollution minor in quantities, but bear significance due to to the harmful substances the release have been agriculture, which is responsible for pesticides, dust from agriculture practices and field burning, and the construction industry.

Nature too adds few natural pollutants like pollen, hydrocarbons released by vegetation, dusts from deserts, storms, and volcanic activity.

The typical composition of unpolluted dry air has, been given in Table 6.3 together with the total masses of the individual gases in the atmosphere. The composition listed has been by volume (or numbers of molecules); mass percentages can be determined by multiplying the volume percentages by the molecular weight of the gas molecule and dividing by 29, the average molecular weight of air. The volume percentages of gases present in trace amounts (under 19 ppm) are not accurately known; the SO_2 concentration has been estimated at from 0.0002 to 0.002 ppm, for example. It will be noticed that the mass of the atmosphere has been so great that the total mass of even a trace gas has been quite large.

The estimated emissions of the five primary air pollutantscarbon monoxide (CO), particulate matter, sulphur oxides (SO_x) expressed as SO_2 hydrocarbons (HC), and nitrogen oxide (NO_x, mainly NO and NO_2) expressed as NO_2—are shown in Table elsewhere in this chapter, with a breakdown according to source. These have been the estimates for 1982 and are based on studies of a great many different sources but do not include some industries and other sources for which emission factors are not known. Some other sources are discussed later in this chapter.

It will be seen by comparison with Table 6.3, the annual emisions are often significant in comparison with total amounts ins the atmosphere.

Table 6.3. The composion of unpolluted dry air and the approximate total masses of the different constituents of the atmosphere. Many trace gases are not listed.

Constituent	*Molecular Formula*	*Volume Fraction*	*Total mass (millions of metric tons)*
Nitrogen	N_2	78.09%	3,850,000,000
Oxygen	O_2	20.94%	1,180,000,000
Argon	Ar	0.93%	65,000,000
Carbon dioxide	CO_2	0.032%	2,500,000
Neon	Ne	18 ppm	64,000
Helium	He	5.2 ppm	3,700
Methane	CH_4	1.3 ppm	3,700
Krypton	Kr	1 ppm	15,000
Hydrogen	H_2	0.5 ppm	180
Nitrous oxide	N_2O	0.25 ppm	1,900
Carbon monoxide	CO	0.1 ppm	500
Ozone	O_3	0.02 ppm	200
Sulfur dioxide	SO_2	0.001 ppm	11
Nitrogen dioxide	NO_2	0.001 ppm	8

Man-made air pollution in urban areas is often referred to as. "smog." The word "smog" was apparently coined about 1905 by Dr. H.A. Des Voeux, an active organizer of British smoke abatement societies, to describe the "smoke-fog" of the London pea-soupers. Today, the London-type smog has been often referred to as "classical" smog, while the Los Angeles-types smog, which is quite different, is referred to as "photochemical" smog because it is formed through chemical reactions involving sunlight. Table 6.4 lists some of the characteristics of the two types of smog.

Methods of Detection and Measurement of Air Pllution

Air pollution is generally measured by sampling of air by thermal and by *electrostastic precipitation*, *Sonkin impactor* and *electrostatic dust collectors*. The practiculate pollution is measured 'by the instrument called *deposit gauge* or by *Owen's dust counter*. The thickness of the smoke is measured by *Liegean sphere* and by *Ringelmann chart*. The rough estimation of SO_2 in air could be made by chemical analysis of the dust collected in a diposit gauge or by a *bubbler method*. Flourides have been estimated by colour reactions.

Table 6.4. Characteristics of "classical" and "photochemical" smogs.

Characteristics	*"Classical"*	*Photochemical*
First occurrence noted	London	Los Angeles
Principal pollutants	Sulphur oxides, particulate matter	Ozone, nitrogen oxides, hydrocarbons, carbon monoxide, free radicals
Principal sources	Industrial and household fuel combusion (coal, petroleum)	Motor vehicle fuel combustion (petroleum)
Effects of humans	Lung and throat irritation	Eye irritation
Effects on compounds	Reducing	Oxidizing
Time of occurrence of worst episodes,	Winter months (especially in early morning)	Around midday of summer months

In order to measure and control the magnitude of air pollution in various industrial centres of India, National Environmental Engineering Research Institute (NEERI) has estiblished air monitoring stations in Mumbai, Kolkatta, Delhi, Chennai, Hyderabad, Kanpur, Jaipur, Ahmedabad and Nagpur. In one of the Survey conducted by NEERI in 1980 to measure the air pollution by sulphur dioxide (SO_2) and suspended particles in some major cities of India. It is found that Chembur-Trombay area of Mumbai is having highest SO_2 pollution, while, New Delhi is having highest air pollution of suspended particulate matter. In another survey, Kolkatta is reported to have highest carbon monoxide pollution during peak traffic hours.

Air Pollutants

Pollutants present in the air are present in gaseous form as well as in the form of particles.

Sulphur Oxides

The most important sulphur oxide emitted by pollution sources has been sulphur dioxide (SO_2), although some sulphur trioxide (SO_2) is also generally produced, in amounts no more than a few percent of the SO_2 produced. SO_2 is a colorless, nonflammable gas which has an acrid taste at concentrations less than I ppm of air and which has a pungent, irritating odour at concentrations above about 3 ppm.

SO_2 readily gets oxidized to SO_2 in the atmosphere by photochemical or catalytic processes, and in the presence of moisture the SO_2 becomes sulphuric acid or a sulphate salt and soon precipitates out of the atmosphere. The SO_2 in the atmosphere lasts only a few days at most and this is the reason that the SO_2 mass in the atmosphere is so small compared to annual emissions by man.

Actually only about one-third of the sulphur oxides in the atmosphere are believed to be produced by man's activities. Robinson and Robbins have estimated that sulphur oxides from man's activities introduce 66 million metric tons of sulphur (or 132 million metric tons of sulphur dioxide) into the atmosphere annually, largely from coal and petroleum combustion,. Natural sulfur sources are biologically produced hydrogen sulphide (H_2S) (arising from decay of organic matter) that is eventually oxidized to sulphur oxides and sulphates from sea spray. About 69% of the total sulphur and 93° of the man-made sulphur arise in the northern hemisphere.

Table 6.5. Gaseous sulphur pollutants from urban sources, in millions of metric tons of sulphur annually

Source	*Amount of sulfur*
Coal combustion	46
Petroleum combustion and refining	13
Copper smelting	6
Lead and zinc smelting	1.3
Total man-made	66
Biological H_2S from land	62
Biological H_2S from seas	27
Sulphates in sea spray	40
Total natural	129
Total	195

Individual SO_2 concentrations exhibited a log-normal frequency distribution (i.e., the logarithms of the SO_2 concentrations exhibited a normal, or Gaussian, distribution) and some very high values were encountered for short periods of time. The data showed that the 1-h maximum values for the year were about 10 to 20 times the annual average and 1-day maximum values for the year were about 4 to 7 times the annual average. Thus a city with an annual average of 0.10 ppm can be expected to have up to 0.4 to 0.7 ppm for the worst day of the year and 1 to 2 ppm for the worst hour of the year. Much higher concentrations can occur near single point sources of SO_2, such as coal-fired power plants, where levels of several ppm are not uncommon.

Sulphur oxides can damage materials and property, mainly through their conversion into the highly reactive sulfuric acid. Discoloration and physical deterioration are produced in building materials (limestone, marble, roofing slate, and mortar) and sculpture. The corrosion of most metals, especially iron, steel, and zinc, is accelerated by atmospheres polluted by SO_2 ; particulate matter, humidity, and elevated temperatures play important synergistic roles. Deterioration and fading are also produced in fabrics (such as cotton, nylon, and rayon), leather, and paper. The drying time, brittleness, gloss, and even color of paints can also be affected.

SO_2 also affects vegetation adversely even at concentrations below 0.03 ppm. High concentrations over short periods of tune can produce acute leaf injury, such as necrotic,(tissue-destroying blotching of broad-leaved plants and grasses or brownish discoloration in the tips of pine needles. Lower concentrations over longer periods causes chronic leaf injury, such as a gradual yellowing (chlorosis) as chlorophyll production is impeded. SO_2 and H_2SO_4 are both capable of irritating the respiratory system of animals and men. The levels needed to produce pathological lung change or mortality in animals are much greater than the levels encountered in urban atmospheres but the latter are capable of producing adverse health effects.

The mechanism by which SO_2 damage plants is not well understood. The gas is absorbed after passing through the stomata of the leaves and is oxidized in the tissues to sulphutic acid or sulphate salts. The damaging action has been ascribed to the result of the oxidizing or reducing properties of sulphur dioxide by itself and not due to the action of acid. Formation of sulphuric acid or sulphate keeps $S0_2$ concentration to a low level. Sulphuric acid aerosols have been generally toxic to plants although emission of large droplets from factories are known to injure vegetation. SO_2 is also involved in the erosion of many building materials like limestone, marble, the slate used in roofing, mortar and deterioration of statues. This specially occurs near SO_2 emitting source viz., petroleum refineries, smelters, kraft paper mills, etc.

Hydrogen Sulphide

It is a colourless toxic gas which is having a penetrating odour resembling rotten eggs.

The principal natural resources of H_2S have been decaying vegetation and animal material, especially in shallow aquatic and marine environments. It has been also produced by sulphur springs, volcanic discharges, coal pits and sewers. It is estimated that about 30 million tons yr^{-1} of MS are given out by ocean and 60 to 80 'million tons yr^{-1} by land. Industrial H_2S emission does not exceed 3 million tons yr^{-1}. The important industrial sources of H_2S include the users of sulphur containing fuels. H_2S normally, does not appear to he the serious pollutant, as it gets oxidized instantaneously to elemental sulphur and sulphur dioxide.

Exposure to hydrogen sulphide results in leaf lesions, defoliation and reduced growth. Sulphur dioxide paralyses or destroys bronchial cilia in air passage of man, constricts bronchiae, damages lungs, lowers resistance to pneumonia and influenza and causes bronchitis, emphysema and irritation of mucous membrane. A low concentration of H_2S causes headache, nausea lassitude collapse, coma and death. An unpleasent odour destroys the apetite of some people at 5 ppm. A concentration of 150 ppm may bring about conjuctivitis and irritation of the mucous membrances. Exposure to a concentration of 500 ppm for 15 to 20 minutes may be serious causing colic diarrhea, and bronchial pneumonia. Brief exposure to H_2S at 700 to 900 ppm has been fatal H_2S readily passes through the alveolar membrane of the lungs and penetrates to the blood stream. Death may take place within a few seconds from even one or two inhalations. Death also occurs from respiratory failure. The MAC for an 8-hour day is 20 ppm.

Carbon Monoxide

Carbon monoxide (CO) is a colorless, tasteless, odorless gas against which man cannot easily protect himself. It originates from the incomplete combustion of carbonaceous materials and is the air pollutant emitted in the largest quantities.

Surprisingly little is known accurately about the sources and sinks of CO in the atmosphere ; these are currently being actively studied. Man's activities are producing perhaps 250 million metric tons annually and there exist some biological sources of CO, although not much is known about them. It has been found, for example, that the oceans are a natural source of CO although they probably produce only 10 million metric tons annually, and that considerable CO is present in rainwater. The average concentration of CO in the atmosphere is not well-known either and the value of 0.1 ppm is only an estimate, which might be several times too large or too small.

CO can be oxidized to carbon dioxide (CO_2), but the rate at, which this occurs seems to be very slow and mixtures of CO and O_2 exposed to sunlight for several years have remained almost unchanged. As the residence time of CO in the atmosphere is at most only a few months, some' removal process must exist. Perhaps the CO gets adsorbed and oxidized on surfaces ; perhaps it is removed and utilized by plants or animals ; or perhaps photo chemical or catalytic processes are involved in its removal. Recent research reports that soils are capable of removing large amounts of CO from the atmosphere, probably due to the activity of soil microorganisms.

The toxic effects of CO on human beings and animals arise from its reversible combination with hemoglobin (Hb) in the blood :

$$HbO_2 + CO \rightleftharpoons HbCO + O_2$$

Hemoglobin is having a much greater affinity for CO than it does for O_2, and when O_2 and CO are present in sufficient quantities to saturate the hemoglobin, the concentrations of HbO_2 (oxyhemoglobin) and HbCO (carboxyhemoglobin) are related by the Haldane equation

$$\frac{[HbCO]}{[HbO_2]} = M\frac{p(CO)}{p(O_2)}$$

where $p(CO)$ and $p(O_2)$ denote the partial pressures (or volume concentrations) of the CO and O, gases and M is a constant that depends on the species. For man, M is about 200 to 300, while in rabbits it is less than half this value. As the ordinary air contains about 21% O_2, the ratio of HbCO to HbO_2 in man is approximately equal to 1/1000 of the CO concentration expressed in ppm.

It generally takes a few hours to reach this equilibrium but the time is decreased by increased respiration rates.

The combination of hemoglobin with CO lessens the oxygencarrying capacity of the blood so that less O_2 is available to the body cells. It also reduces the dissociation of oxyhemoglobin (HbO_2) into hemoglobin and oxygen so that anoxia (oxygen starva tion) may result even though the blood is carrying several times as much O_2 as the body requires. It is thought that CO may also impair cell functioning by blocking oxidation in other ways as well.

The approximate HbCO levels (compared to total HbCO+ HbO2) at which different symptoms occur are as follows

0.0-0.1 No observable symptoms, but some evidence of physiologic stress may be detectable.

0.1-0.2 Labored respiration during exertion.

0.2-0.3	Headache.
0.3-0.4	Muscular weakness, nausea, dizziness.
0.4-0.5	Slurring of speech, tendency to collapse.
0.5-0.6	Convulsions.
0.6-0.7	Fatal coma if duration of poisoning is prolonged.
0.8	Instantaneous death.

CO levels low enough to give only 20% HbCO have been known to kill when the victim remained in the poisonous atmosphere and this corresponds to only about 250 ppm CO. The most effective treatment for CO poisoning is to place the victim in a hyperbaric (high-pressure) chamber with 2 to 2.5 atm of O_2 ; this speeds up elimination of the CO and, more importantly, it also corrects tissue anoxia by providing large amounts of dissolved O_2 in the blood plasma, permitting the body to bypass the hemoglobin mechanism.

Smokers who smoke a pack of cigarettes daily and inhale the smoke may have blood HbCO levels of 5% or more. Although these levels do not lead to clinical symptoms, they have been associated with impairment of mental performance and visual acuity and other functions, and little is known of the affects of chromic exposure to low levels of CO on human health, behaviour, and performance. There is some epidemiological evidence suggesting that weekly average CO concentrations of around 10 ppm may produce increased mortality among hospitalized heart patients and that blood HbCO levels above 5% in patients with heart disease is associated with physiologic stress.

At present, the most dangerous results of exposure to carbon monoxide have been the serious intoxications and even death that occur from CO production in closed areas-from automobile exhausts in garages (or exhaust fumes leaking into the interior of the automobile), blocked furnace flues in homes, etc. Several hundred die from CO poisoning each year ; many of them are suicides.

In the developed countries cigarettes have been linked to atleast 80% of all deaths from lung cancer, to 75% from chronic bronchitis and emphysema, and to 25% from ischaemic heart disease. On the contrary, Dr. M. Sandler, a renowned neurologist says that cigarette smoking helps to develop immunity to the dreaded Parkinson's disease, affecting nervous system and characterised by tremors, muscular rigidity and emaciation. "*Pyridine*", one of the numerous substances released into the body while smoking, acts as protective agent against Parkinson's disease, probably by competing with other toxic substances and blocking the impact on neuroreceptors.

Non-smokers, who work or live in company of a smoker run a substantial risk of having heart attack or developing cancer. Swadish experts evidenced this. Mrs. Gun Palm, a non-smoker developed lung cancer and also tumour and metastases in the brain in 1980, who shared a poorly ventilated office in Stockholm with smoker-collegues, says "world Health" magazine of the WHO. She died in Fabruary, 1982 of passive smoking at age of 55.

Most plants are insensitive to CO levels known to affect man, but at higher concentrations (100 to 10,000 ppm), it affects leaf drop, leaf curling, reduction in leaf size, premature aging, etc. CO is supposed to inhibit cellular respiration in plants by reacting with cytochrome oxidase enzyme system.

Hydrogen Fluorides

Active volcanoes have been the natural sources of fluorides in the atmosphere. These have been also emitted from aluminium, steel and electrochemical reduction plants, blast furnaces, brick, the and superphosphate fertilizer industries and from the combustion of coal.

Fluroride burns the tip of leaves. Low amounts impair plant growth, give rise to excessive dropping of bloom and fruits, developmeat of small, partially or completely seedless fruits, and premature formation of soft red flesh and spliting of peach.

Hydrogen Chloride

It is infrequently given out by accidental spills from chemical manufacturing plants. Besides, it gets released from combustion of coal, paper, plastics and chlorinated hydrocarbons, and ignition of solid-fuel rocked engines.

Hydrogen chloride has been reported to be responsible for the abaxial glazing of leaves caused by collapse and plasmolysis of epidermal cells. High concentrations give rise to nectrotic lesions.

Hydrocarbons

Hydrocarbons are chemical compounds having only carbon and hydrogen. The light hydrocarbons are gaseous at ordinary temperatures. Methane occurs naturally and is the principal-constituent of the fuel known as natural gas ; it is colorless and odorless (the odor of natural gas is due to sulfur compounds added so that humans can detect it). Ethylene and propane are also gases.

Biological decomposition of organic matter, seepage from natural gas and oil-fields and volatile emissions from plants have been the major causes for the release of hydrocarbons such as methane, ethylene and aniline. Incomplete combustion of fuels, motor vehicles exhaust, petroleum-refineries, agricultural burning, motor fuel marketing, manufacture of explosives and cracking of natural gas in petrochemical plants have been, the anthropogenic sources that emit hydrocarbons.

Ethylene makes yellowing and occasional necrosis of leaves, chlorisis of floral buds, inhibition of terminal growth, shortening of internodes, thickness of stems, lack of apical dominance, reduced growth, dry sepal diseases of orchids and decrease in amount of chlorophyll and cardenoids. In man, hydrocarbons causes irritation of mucous membrance, bronchial constriction and eye irritation ; some of these are reported to trigger development of lung cancer in experimental animals. We are also aware of the harm done by methyl isocynate which accidently leaked out from the storage tanks of the pesticide factory in Bhopal on December 2, 1984 killing over 4000 people and seriously affecting lakhs of residents.

Ammonia

Refrigerator pre-cooler system of cold storage, manufacture of anhydrous amonium fertilizers and nitric acids, domestic incineration have been the prime generators of ammonia.

It is able to induce bleaching of leaves, rusty spots on leaves and flowers, reduction of root and shoot growth, browning and softening of fruits, development of dark, corky lenticels in apples and reduction in the rate of seed germination.

Nitrogen Oxides

Although many different oxides of nitrogen are known (including laughing gas, which is nitrous oxide, N_2O), only nitric oxide (NO) and nitrogen dioxide (NO_2) are emitted to the atmosphere by man in significant quantities. They are formed by reaction of the nitrogen and oxygen in the atmosphere when combustion takes place at high temperatures (typically exceeding 1100°C) and cooling takes place fast enough to prevent decomposition

$$N_2 + xO_2 \rightleftharpoons 2NO_x$$

Usually less than 0.5% of the NO_x is initially emitted as NO_2.

Robinson and Robbins have estimated that biological production of NO and N_3O amounts to about 1 billion metric tons annu- ally, while man's combustion processes produce about 48 million metric tons of NO_x (expressed as NO_2) annually. These emissions are important parts of the environmental nitrogen cycle, although biological ammonia (NH_3) production of over 1 billion metric tons annually is also significant.

The concentrations of NO and NO_2 in nonurban areas are only a few parts per billion, however, and these gases have a residence time in the atmosphere of only 3 or 4 days.

Man-made NO_x pollution has been significant in urban areas because peak NO concentrations are often above 1 ppm and NO_2 levels occasionally exceed 0.5 ppm. These oxides both play an important role in the production of photochemical smog.

Nitrogen oxides have been reported to produce fading dyes and additives deterioration of cotton and nylon, and corrosion of metals due to production of particulate nits. The concentrations at which significant effects occur have not been determined, however.

Several sensitive plants are reported to be adversely affected (by leaf injury and reduction of growths by NO_2 concentrations of 1 ppm for a day or as little as 0.35 ppm for several months.

NO is not an irritant and it is not believed to have any adverse health effects on humans at concentrations that occur in the atmosphere, even in highly polluted areas. These concentrations are dangerous, however, because of the possibility of oxidation to NO_2. Hemoglobin has an extraordinary affinity for NO (about 1500 times its affinity for CO) but fortunate) atmospheric NO appears to be unable to enter the bloodstream to react with the hemoglobin.

NO_2 is a reddish gas whose odor could be detected at concentrations of about 0.12 ppm. Its importance in photochemical reactions has been due to its strong absorption of ultraviolet radiation. Concentrations of 100 ppm or more for a few minutes can prove lethal to humans and animals, and exposures to 5ppm for a few minutes leads to effects on the respiratory system. Exposure of monkeys to 15 to 50 ppm for 2 h damaged the lungs, heart, liver, and kidneys and prodaced pulmonary changes similar to those occuring in human emphysema. Long-term exposures to 0.06 ppm have been related to an increase in acute respiratory disease in humans. It is thus clear that NO_2 levels in polluted urban atmospheres are associated with adverse health effects.

Serious illness and death has resulted from short exposures to NO_2. For example, it was responsible for 124 deaths in a fire at Cleveland's Crile Hospital on May 15, 1929, when X-ray film having nitrocellulose accidentally caught fire and produced NO_2.

Photochemical Oxidants—Photochemical Smog

Sometimes, in the presence of sun light, atomic oxygen from the photochemical reduction of NO_s also reacts with a number of reactive hydrocarbons (such as methane, ethane, toluene etc., all of which originate from burning of fossil fuels or directly from plants) to form reactive intermediates called radicals. These radicals then take part in a series of reactions to form still more radicals that combine with oxygen, hydrocarbons, and NO_2. As a result nitrogen dioxide is regenerated, nitric oxide disappears, ozone accumulates and a number of secondary pollutants are formed such as formaldehyde, aldehydes and peroxyacetyl nitrate or PAN ($C_2H_3O_SN$). All of these collectively form *Photochemical smog*.

Small amounts of ozone are also added to the atmosphere by electrical discharge like as lightning flashes, by vertical flux of stratospheric ozone and by tropospheric electric storms. Ozone is a natural constitutent of upper atmosphere i.e., stratosphere, where it is formed and gets destroyed in a cyclical process with sunlight as the driving force. Most of the solar ultraviolet radiation gets absorbed by stratospheric ozone before it reaches the lower atmosphere i.e., troposphere, where approximately ten per cent of the atmospheric concentration of ozone is found. Ozone is also formed in rest quantities in the atmosphere of every big city by the action of sunlight on various waste products of combination. Ozone concentrations have been increasing at an alarming rate, threatening man's health and the productivity of his crops. It is calculated that doubling the troposheric ozone content may raise the surface temperatures by 1°C, which is substantial compared to the 2°C-3°C temperature rise calculated for a doubling of carbondioxide. It has also calculated that man's activities may cause the doubling of the troposheric ozone content by the end of the century. Ozone filters the ultraviolet rays coming from cosmicrays to earth.

The truly significant quantities of ozone present in our immediate environment are formed chemically by the action of ultra violet light on Nitrogen oxide. A multitude of combustion processes, especially the inefficient internal combustion engines of automobiles daily emit tonnes of waste; hydrocarbons and nitrogen oxides into the atmosphere. Heat from any source may make atmospheric nitrogen and oxygen to react into nitrogen oxides. The hotter the source, the greater the production of nitric oxides. The nitric oxide gets oxidized to nitrogen dioxide by atmospheric oxygen but energy from sunlight quickly splits the nitrogen dioxide back into nitric oxide and atomic oxygen, which reacts with the molecular oxygen of the atmosphere to form ozone.

Ozone causes necrotic flecking of upper surface of leaves, general chlorisis and bronzing, precious dropping of olderleaves, reduced growth of shoots and roots, suppression of nodulation, reduction in seed set and depression of marketable yields. It causes shrinking of nuclei and cytoplasm of mesophyll cells which becomes granular, causing an increase in inter cellular space.

Ozone is now reported to be responsible for the several widerspread diseases like weather fleck of tobacco, leaf tip burn of carnations, tip burns of onions bronzing of beam, speckle leaf of potato, and brown leaf of grapes. PAN causes bronzing and glazing of abaxial leaf surface which is due to plasmolysis and collapse of mesophyll cells around substometal chambers. Epidermal and guard cells donot get injured. In human beings, oxidants bring about stinging of eyes, coughing, headache, severe tired feeling, pulmonary congestion, oedema, haemorrhage, dry throat, disorientation altered breathing patterns, narrowing of airways and ageing of lung tissues.

Ozone, PAN and nitrogen dioxide severely injure many forms of plant life, destroying the cells of leaves, damaging the chioroplasts, and interfering with the plant's metabolic processes.

Tobacco smoke

It is mainly generated by smoking cigarettes and bidis. It is gradually becoming a potent pollutant especially in closed atmospheres such as buses, trains, auditoria and so on. It is also believed to be causing lung cancer, pulmonary and coronary heart diseases. It causes thickening of bronchial epithelial layer, loss of ciliated cells, and appearance of cells with bizzare nuclei, which are probably the percursors of cancerous cells.

Particulate Matter

Solid and liquid aerosols suspended in the atmosphere are termed as particulate matter. They come either from condensation processes or from dispersion processes (erosion, grinding, spraying, etc.). Although "smoke" is popularly used to denote mixtures of particulate matter, fumes, gases, and mists, it properly refers to solid (or solid and liquid) condensation aerosols. "Dust" refers to solid dispersion aerosols and "mist" to liquid aerosols.

Table 6.6 includes list of some of the characteristics of these particles. Most of their mass in the atmosphere is accounted for by the "large" and "giant" particles. The giant particles arise mainly from dispersion processes, and combustion processes appear to generate most of the small particles. Most particles are removed from the atmosphere by gravitational settling.

Table 6.6. Characteristics of atmospheric particles.

Typical size	*<0.1 μm*	*0.1 μm—1 μm*	*> 1 μm*
Name	Aitken particles	Large particles	Giant particles
Principal neture	Combustion aerosols	Combustion products and photochemical aerosols	Natural and industrial dust
Settling speedsa	Less than 8×10^{-7} m/s	Intermediate	Greater than 4×10^{-5} m/s

Since particulate matter is by definition nongaseous, concentrations in the atmosphere cannot be expressed in volume units, and the favored unit is the microgram per cubic meter (Lg/m^3). Nevertheless urban areas consistently show particulate matter concentrations several times as high as nonurban areas. The data also show a slight tendency for downtrends in urban areas over the years and uptrends in nonurban areas, prehaps due to the increasing "urban sprawl." Atmosperic particles can scatter and absorb sunlight, thus reducing visibility. In general, cities receive about 15 to 20% less solar radiation than rural areas and the reduction of sunlight can become as high as one-third in the summer and two-thirds in the winter. The reduction in sunlight is strongly correlated with fuel combustion for industrial and household heating purposes. Particles also reduce visibility by attenuating the light from objects and illumuiating the air, reducing the contrast between the objects and their background. The visual range is approximately inversely proportional to the concentration of particulate matter, with 100 μg/m^3 corresponding to a range of 12 km on the average (though sometimes it might be as much as 36 km or as little as 6 km since other factors, still unknown, are apparently important). Reduced visibility is aesthetically undesirable and it is also dangerous for aircraft and motor vehicles.

The effects of particulate matter on materials includes corrosion of metals when the air is humid; erosion and soiling of buildings, sculpture and painted surfaces; and the soiling of clothing and draperies. A new problem produced by particulate matter is its corrosion and damage of electronic equipment, especially through chemical or mechanical action on electrical contacts. Many of these problems arise from particles that have settled out of the air and it used to be common to give dust-fall measurements in terms of mass of particles settling on a given area each month or each year. Dust-fall values are not an accurate indication of corrosion or other type of damage, however and are no longer commonly given.

The toxic effects of particulate matter on animals and humans can be classified as (1) intrinsic toxicity due to chemical or physical properties, (2) interference with clearance mechanisms in the respiratory tract, or (3) toxicity due to adsorbed toxic substances, Many toxic particles have been discovered in polluted urban atmospheres, including metal dusts, asbestos, and aromatic hydrocarbons such as the carcinogen 3, 4-benzpyrene; their concentrations are generally extremely small but they may play a role in the higher cancer rates that occur in urban areas as compared to rural areas even after correcting for the greater amount of smoking that occurs, in urban areas.

Recent studies carried out shows increased mortality and illness accompanying higher levels of particulate matter. Respiratory illnesses, especially from chronic diseases such as bronchitis and emphysema, show the most pronounced association with levels of particulate matter and adverse health effects have been noted for annual geometric mean levels of as little as 80 μg/ma. In these studies, higher particulate matter concentrations are usually associated with higher sulphur dioxide levels, however, and it has been not easy to separate the effects due to the two pollutants.

Dust pollution

'Dust is found ' to travel several thousands of kilometres, across deserts and seas. Air-borne particles of the Saharan sand cross the Arabian sea and reach India. Though dust particles offer nuclei for cloud formation, they can be nuisanc tc certain industries needing aseptic and clean environment like drug-industries and food-processing plants. They sometime become health hazards as they may lead to diseases like allergic asthma, bronchitis, emphysema and even fibrosis of the lungs.

However, dust pollution of air could be controlled by certain evergreen plants, grasses and epiphytes like orchids. Pollution Research Laboratory, College of Agriculture. University of Kolkatta has reported that certain plants have remarkable dust-filtering, air-cleaning and air-purifying capacities. In one of the study, it has been reported that certain plants with simple leaves such as peepal (*Ficus riligiosa*), pakur (*Ficus infectoria*), banyan (*Ficus benghalensis*), teak (*Tectona grandis*), sal (*Shorea robusta*), arjuna (*Terminalia arjuna*), mast (*Polyalthia longifolia*), mango (*Mangifera indica*); etc., are better dust collectors than the plants with compound leaves like gul mohar (*Poinclana regia*), tamarind (*Tamarindus indica*), *Cassia fistula*, neem (*Azadirachta indica*).

Some Other Particulate Pollutants

Fluorides

The particulate fluorides are believed to originate in the same way as the gaseous fluorides. However, these have been found to be less phytotoxic harmful or toxic to plants. They bring about an increase in the fluoride content of the leaves and occasional tip burn. But the growth and yield hive been not greatly affected. The ingestion by cattle of various fluorine compounds falling on for ages, make abnormal calcification of bones and teeth called flurosis, eventually resulting in loss of their weight, etc.

Lead

Lead enters the atmosphere mainly from automobile exhaust and it causes long-term environmental pollution. Automobile gasoline is having tetra-ethyl lead [$(CH_3CH_2)4Pb$] which when is burned enters the atmosphere. In the rainfall and soil samples of urban areas large concentrations of lead have been reported. Roadside plants and meadow mice living along major highways are found to contain high concentrations of lead in their tissues, and this has a sublethal effect on the health and longevity of the animal. Traffic policemen and others who are exposed for long periods to heavy traffic are having higher than average levels of lead in their blood. It has been reported that 30 to 50% of the lead inhaled gets absorbed into the body and these airborne lead compounds are found to cause lead poisoning. Further, the use of lead-lined vessels for cooking and the storage of wine have resulted in. heavy lead burdens in the bodies of those who are using then.

Lead has been widely used as a material of choice for shielding against x-rays and other nuclear radiations. Lead arsenate is used in insecticides and lead borate in plastic industry. Significant deposition of lead is also coming from smelting complexes, ceramics, paints, pesticides and solder used for sealing. Lead gets accumulated in considerable amounts in the leaf tissues as also in the tissue of human body.

Also, certain paints and putty are having major components of lead and there are cases in which lead poisoning take place due to occupational exposure of painters and also to children who habitually or accidentally nibbled cracks and peels of old paints. Although 90-95% of the lead that is ingested is insoluble and is quickly ell minated, the remainder does enter the blood and tissues, including bone. Lead levels of 20-40 μg per 100 g of blood (0.2-0.4 ppm) are regarded as normal and harmless for city dwellers. Both 0.8 ppm lead levels in adult human blood causes over symptoms such as anaemia, kidney disease and convulsions. However, in children 0.6 ppm level of lead in blood may cause lead poisoning and ultimate death. Being a cumulative posion it disrupts the functioning of cells and organs of the musular circulatory and nervous system for binding with the cellular enzymes also causing coagulation of proteins. It damages liver, kindey and gastro intetine and induces abnormalities in fertility and pregnancy.

Cement Kiln and Other Dust

Particulates released by cement manufacturing units are responsible for the premature fall- of needless, higher pubescene of leaves, formation of more stomata and trichomes reduction in number and sizes of cobs and weight of seeds and increase in number of infertile seeds. Dusts from stone crushers, lime kilns, slate making units and quarries have been not less hazardous.

Potassium Salts

These are derived mainly from potash mines, they bring about branch tip death, chlorosis and necrosis of leaves.

Sodium Chloride

The de-icing salts, mainly sodium chloride, have been used to remove ice and snow in winters. These salts have been recognised to cause damage to the roadside trees in the form of leaf necrosis, defolitation, supression of flowing, and die back of terminal shoots in apple.

Agricultural Chemicals

These are many chemicals such as insecticides, herbicides, fungicides and pesticides which are used widely in agriculture and are known to produce foliar lessions, chlorosis and abscission of leaves and reduction in fruit seeds. Several other types of particles in air such as coal dust and asbestos could be linked with necrotic lessions, reduction in fruit seeds in plants, silicosis and lung cancer respectively.

Living organism are rarely, if ever, exposed to single pollutant in nature. The influence of mixture of pollutants has been found to be usually synergistic i.e., greater than the additive effect of the different pollutants alone.

Other Air Pollutants

There are other air pollutants besides the major types just discussed. In certain areas these may be significant contributors to the total air pollution burden. Some particulate matter is produced by abrasion (such as the wearing away of rubber tires and footwear); some organic vapors result from cosmetics and aerosol cans; and of course there is the smoke from tobacco products that is so annoying to many nonsmokers.

Table 6.7. Minor air pollutant emissions in millions of metric tons annually.

Pollutant	*Amount*
Ground dust from natural sources	27
Aerosols and vapors from aerosol cans	0.26
Rubber particuiates from vehicle tires	0.28
Smoke from cigarettes	0.21
Foot% gar use	0.05
Smoke from cigars	0.04
Organic compounds from perfumes and colognes	0.03
Naphthalene from mothballs	0.005

Another class of air pollutants have been the aeroallergens, the most important being ragweed pollen, although grass or tree pollen can cause allergic responses in some persons. This is an important problem since 10 or 15 million persons are adversely affected. Ragweed is crowded out by grass and other vegetation except in places where the soil has been disturbed (railroad tracks, developed land) so ragweed pollen is really more a man-made pollutant than a natural one.

Industrial processes, especially in the chemical industry, can produce special air pollutants-sulphuric acid, hydrogen chloride (HCI), formaldehyde, various alcohols, and many other sophisticated chemical compounds characteristic of our technological society. HCI can also be produced by the incineration of polyvinyl chloride plastic. Various fluorine compounds (HF, F_2, SiF_4, $H2SiF_6$, etc.) are emitted by phosphate fertilizer manufacturing plants (since large amounts of fluoride are present in phosphate rock, typically 3%), aluminum reduction [which is accomplished by electrolysis of alumina ($AI2O_3$) in a bath of molten cryolite, Na_3AIF_6], steelmaking, ceramic firing, and some chemical processing. Fluorides readily get absorbed by vegetation and can cause leaf injury and reduction of growth and yield even in very low concentrations, as low as 0.1 ppb. In addition, livestock have fallen victim to fluoride poisoning from ingesting contaminated vegetation ; moderate adverse effects can occur in dairy cattle whose feed contains 40 to 60 ppm fluoride (as F^-).

A particulate air pollutant that has attracted special interest in recent years is asbestos. Its occupational hazards are wellknown. All persons in urban areas are exposed to asbestos in the air from the wearing down of automobile brake linings and from, the practice of spraying insulating asbestos during the construction of new buildings. In an effort to protect the public and the asbestos workers, the government has issued regulations governing asbestos spraying, requiring that the area be enclosed in tarpaulins during spraying and that workers be provided with respirators and coveralls. Any given locality is likely to have other, specialized air pollution problems. In Iowa, for example, the use of anhydrous ammonia as an agricultural fertilizer has meant the presence throughout the state of anhydrous ammonia tanks that occasionally rupture or release ammonia during filling operations ; many times each year nearby residents are forced to flee their homes very suddenly and remain elsewhere for many hours.

Green House Effect

A large amount of carbon dioxide gets introduced into the atmosphere from fossil fuel burning, furances and breathing of animals. From fossil fuel alone, more than 2.5×10^{13} tonnes of CO_2 is being emitted into the atmosphere each year. Not all of the CO_2 injected into the atmosphere remains there ; about half of it gets utilized by plant life or absorbed by water of the oceans. Part of the CO_2 dissolved in the ocean may get precipitated or incorporated in marine organisms. In this respect aquatic plants in the ocean are playing an important role in maintaining CO_2 equilibrium between the atmosphere and the surface layers of the ocean (up to 100 meters deep). Part of the CO_2 taken up by terrestrial plants gets deposited in dead vegetation and humus on the forest floor. some of it, in the form of organic plant parts, has been eaten by herbivorous animals and gets deposited on or in the soil. However, much of CO_2 is still left in the atmosphere. An increase in atmospheric carbon dioxide will influence the photosynthesis, and consequently on plant growth by its direct fertilising effect, especially in hot tropical environments and a longer growing season in temperate regions. This potential fertilising effect should be exploitable by using modified crop varieties and agriculture practices to compensate for the disadvantageous effects of temperature increase. Carbon dioxide emitted by volcanoes during several billion years was at let 40.000 times that still present in the air.

On a global time scale, the known amounts of CO_2 in limestone and fossil sediments suggest that normal residence time of CO_2 in the atmosphere has been probably around 100,000 years.

Carbon dioxide gets confined exclusively to troposphere. In dense concentration it can act a serious pollutant.. The temperature at the surface of the earth has been maintained by the energy balance of the sun's rays that strike the planet and the heat that gets radiated back into the space. Some of the sun's ray's that penetrate the thick layer of CO_2 are able to strike the earth and get converted into heat. The heated earth is able to readiate this absorbed energy as radiations of longer wavelengths. Much of this does not pass through CO_2 layer to outer space but gets absorbed by the CO_2 and water in the atmosphere and adds to the heat that has been already present. Thus the earth's atmosphere heats up. This phenomenon is termed as the green house effect. Carbon dioxide thus acts like the glass of a green house and on a global scale; tends to warm the air in the lower levels of the atmosphere. An increased heating of earth would cause recede of glaciers, disappearance of ice caps such as those found over Antarctic and Greenland, and rise in ocean level. Infact, it has been estimated that if all the ice on the earth should melt, 200 fet of water would be added to the surface of all oceans,' and low-lying costal cities such as Bangkok and Venice would get inundated. Only a rise in sea level of 50 to 100 cm caused by ocean warming would be able to flood low-lying lands,

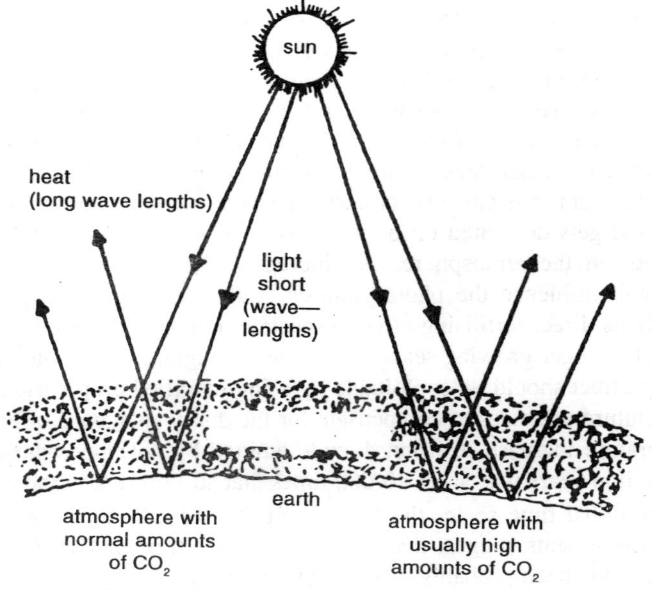

Fig. 6.1. Greenhouse effect of carbon dioxide.

in Bangladesh and West Bengal. Further, due to the much warmer tropical oceans because of increased carbon dioxide, there have been likely to be more hurricanes and cyclones and early snow melts in mountains causing more floods during mansoons. According to Mr. Stephan Keckes, at Yugoslavian marine biologist, head of the United. Nations Environment Programme's Centre on ocean and costal areas, within 30 years, rising seas will be able to wash away entire countries and flood cities from Boston to Mumbai. He calculated that seas will rise by 1.5 to 3.5 meters within three decades. In Bangladesh alone 15 million people will have to move or drown. He says that little can be done about rising, oceans beyond studying the phenomenon and preparing for the worst.

According to G.N. Plass, if the carbon dioxide content of the atmosphere gets doubled, the average surface temperature of the earth would rise 6.5 °F. However, this would not happen because of reflection of some of the sun's heat back into the space by densely accumulating particulate contaminants such as smoke and dust from industrial and automobile exhaust. If carbon dioxide continues to accumulate, it may disallow the cooling effect of particulate contaminants, and as a consequence the earth's temperature may rise again.

There is sufficient evidence that the temperature of the entire earth has risen slightly during recent decades. Glaciers in both hemisphere are receding. Between 1885 to 1940, there occurred an increase in mean annual temperature of about 0.9°F of the earth. After 1940, global warming subsided. Warming of Northern Europe and North America continued between 1940 and 1960, but the mean annual air temperature on global scale as well as for the Northern Hemisphere got decreased slightly (0.2°F). More than 40 per cent of the total increase in carbon dioxide content of the atmosphere from combustion occured during that period. It might be possible that increased particulate pollutants from industry and automobile exhaust nullified or masked any effect of temperature from carbon dioxide content of the atmosphere, but this has been not. There was an overall temperature rise of 0.7°C over the past 134 years with the three warmest years in the whole record being 1980, 1981 and 1982. In addition, five of the nine warmest years even have occured since 1978. There have been however, some unexplained fluctuations within this long term trend, between 1980 and the mid-1980 but overall conditions were relatively steady, with land-based readings actually showing a slight fall. The latest predictions for global warming given at European meetings of climatologists and policy makers say that the temperature of the earth could increase by 1.5 to 4.5°C by the year 2050.

OZONE

Ozone is present in minute traces in the atmosphere. It has a peak concentration (10 mg kg^{-1}) around 25 km above the surface of the earth (stratosphere), and then decreases again. At no level below maximum, its concentration has been more than a millionth part of the atmosphere. Normally, it has been present in the atmosphere at about 0.5 ppm at sea level. However, it shows remarkable variation from an average of about 0.02 ppm in winter to about 0.07 ppm in summer. It has been produced mainly from oxygen containing molecules such as SO_2, NO_2 and aldehyde on absorption of ultraviolet radiations

$$\underset{\text{Nitrogen dioxide}}{NO_2} \xrightarrow[\text{UV-Radiations}]{\text{Absorption of}} \underset{\text{excited molecule}}{NO_2} \rightarrow \underset{\text{Atomic oxygen}}{O^*}NO$$

$$\underset{\text{Atomic oxygen}}{O^*} + O_2 \longrightarrow \underset{\text{Ozone}}{O_3}$$

An umbrella of ozone is able to protect us from the harmful solar radiations. Inspite of being in such a small proportion, it plays a vital role in the climatology and biology of the earth. It filters out all radiations below 3000 Å (UV-B-radiation) which 'are biologically harmful, and thereby controlling the thermal budget of the earth. The amount of ozone, therefore, must have been intimately connected with the life-sustaining process. Any large scale depletion of ozone content therefore, will exert catastrophic influence on biotic systems including plants.

Over last few years it has become evident that the ozone concentration of the earth's atmosphere is decreasing largely due to increasing use of CFCs by man. These obnoxious compounds emitted mainly by aerosol escape to stratosphere and react with ozone. A sharp drop in the protective ozone layer (about 40%). over Antarctica could have been caused by human produced pullutants. If the nothing is done to slow ozone depleting air pollution, temperatures around the world may rise as much as 5.5°C. A gradual warming of the earth threatens increased melting of polar ice caps, flooding of coastal regions and skin cancers in a few years, and if it is not checked, eventual extension of human species occurs.

On the contrary, when ozone is occurring in concentration above normal, it makes pollution. It is known to be damaging the human health.

Table 6.8. Effects of ozone on human health.

Ozone level (ppm)	*Observed effects*
0.2	No ill effects
0.3	Nose and throat irritation
1.0-3.0	Extreme fatigue after two hours
9.0	Severe pulmonary edema

The data shows that above 1 ppm of concentration, ozone becomes extremely fatigued. It can bring about damage to plants too.

Table 6.9. Effects of ozone on plants.

Plant	*Concentration of ozone (ppm)*	*Exposure Time*	*Observed effects*
Radish	0.05	20 days (8hr/day)	50% reduction in yield
Tabacoo	0.10	5.5. hr.	50% reduction in poller germination and pollen tube growth

At levele of 0.2 ppm, ozone damages tobacco, tomato, bean pine and most other plants. It may be able to depress growth rate without producing any obvious lesion. However, in very high concentrations (15 ppm to 20 ppm) it makes visible damage as leaf blotche. It may also be responsible for white markings on the leaves of certain grain crops and the searing of the tips of white pine seedings, known as tip burn.

Ozone is also able to with many fibres especially cotton, nylon and polyster, and dyes. The degree of damage appears to be correlated with light and humidity. It hardens rubber.

Table 6.10. Effect of ozone rubber.

Ozone concentration (ppm)	*Time for first crack to appear (minutes)*
0.02	65
0.06	5
0.45	3
20000.00	1 second

Ozone may comprise as much as three-fourths of the total oxidant in killer smog.

Peeling of ozone umbrells by CFMs. Certain fluorocarbon compounds which are called chlorofluoromethanes or CFMs or "freon" are used as propellants in pressurized aerosol cans. They are inert in normal chemical and physical reactions, but they get accumulated in greater amounts at high altitudes and there in the stratosphere these inert gaseous compounds (i.e., CFMs) release chlorine atoms under the influence of intense short-wave ultraviolet radiation. Each atom of chlorine chain then reacts with more than 1,00,000 molecules of ozone, converting ozone to oxygen: The reduction in stratospheric ozone disallows greater penetration of ultraviolet light, which intensifies UV radiation at the earth's surface. Some scientists such as Ahmed (1975), Brodeur (1975), and Russell (1975) feel that this intensified radiation will cause a significant increase in skin cancer and eventually have a lethal effects on many organisms, including man.

The protective ozone layer of the stratosphere is also considered by many ecologists to be endangered by supersonic jets, the SSTs. The jet engines of supersonic aircraft flying at high altitudes release nitrogen oxide (NO_x) which catalytically destroy ozone molecules.

Aircraft Emissions

Pollutant emissions from aircraft are a small but noticeable component of the total air pollution problem in the world. Aircrafts are responsible for about 2.5% of the carbon monoxide emissions and about 1% of the hydrocarbon emissions, but only negligible amounts of the other major air pollutants. These emissions, unlike most air pollutant emissions, do not occur mainly in urban areas. The amounts of pollutants emitted by jet aircraft per kilogram of fuel consumed or per passenger-mile are considerably lower than the corresponding values for motor vehicles.

The visibility of smoke from jet aircraft has proved a frequent source of complaints. This smoke is composed largely of fine carbon particles approximately 0.5 μm in diameter, which were not burned properly. Since these small particles scatter light quite well, they reduce visibility and are thus quite conspicuous. Modern turbofan engines have combustion chambers ("smoke burrner cans") for smoke reduction that provide a leaner (higher air-to-fuel ratio) mixture and reduce carbon formation. These avoid the visible smoke but the other emissions, which were more serious to begin with, still remain.

Although they do not constitute an important pollution source from the point of view of public health, space rocket engines produce many dangerous exhaust products. One study found that the engine of the

Apollo Lunar Module, which took two astronauts to the surface of the moon and brought them back to the command ship circling the moon, produced ammonia, water, carbon monoxide, nitrous oxide, oxygen, carbon dioxide, and nitric oxide as major exhaust products and a wide variety of different minor exhaust products. These constitute a possible source of contamination of the lunar surface and of the lunar samples returned to earth.

ACID RAINS

Acid rains means in common language the presence of excessive acids in rain water. It has been one of the effects of air pollution. Every source of energy that we use-be it coal, fuelwood or petroleum products, has sulphur and nitrogen. These two elements when burnt in the presence of atmospheric oxygen are converted into their respective oxides-sulphur dioxide and nitrogen dioxide, which are highly soluble in water. During rain these oxides react with large quantities of water vapour of the atmosphere to form acids like sulphuric acid, sulphurous acid, nitric acid and nitrous acid which then return to the earth's surface, with rain water or may remain in the atmosphere is clouds and logs.

Acid rain causes a number of adverse implications. It tends to increase acidity in the soil, -threatens human and aquatic life, destroys forests and crops reducing agricultural productivity. Besides, it is able to corrode buildings, monuments, statues, bridges, fences and railings, that costs the world 1450 million dollars a year. At St. Paul's cathedral some stonework is being eaten away at the rate of an inch every 100 years. Even the British Parliament building has suffered serious damage from the presence of sulphuric acid in rain fall. It creates a serious threat to human health also, since it contaminates not only the breathing air but also the drinking water and even food.

The acids have been found to be very dangerous to the living organisms as they can destroy life. Acid rain can play havoc with the human nervous system by making the person an easy prey to neurological diseases. This happens because these acids produce highly toxic compounds which contaminates the potable water and enter our body.

Acid rain has been already an acute problem in North America and Europe. Crops and forests in Canada are being destroyed by acid rain due to pollutants emitted by industries in Northern USA. Acidity Kills fish, bacteria and algae and the acquits eco-system is destroyed.

Winds are known to carry air pollutants from one country to another. Air pollution in England now descends upon sweden as acid rain.

Acidification of soil changes its biology and chemistry. When the soil gets acidified, plants can absorb cadmium more easily and high levels of cadmium in plants has been dangerous for animals and human beings.

Acid rain in Japan has damaged 5,000 sq. kms of cedar trees in Kanto plain which lies to the north of Tokyo. This area is having high acid deposition brought about by air pollutants.

Acidic air pollutants have been responsible for many other damaging effects like corrosion of metals, weakening or disintegration of textiles, paper and marble. Investigations are going on to know whether Taj Mahal is being affected due to pollutants released from Mathura refinery. Hydrogen Sulphide tarnishes silver and blackens leaded house paints, ozone produces cracks in rubber ; its economic significance has been apparent.

Air pollution may cause or contribute to a variety of safety hazards, e.g., hazards associated with reduced visibility due to smog etc. Air contaminants that have been detectable by the sense of sight, touch, smell or taste can be nuisance in many ways even if they do not result in direct adverse economics or health effects.

In the near future the developing countries like India will soon have to cope with this problem of acid pollution. Industrial areas with the pH value of rain below or close to the critical value had been recorded in Delhi, Nagpur, Pune, Mumbai and Kolkatta: Nadia acidity has been largely due to sulphur dioxides from coal fired power plants and petroleum refinery, emitting nearly 85% tonnes annually. The phenomenon of acid rain is becoming more and more common in Mumbai with several industries discharging sulphur oxides in the air making rain water more acidic. The average pH value of acid rain at Kolkatta has been 5.80, Hyderabad. 5.73, Chennai, 5.85, Delhi, 6.21, and Mumbai, 4.80.

The situation, in India has been likely to worsen in the near future with the increased tempo of thermal power plants.

Variables Affecting Severity of Pollution

The meteorological variables which influence severity of a pollution are as follows

1. Wind speed and direction;
2. Atmosphere diffusion;
3. Temperature variation with height, includes lapse rate and inversion;
4. Mean maximum depths;
5. Precipitation.

The non-meteorological variables which influence severity of a pollution are as follows ·

1. Topographical Feateres;
2. Quality and quantity of pollution

let us discuss these one by one.

Wind Speed and Direction

Pollution gets dissipitated in the atmosphere by involving both the horizontal and vertical movements of the wind. In general, greater the wind velocity, the greater will be the dilution. Turbulence has been a stirring action of wind and, therefore, gets related to the vertical movement of wind gloving across the surface of earth i.e., fluid moving along the surface of the containing structure. The drag against the surface of the earth will make the wind near the surface to blow at very slow speed. Wind speed tends to increase very rapidly with height upto 10 metre. Above this, it continues to increase in speed with height but at a much lower rate.

Atmospheric Diffusion

Atmospheric diffusion means the movement of large parcels of air from one point to another.

Temperature Variation

The temperature distribution of the atmosphere has been found to depend upon the rate at which energy being received from the sun and from various transport mechanism i.e., electromagnetic radiation, convection, evaporation, etc. Because of this, the temperature does not remain constant but varies with height, season, time of day, amount of cloud cover and many other variables.

Lapse Rate

Lapse rate may be defined as equal to the adiabatic lapse rate minus the temperature lapse rate. Temperature lapse rate may be defined as the ratio of change in temperature to change in height in 100s of metres. The adiabatic lapse rate may be defined as the rate of cooling with lofting (or heating upon discent) of a parcel of air with no heat exchanges. A parcel of dry air expands upon rising. When air expands, it cools at the adiabatic lapse rate if no heat exchange occurs. If the surrounding air becomes cooler, the parcel will continue to rise and therefore, unstable conditions or strong lapse rate exists. A strong lapse rate reveals unstable conditions and therefore, good air mixing. More positive lapse rate reveals stable air, which implies that air pollution will not be removed because there has been not sufficient atmosphere turbulence or mixing. Inversion of the temperature lapse rate i.e.,· from positive to negative, resulting in stable atmospheric conditions is termed as 'Inversion'.

Temperature Inversion

Temperature inversion may be considered to be a meteorological condition in which air pollutants are not able to rise and get disbursed in the atmosphere and produce high concentration of pollution.

A temperature inversion is said to exist when the normal lapse rate in the lower atmosphere gets inverted and the temperature actually increases with height, i.e., exhaust gases and pollutants which rise only a certain distance under these conditions and persistent inversion that last several days can be dangerous.

Inversion takes place frequently during the night or early morning hours. Low wind speeds, equal or less than 10 kmph usually accompany inversions, so there occurs very little horizontal dispersion of pollutants. Inversion temperatures usually get limited to the first 500 metres and this, therefore, has been the maximum inversion heights.

Mean Maximum Depths

The mean maximum depth (MMD) may be defined as the height to which the unstable air mixes. In the absence of radio sound observations, the maximum mixing depth could be estimated as being the height of the loop of the low altitude cloud layer. The maximum mixing depth has been found to vary during the day' as well as varies from season to season. Variation is also dependent upon the topographical features. Vertical depression of pollutants gets limited by the ground and the MMD. Therefore, mixing depths have been essential in estimating the amount of vertical diffusion of pollution in the atmosphere.

Precipitation

Pollutants may get washed out of the air by the natural secrubbing action of rain, snow and all other forms of precipitations when it falls to the ground. Gases that are soluble in water get removed by adoption when the particles stick to the precipitations after being impacted by it. Not only can precipitation influence the atmospheric pollution, but the pollution can affect the precipitation.

Topographical Features

Topography can very seriously alter local atmospheric conditions. Most important of these have been valleys, shore-lines and hills. Most of the famous air pollution episodes occurred in locations with adverse topographical conditions. Valley affects take place due to the channelling of winds. Valleys tend to make the windflow in the general direction of the valley axis. Slope winds take place in valleys in the evening when the air near the ground is cooled. Any air pyllution relased on the slopes or in the bottom of valleys will stay in the valley if there exists an inversion. Shore-line winds get created due to the differences in heating rates of the earth and the water under the same amount of the sun shine land absorbs heat faster than water. Hence, on a sunny day, sea breezes get created which come from water to the land. Land also cools faster than water creating on cloudy days or at night times land breezes. Land breezes are generally lower in velocity and shallower than sea breeze.

Hills can make a varying degree of influence on air pollution removal. A smooth hill makes the least affect of the flow of air.

Rough hills conversely make turbulence eddies and good mixing which promote improved air pollution removal.

Quality and Quantity

Quality and Quantity of air pollution could be estimated with regard to different sources of pollutions such as transportation, industry, power generation, space heating and refuse burning. Nearly 90 per cent by weight of this pollution has been gaseous and 10 per cent particulate matter. The pollutants from the different sources can be further classified according to their physical and chemical composition like inorganic or organic gases and particulates. However, there have been no correct measurements that can tell about the emission of pollutants from the same source under different processes. The ability to determine the effectiveness of controlling a number of pollutants has been likely to depend on our measurements.

The air pollution problems of one city or country may differ greatly from those of another city or country. It is true even if the sources of air pollution are similar. Meteorology has played a very reital role in determining the significant level of air pollution.

General Pathological Effects of Air Pollution

Severe air pollution affects human health and causes many fatal diseases in them. For instance, there occur lung diseases in workers exposed to occupational hazards, such as black lung disease among coal miners who inhaled mine dust for many years or asbestosis among pipe fitters and insulation workers, exposed to .irborne asbestos fibers. As listed in table 2.8, a variety of air pollutants have been reported to cause many human disease like emphysema, chronic bronchitis, pollen allergies, lung cancer, especially in city dwellers. Mountain et al., (1968) reported that air pollution due to particulate matter and carbon monoxide in New York city causes respiratory problems in children under 8 years of age. Becker et al., (1968) reported that in many American cities along the Eastern Seaboard increasing frequencies of bronchitis, cough, sore throat, wheezes, eye irritations, and general ill health in people occurred as air pollution level increased.

Ecology of Air Pollution

Once gets injected into the atmosphere, pollutants enter the biogeochemical cycles by different routes. The air above many cities can assimilate and disperse great quantities of fine particulate and gaseous pollutants as long as air can move and disperse. But when air masses over cities become stagnant, pollutants accumulate. quickly and deteriorate air quality which cause many respiratory diseases in man and other animals. Air pollutants also accumulate during temperature inversions, when cooler surface layers of air get trapped under warmar upper layers. In these situations, the upper layers of warm air prevent the vertical rise and dispersal of pollutants which are held near the ground. Temperature inversions commonly occur in cities surrounded by mountains or bordered by mountains on the leeward side.

Further a portion of air pollutants reaches land as dry fallouts; it may then enter various nutrient cycles and food chains through water and soil. Other contaminant of air react chemically or photo-chemically with each other and produce such secondary pollutants as sulphuric acid, ozone, and peroxyacetyl nitrate or PAN. Aerosols and other forms of fine particulate matter act as condensation nuclei, to which water vapours present in the air are quickly surround to form droplets of fog or rain.

Moreover, different air pollutants adversely affect flora, fauna and climate of a given area variously.

Effects of Pollution on Climates

Pollution in the atmosphere is capable of very important effects on the climate in localized areas, especially urban areas. The effects in urban areas include the following:

1. *Higher temperatures*. Minimum daily temperatures in urban areas are often 5 to 10°C higher than those in the surrounding rural areas and annual mean temperatures are typically 0:5 to 1.3°C higher. In summer, this is due to the fact that the tall buildings

and pavements of cities absorb more solar radiation (and reflect less) than the vegetation and soil of the rural areas in daytime and release more heat in nighttime because of their higher specific heat. In addition, less heat goes into evaporation. Increased fuel consumption, especially in wintertime, is also responsible for artificial heat production. These effects result in the production of an "urban heat island" that has been the object of many scientific studies. Increased convection above cities is one notable example of how mateorological conditions are affected.

2. *More rapid runoff of water*. Cities are characterized by more rapid runoff of water, which in a rural area would normally be largely absorbed in the soil. Well-documented consequences are a reduction in evaporation of water in the city and lower relative humidity (typically 2 to 8% lower).
3. *Attenuation of solar radiation*. The particulate matter in the atmosphere, whose urban concentrations are typically 10 times those of rural areas, is capable of reducing the amount of solar radiation falling on the city by 15 to 20%. These concentrations also get accompanied by a reduction in visibility.
4. *Lowering of wind speeds*. The presence of urban construction gives rise to increased turbulence because of the increase in surface roughness and wind speeds near the surface of the earth are reduced.
5. *Increased dowdiness*. This is probably due to the updrafts produced by the urban heat island and partly to the large number of small particles produced by man's activities, which are capable of serving as condensation nuclei for water vapor in the atmosphere. Urban areas appear also to have 5 to 10°h more precipitation than nearby rural area but this is just about the limit of accuracy of precipitation measurements. Some much larger precipitation effects have been reported but their existence is a matter of controversy in the scientific literature.

Even in nonurban areas, man's activities have led to climatic effects. Conversion of forests to pasture has often been followed by overgrazing, with increased soil erosion by water and wind being the end result. Similarly, conversion of grasslands to agricultural crop production has led to erosion. Irrigation practices also affect the water and heat balance. Large Milan-made reservoirs have led to reduction in temperature extremes, increase in humidity, and effects on wind patterns. In some cases, man is deliberately attempting to affect the climate. Several methods of dispersing fogs at airports have been tried.

Weather modification has included cloud seeding is increase precipitation and seeding of hurricanes to reduce their wind and storm damage. The results have not been too successful and cloud seeding may not increase precipitation but just redistribute it.

The Cost of Air Pollution

What are the total costs in damages due to air pollution ? What will be the cost in investment and operation for adequate controls ? Neither of these questions can be answered very accurately but there have been some pioneering studies carried out to provide estimates.

Amounts were unknown for replacement and protection of precision instruments, maintenance of cleanliness in production of foods and beverages, soiling of homes and their furnishings, medical costs, the cost of absenteeism from work due to illness, and the cost of fuels wasted in incomplete combustion. Lave and Seskin have tried to determine the medical costs and they estimate that a 50% reduction in air pollution levels in major urban areas would save $ 2.08 billion annually in terms of decreased mortality and morbidity-or 4.5% of all economic costs associated with of these health effects might run as high as $ 29 billion. In conclusion, there is evidence that investments of air pollution control are warranted and that the will be much less than 1% of our gross national product.

State of Air Pollution

In Mexico city, just breathing means equivalent of smoking two packs of cigarettes a day. This city is having some three million cars and 30,000 factories which are releasing 20 tons of lead, carbon monoxide and other contaminants into the atmosphere of this city of 18 million making t one of the most polluted places or earth.

Like Mexico City

Indian cities are not as yet so badly affected, though in the count of suspended particulate matter (SPM), Kolkatta has been ranked as the top position among the major metros of the world.

There are more than 300 million passenger cars, trucks and buses the world over and their numbers increasing rapidly, keeping pace with the industrial and social progress. India is likely to have about 2.7 million vehicles by 19)0, out of this, 2 million would be . two-wheelers operating on petrol. It is reported that in all the .big cities in the country about 800 to 1000 tonnes of pollutants are being ejected into the atmosphere everyday, of this 50% is accounted for automobile exhaust. In the major meteropolitan cities, vehicular exhaust accounts for 70%

of all CO, 50% of all hydrocarbons, 30-40% of all oxides and 30% of all particulate: matte. In Delhi alone there happens to be 8,50,000 vehicles which release 325 tones of CO, SO_2, NO_2, hydrocarbons, and other polltutants into the atmosphere everyday. If these emissions are not controlled then by 1991-92, they would be contributing upto 50% of the CO and 80% of the total hydrocarbons in the air. It has been ensimated that a car (without cleaning device) on burning 1000 litre of fuel releases 350 kg CO, 0.6 kg SO_2, 0.1 kg lead and 1.5 kg particulate matter.

All the two and three wheelers in the country run on two stroke engines that burn a mixture of petrol and oil. The combustion has been never complete and all of them, therefore, give out a cloud of blue smoke. Buses and trucks in India are now powered almost exclusively by diesel engines, and in theory at least the exhaust from them should be far less toxic than that from petrol burning vehicles. By the end of the decade, India should be producing 2,00,000 cars a year. Permission for the manufacture of 3.5 million two-wheelers has already been granted. Naturally a direct result of this surge has been going to make an increase in air pollution.

According to Prof. J.M. Dave, Dean of the School of Environmental Sciences at JNU and his team of researchers, 400 tonnes of pollutants are emitted everyday in Delhi by nearly 5,00,000 vehicles amounting to 34 per cent of the smoke and dust emitted in the city. The team also reported the pollution generated by the different vehicle categories.

The major constituents of vehicular emission have been carbon monoxide, lead, hydrocarbons, oxides of nitrogen and smoke.

According to a report prepared by the Institute of petroleum, Dehradun, if vehicle pollution remains unchecked, by 1991-92 the vehicles in Mumbai will release 1,07,000 tonnes of carbon monoxide and 37,000 tonnes of hydrocarbons per year in the atmosphere . and in 2,000 A.D. 1,85,000 tonnes of carbon monoxide and 6,93,000 tonnes of hydrocarbons will be released in Mumbai city's atmosphere.

All north Indian cities are under going the thermal inversion that makes the air nearest the ground colder than the air higher up. This makes the noxious gases, which are driven up by the heating of the earth in the day time, descend once again at night. What descends, however, have been not the emission of those night time hours alone but of the entire day.

In the State of India's Environment 1984-85, published by the Centre for Science and Evironment, New Delhi, it was reported "of the 48 thermal power stations, officially surveyed in 1984, 31 had taken no pollution control measures and only 6 had their pollution control equipment functioning properly." All Indian power houses use, inferior coal, in terms of its ash content, and most of use power stations are not having de-sulphuration or nitrification equipment. Most of them do not using electrostatic precipitators, their notions of pollution control being confined to building tall chimmey so as to disperse the flue gases over a larger area and thus to distribute it to what the authorities hope is more tolerable level.

Another major, problem of the metropolitan areas has been smog. Besides being a health hazard, it has been sometimes so thick that visibility gets reduced to such a level that airports have to be temporarily closed. Even the vehicular traffic moves very slowly.

Now India has learnt that further "neglect of the environmental aspect has been going to be catastrophic. The worst industrial accident on record in India occurred on December 1984, when a deadly cloud of methyl isocyante escaped from a union carbide pesticide plant in Bhopal, in Madhya Pradesh, Killing over 2,500 people and severely disabbling and injuring thousands.

Even, otherwise, the environment has been today endangered from industrial pollutants. A case in point here is the Tai Mahal which is threatened by industrial enterprises built up in Agra-Mathura region. With increasing congestion the roads and a host of factories blenching smoke, air pollution too is beginning to reach choking levels. In Kolkatta, in areas like Dalhousie, Kalighat and Bhowanipur, air pollution has been three times the tolerance limit. In Delhi in winter season, it has been not mist that blocks the sunlight, but a thick dense smog which settles down for hours.

Prevention and Control of Air Pollution

Air pollution is regarded a grave danger for the healthy sustenance of all forms of life on this earth, the foremost thing which deserves to be carried out has been to educate the people that the atmosphere has been not meant to be dump for all kinds of pollutants. Importance of preserving the health and welfare of man, protection of plant and animal life, prevention of damage to property, ensuring visibility for safe air and ground transport, and maintenance of cleaner atmospheric environment should also be explained. This theoretical effort is complemented by practical measures to control air pollution.

First of all, desirable and harmless air quality standards have to be established. Once done, adequate legislation has to compel control of pollutants at their sources. Source control in the pure sense deals with the elimination before or during ultimate consumption of potential air contaminant contained in raw materials. Unfortunately lack of technical knowledge and economic incentive disallows full practice of this classical method. Source control and abatement of formed contaminants have been complementary practices in the campaign against air pollution. Source control disallows the emission of contaminants to the atmosphere; abatement renders the emission of contaminants to the atmosphere; harmless and inoffensive. The two controls overlap at many points. For example, various devices such as the positive crankcase ventilation valve and catalytic converter, have been developed to reduce exhaust emissions by automobiles, but these devices are not always fully maintained by the public. Likewise, particulate pollution from industry and power generation can be controlled by electrostatic precipitators which are capable of dramatically reducing smoke and dust. Gaseous pollutants of industry and power station can be removed by chemical means, i.e., differential solubility of gases in water. A fine spray of water in a device known as a "scrubber" can effectively separate many gases such as ammonia and sulphur dioxide. Other gases may be removed by filtration or absorption through activated carbon, and still others by chemical conversion to inert or innocuous materials.

There arc some higher vascular plants and many non-vascular plants such as mossess and lichnes that respond to gaseous and particulate air pollutants at concentrations much lower than those that elicit responce in animals and human beings. These plants are used as indicators of pollutants in air and to monitor their concentrations (biomonitors). Certain weeds like water hyacinth are able to check the heavy metal contamination caused by industrial effluents. The stem and leaves of this weed have been shown to selectively absorb and retain heavy metal such as lead, cadmium and chromium from industrial sullage and thus help in reducing contamination.

Technology for control of emission needs to be adopted for all types of vehicle using petrol or diesel and servere punishment should be specified to the defaulters. Mumbai Motor Vehicles (Amendment) Act, 1984 empowers authority to suspend, after a grace period of 14 days, the registration of vehicles which are emitting pollutants beyond a certain specified limit.

Pollution caused by two-stroke engines can only be got rid of by using the technology for four stroke engines. In case of three wheelers, the government can insist that their' engines be designed to run on liquified petroleum gas (LPG). In Bangkok three-wheelers are obliged to have four stroke engines or to run on gas, and in South Korea more and more taxis have been running on LPG. That is possible in the developing countries like India.

The surest and easiest way to reduce the pollution caused by burning petrol has been able to produce unleaded petrol only. The octane rating of Indian gasoline has been so low that this will pose few problems to either the refineries or to the present generation of cars, all of which are having low-compression cylinder heads. The most intractable problem will be to reduce the pollution caused by diesel burning buses and trucks. If all of them had been properly maintained and not overloaded, this would solve it self. But that is not practically possible. Thus, the only long term solution is to find a substitute to diesel. It is in any case highly desirable, for the demand for diesel is going up by leaps and bound and at least for the present it cannot be easily replaced in tractors and locomotives.

Research carried out in recent years has revealed that with only minor modifications a diesel engine can be able to run on a mixed fuel containing up to forty per cent methanol. As methanol is a completely clean burning fuel that forms only steam and water and further its flame speed has been higher than that of even gasoline.

In order to curb the other main source of air pollution i.e., the gases of the power stations, complete flue gas treatment plants have to be installed. The experience of European power stations reveals that such equipment will increase the capital cost of the plant by around 22 per cent.

The percentage of SPM concentration in our country has been highest in Kolkatta. This has focused international interest on the city's pollution with the World Health Organinsations Global Environmental Monitoring System (GEMS) choosing Kolkatta as one of its 'comparison stations'. A continuous monitoring of SPM, as also Sulphur dioxide and oxides of Nitrogen Concentration in three areas of the city i.e., Cossipur, Dalhousie Square and Bhowanipur, has been carried out by the National Environmental Engineering Research Institute (NEERI) under the GEMS programme and reports sent every quarter to the WHO headquarters at Geneva. Two other Indian cities are now added to the GEMS list of 'comparison stations' Mumbai and Nagpur, where NEERI has been situated and which among the least polluted metropolitan cities in the country.

In India, air pollution control act envisages the formation of air pollution boards at the Central and State levels "with powers to issue and revoke licences to polluting industries, enforce emission standards and frame rules and regulations for the control of air pollution". The act is primarily directed to the highly polluting industries such as iron and steel, textiles and power plants. The Boards have power to prohibit certain trades and manufacturing processes in notified areas and prescribes emission standards in scheduled premises. The legislation is also understood to ban the burning of garbage and other waste products in urban areas as well as the fluting up of air by burning smoking fuels for domestic purposes.

7

POLLUTION MONITORING

Efforts to monitor, map and abate pollution through biosystem approach have gained importance in recent years. It has been realized by the environmental protection agencies (EPAs) world over that this new alternate technology holds tremendous potential in the restoration of environmental quality and its management. Bio-monitoring or screening of xenobiotics in the environment with living test systems is one such facet. It has now been recognized that no water pollution studies are complete until biological aspects are included. Bioassay is not just a tool, but a very important criterion to allow/disallow the discharge of a toxic substance.

BIOTECHNOLOGICAL APPROVED

The availability of diverse techniques have now placed toxicologists and environmental scientist in a better position to monitor the environmental health from diagnostic, preventive and remedial points of view. However, till recent years the conventional surveillance was largely based on physical and chemical methodologies. But in any pollution study, knowledge of the mechanism of biological response plays a crucial role as the ultimate damage is effected on the living system. Moreover, it often becomes difficult to detect the intermittent and chronic pollution effects through conventional technologies. This is because damage to the biological systems may be brought about at a very low concentration of the pollutant, much below the so-called permissible limits (MATC = maximum allowable toxicant concentr-ation) as recommended by conventional strategies. These 'hidden' injuries can often be resolved only through biosystem approach. Other advantages include its cost-effectivity in the long run, while the knowledge of 'ecological equivalent' may offer the possibility of extrapolation of data from one region to the other. Bioassays do not require assumptions and they provide the means of quickly screening samples for toxicity assessment. Thus bio-monitoring can serve in a complementary fashion with other strategies in defining toxicity threshold.

In this regard, several groups of plants, microbes and animal test samples have been utilized at different organization levels. This chapter attempts to highlight some of the techniques developed so far to trace pollution-induced responses and the possibility of their utilization in monitoring programmes.

Parameters

The parameters are crucial in bioassay studies as to the reliability, predictivity and universal acceptance. This is more apparent when one takes into account the possibility of inherent variability in living systems coupled with the influence of environmental factors upon them.

However, the techniques of bioassay largely encompasses three types of criteria, viz. symptoms of visual damage, genotoxicity test and assessment of the responses at the metabolic levels.

Visual rating

At the initial stages of bioassay, it was largely based on visual rating only. Hence the concept of LD_{50} or LC_{50} emerged for fishes, i.e. the dose at which 50% of test organism is affected. Computer programmes for the determination of these values have also been developed. The growth rate, productivity or phenology are considered. For the microbial growth, turbidometric analysis or electronic particle counters are used more often nowadays. In case of higher plants seed viability, germination frequency, growth rate of different parts and any visual damage symptom of leaves and other parts are considered. Presence or absence of a particular species in a polluted environment (*indicator*) is also another good criterion. However, no single indicator species can fulfil all the purposes equally well. Hence multispecies testing concept has emerged.

Genotoxicity test

This involves the assessment of damage at the cellular and sub-cellular levels. Cells are the primary sites of interaction between chemicals and biological systems. The importance of toxicity assay at this level is based on the assumption that cellular changes are finally reflected in the metabolic and morphological disorders at the organismic, species or population levels. The parameters at the cellular level include different biomolecules, organelles, immune reactions (immunio-assay) and membrane processes. These involve simple and inexpensive tests.

Cytotoxic tests depend on the estimation of chromosome damage including breakages, sister chromatid exchange (SCE) or micronuclei counting. Disfunction of plasma membrane is mainly caused by lipid peroxidation affecting its fludity and structural integrity. It can be measured by conductivity studies indicating ion leakage or trypan blue uptake or leakage of enzyme like LDH (lactose dehydrogenase). While lysosomal viability (as an indication cell viability) is rated through the neutral red dye retention assay. Lately DNA probe is also being considered as a corollary to these parameters, particularly helpful in the identification of pathogens in water samples.

Table 7.1. Toxicant effects and bioassay levels.

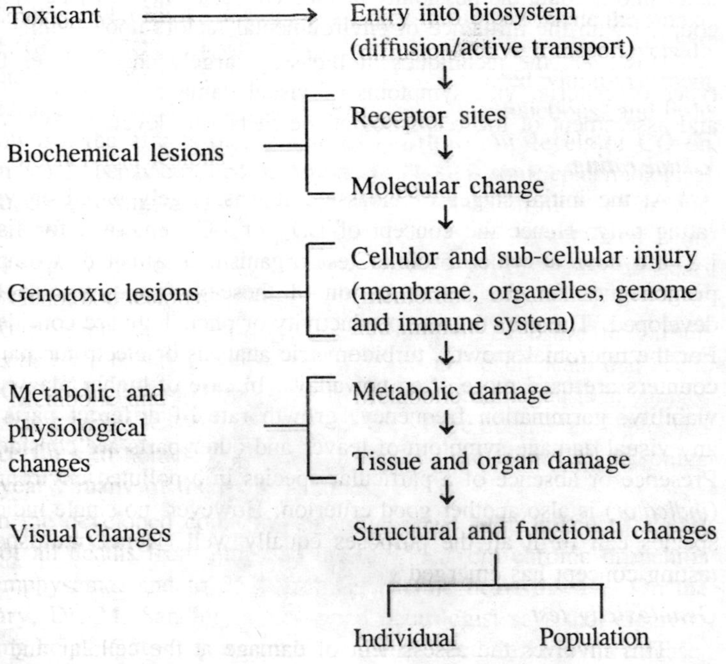

Metabolic rating

With the advancement of knowledge of the physiological and biochemical mechanisms of metabolic processes, it was thought worthwhile to consider the changes in some of these parameters induced by pollution stress as unquestionable 'biomarkers' and thus help in visualizing the impending danger.

Biomonitoring involves both qualitative and quantitative assessment of these markers. They include changes in the contents of chlorophyll molecule and its fluorescence kinetics, contents of soluble protein; nucleic acids; changes in the activities of key enzymes, their reaction kinetics and electrophoretic assessment of isozymes or the induction of some stress proteins.

Utilization

Plant test systems

Among the test systems in plant groups, *algal bioassay* have been fairly used since 1970s. This is due to their high sensitivity, easy availability and culturing facilities in limited areas. They are considered as good indicators of pollution. The primary criteria considered are growth rate, productivity (biomass yield) and LC_{50} values. At the metabolic level, the photosynthetic efficiency has also been taken into account using C^14 assimilation, O_2 evolution and by noting the degradation of *in vivo* chlorophyll fluorescence. Inhibition of some key enzymes has been considered as well.

Some of the algae, commonly considered as test materials, are *Chlorella*, *Scenedesmus*, *Selenastrum*, *Navicula*, *Spirulina*, *Anabaena* and *Microcystis* among the microalgae, while among the marine macroalgae *Ulva*, *Fucus*, *Laminaria*, *Macrocystis*, and *Codium* are worth mentioning.

Experimental methods of algal toxicity have been reviewed by many. For quantifying the responses LC_{50}, Cu-equivalent approach and 'toxicity unit' (TU = $100/LC_{50}$) concepts have been utilized. Palmer's *pollution index* helps composite rating of organic pollution. In case of marine macroalgae, changes in frond structure and biomass have been

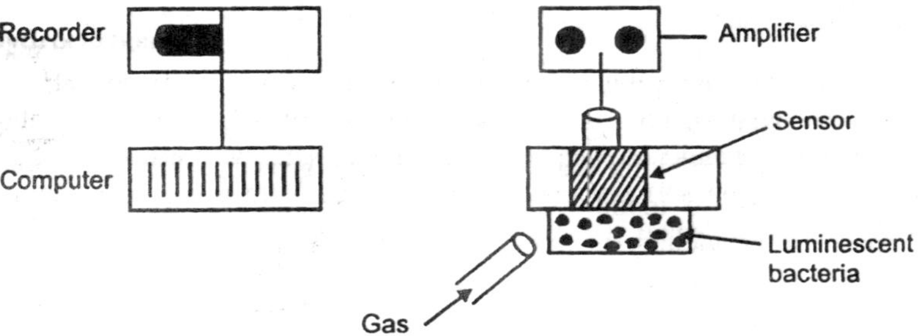

Fig. 7.1. Schematic representation of a photodetector.

used as pollution detection criteria. Benthicc community diversity has also been considered.

Algal species are often used as bio-indicators of pollution. Dominance of Cyanophyceae (blue-green algal group) in the phytoplankton community of a water body indicates its eutrophic nature. *Microcystis* (blue-green algae) causes 'waterbloom' by producing reddish scum of luxuriant growth in aquatic systems due to availability of organic phosphates in abundance. *Navicula*, on the other hand, indicates metal pollution in lakes, being the dominant community where metals like Pb, Zn and Cu are present from mine effluents.

Bacterial bioassay have been used since long for the detection of faecal pollution in potable water through the well-known 'coliform' test. At present, obligate anaerobic bacteria and their phages (viruses) are considered to be most suitable indicators of water pollution. While the bacterium *Salmonella* has been used in *Ames Test* to detect atmospheric mutagens with the help of its different mutant strains. Bacteria are good indicators of organic pollution.

Again the phenomenon of bacterial *bioluminescence* has been used as an indicator in the analysis of atmospheric gases and other compounds like SO_2, formaldehyde, ethyl acetate etc. Bioluminescence is an enzymatically catalyzed light-emitting reaction in living cells. *Photobacterium phosphoreum* colonies are used in a special photodetector, where change in the emission of light due to pollutant effect is detected by a sensor, then amplified and recorded in a computer. These photo-bacteria can also be utilized for investigating the pollution potential of waste waters including that of marine ecosystems.

Lichens (which represent commensalism between algae and fungi) are now commonly used in 'mapping' cities for atmospheric SO_2 detection. They dwindle in areas where the SO_2 concentration in the air is relatively high. Lichen serves as a litmus towards atmospheric gas pollutions. A number of forest and aquatic mosses such as *Bryum*, *Stereophyllum*, *Frontinalis* and others have been used to monitor metal pollution in rivers by measuring their shoot tip growth, while *Sphagnum* has been used to monitor atmospheric deposition of As and Se in Canada in the vicinity of mining and smelting areas.

Aquatic ferns like *Azolla* and *Salvinia* have shown promise in metal pollution monitoring.

While among the vascular *macrophytes*, aquatic plants have more frequently been used for waste water monitoring. Many crop plants and road-side trees have helped monitoring atmospheric deposition of pollutants. Water hyacinth (*Eichornia crassipes*) and Duck weed (*Lemna minor*) have been widely used to monitor aquatic metal pollution. Other aquatic plants that have been found to be useful in this regard are *Pistia stratiotes* or water lettuce, another duckweed *Spirodela*, *Vallisneria*, and *Hydrilla*. In all these cases physiological and biochemical parameters like soluble protein, nucleic acid and enzymes like peroxidase and catalase, besides chlorophyll estimation, have proved to be excellent bioassay parameters. Photosynthetic and respiratory activities can also serve as vital criteria. In case of peroxidase activity, it has been noticed that there occurs a sudden flux when subjected to metal pollution. So it can serve as a 'biomarker' of pollution. While mercury inhibits nitrate reductase activity. Other key enzymes which were tried in bioassay test system include polyphenol oxidase, dehydrogenases and esterases. Mukherji estimated a number of physiological parameters in road-side weeds like *Calotropis*, *Lantana*, *Solanum* and *Croton* to assess Calcutta city air pollutant effects and clearly noted that plants away from the main roads have less disturbances in their metabolic activities.

In case of forest trees having long life-span, long-term effect of pollution are measured by noting changes in leaf shape, while colour is tested by Infrared colour film shots (vigorous leaves reflecting more light) and by measurements of the width of annual growth ring of stem.

Latest and most important biochemical parameter added to the list is the detection of pollution-induced small peptides within the cells called *Phytochelatins* in plants and *Metallothioneins* in animals. They are induced as metal pollution responses alongside the reduction in cellular glutathione content. They are not only reliable markers of pollution, but are also assumed to help metal sequestration and detoxification.

For monitoring ecotoxicity at population level, using demographic techniques where parameters like biomass turnover, survival, and phenology are considered, organisms with short life-span are more desirable. For this purpose, among the plant kingdom, algal system for microbial toxicity testing and *Arabidiopsis thaliana* (a cruciferous plant with very short life-cycle) for higher plant toxicity have been utilized.

Animal test systems

Among the faunal species, toxicity to fishes have been considered since 1950s as a good criterion of xenobiotic bioassay to provide the basis for strategy formulation in the release of toxicants. It has provided the basic tool in monitoring pesticides, phenolic compounds and wastes from tanneries and textile industries. In fact, the concept of LD50 first emerged from studies on fishes. Toxicity assessment has been done on morphology, behaviour, changes in different organs, muscles and metabolism as well. Lately inhibitory effects of xenobiotics on fishes have been investigated on the enzyme AChE (acetylcholine esterase), which is a neurotransmitter and has been found to be a good marker of pesticide pollution. Some of the common fish types in bioassays are *Catla*, *Labeo*, *Channa*, *Teleost* and *Tilapia*.

Other faunal groups include *Protozoa*, particularly the ciliated ones, as good bioindicators through changes in their behavioural patterns, and thus the concept of *ethogram* has developed. A number of zooplanktons, like phytoplanktons, have helped much in evaluating toxicant effects in aquatic systems. They include the well-known *Daphnia monga* and other crustacean species. They also accumulate and concentrate a variety of harmful materials including heavy metals, qualifying them as effective indicators of metal pollution in aquatic environment.

Rotifers are a kind of helminths among the zooplanktons and grow mainly among aquatic vegetation. They constitute another class of fauna which have proved to be good indicators of saprobity and trophic levels of water indicating the contents of putrid organic matter as given by BOD_5. The genus *Brachionus* is connected with eutrophic water. The quotient QBT (i.e. *Brachionus*: *Trichocerca* quotient) has been considered to be a good index of trophic levels, viz. oligotrophic when QBT is <1, mesotrophic 1-2, and eutrophic > 2. However, all these attempts are still based on laboratory tests and yet to be included in field bioassay. The advantage of applying rotifers in biomonitoring of water lies in their easy recognition, easy cultivation, slow growth rate and year-round availability.

Although environmental biotechnology is still in the 'information stage', there is no question now with respect to its utility as pollution monitoring parameter along with the conventional techniques. It is hoped that when some of these test systems and the parameters are standardized, pollution biomonitoring will become more sophisticated and will be placed on a sound footing. But a single bio-test or a single test organism may not always satisfy the criteria, and for which a battery of tests and multi-species system may be desirable. However, the standard test organism should meet certain criteria, which are as follows.

1. It should be sensitive to a pollutant,
2. It should be able to readily âbsorb/adsorb the toxicant,
3. It should be readily available throughout the year and is of common occurrence,
4. It should have features which are directly measurable and predictive,
5. It should be useful in providing inexpensive or cost-effective measure.

The vital question in bio-monitoring is whether the tests based on single species is adequate enough to draw a reasonable conclusion. Cairns has advocated multiple species toxicity testing. Even within a genus, some species may behave as more responsive indicators than others.

Environmental Monitoring

Cell Biology is a specialized branch of Biology encompassing the structural and functional aspects of cells and their components. Recent developments in allied sciences like biochemistry, biophysics, genetics and molecular biology coupled with instrumentation have widened the scope of cell biology. It is being effectively used as an important parameter of screening environmental mutagens and carcinogens.

Cytological Techniques

Cells are the sites of primary interaction between toxicants and biological systems and cell biological methods act as 'biological dosimeters' at cellular level damages.

The tests coming under the orbit of cell biology aim to trace the damages caused by different environmental toxicants on different cellular parameters like cell membrane, cell organelles and chromosomes, carrying the genetic materials like nucleic acids (DNA/RNA) and proteins. They also help in the understanding of the basic mechanism of toxicity, mutagenecity and carcinogenecity.

The utility of this aspect of study has assumed such an importance that a separate discipline called Environmental Mutagenesis has been instituted. It got a major thrust with the exponential growth of industrial chemical production and realization of their effects on human genetic system. Like any other scientific discipline, mere identification of the phenomenon led to the technological innovations of detection at both *in vitro* and *in vivo* levels to find out the remedial measures. One such example being the possibility of amelioration of radiation damage in human genetic system to a great extent by cysteamine injection. It forms disulphide (—s—s—) bridge with cellular protein and offers protection . If the source of the damage is known, then the test systems may help quantitasion and prediction of further consequences. Thus they can act as warning systems. The tests are simple and inexpensive too.

Statistical Damage

Since 1940s, various test systems have been developed using microorganisms, plants, laboratory animals and human cell cultures to assess the toxic and mutagenic potency of numerous chemicals and radiations and even 'living mutagens' or virus and bacteria-induced mutations.

Ames test

The tests based on cell-biological principles include the classical Ames Test. It involves the utilization of a series of strains of the bacterium *Salmonella typhimurium* with the specific ability to detect certain types of chemical mutagens. It is a very widely used preliminary short-term testing and screening of drugs, agricultural chemicals, cosmetics, food additives, inorganic metals and other pollutants. It is based on the principle of the frequency of reversion of mutations at the histamine locus (His^- to His^+). Common yeast cells (*Saccharomyces cerevisae*) have also been used for such type of detections.

Cytogenetic assay

In higher plants and animals detection of permanent genetic damages takes longer time depending on the life-span. Thus in these cases chemical induced disruptions in the chromosome system, be it in vegetative or reproductive cell, is taken as the criterion of assessment of mutagenecity or carcinogenecity, as they constitute the basic hereditary materials. However, insects with shorter life-cycle (*Drosophila*) or "*Arabidiopsis*" system among plants (a member of the mustard family with very short life-span) permit the analysis of events through the entire life.

Other plant systems that have helped reliable screening and monitoring hazardous environmental chemicals are pea, maize, soybean, *Crepis* and *Tradescantia*. *Tradescantia* has unique characteristics which provide two ideal genetic endpoints for mutagenecity testing, viz. 'stamen hair' assay and micronucleus test. The stamen hairs are highly sensitive to gaseous chemicals like Freon-22, Benzene, Ozone, NO_2, SO_2 and they serve as indicators by changing their colour.

Chromosome damage

The most common method of toxicity testing of chemicals is the so called '*Allium test*' or the use of broad bean *Vicia faba* to check the extent of induction of chromosome aberrations in form and behaviour. These may be of different types including fragmentation of chromosomes, bridge formation and disruption of the normal cell division. They serve as clear 'hazard indicators' and can even be quantified.

The severity of the damage may depend on the chemical make-up of the toxicant. In case of phenolic compounds, it has been observed that the toxicity is influenced by the number and position of -OH groups. Genotoxic potencywise they can be put as Pyrogallol > Resorcinol > Gallic acid > Phenol > Guaiacol.

Micronucleus test (MNT)

This is another method where very small nuclei are scored within the cell, formed by large-scale fragmentation of chromosomes. The extent of such nuclei (MN) formation can be directly cor-related to the severity of damage. This is now routinely used for screening mutagenic compounds due to relative simplicity and rapidity. It is most practical for analysis of bone-marrow cells of animals *in vivo* after exposure to chemicals.

Sister-chromatid exchange (SCE)

This is an effective parameter of cytogenetic assay. It is based on the damage caused to DNA molecule and misexchange of chromosome segments. This is characteristically revealed first by using Bromodeoxyuridine (Brd-U) dye and then stained with a fluorescent dye technique. The potentiality of this test is that even after a short exposure it can be easily detected.

Membrane damage

Besides the aforementioned nuclear parameters, damages to cell membrane and cellular organelles can be detected in a number of ways.

The plasma membrane is the first structure encountered by a toxic agent upon reaching the cell. The membranes are the sites of uptake, deposition and elimination of chemicals. The lipoprotein composition of the membrane act as selective barrier due to its semi-permeable nature. Many toxic compounds can modify the membrane structure and its fluidity by the so-called 'lipid peroxidation', i.e. oxidative destruction of the membrane. Dysfunction of the membrane can ultimately lead to cell and organismic death. Inside the cells, other membrane systems including those of mitochondria, nucleus, vocuoles, lysosomes, etc. act as effective sites of compartmentalization.

The loss of semipermeability of the membrane can be measured by the leakage of enzyme like LDH (lactose dehydrogenase) or efflux of electrolytes or through the uptake of *trypan blue*. Fragility of Lysosome can also be assayed by *Neutral red* retention test, i.e. loss of capacity of the lysosome to retain this cationic dye after being damaged. This has been used as a biomarker of cell viability.

The physical damage to different types of membrane systems or the deposition of toxicant granules in different cellular compartments can be detected through the light, electron and phase contrast microscopy including imaging techniques.

Recent developments in the technique of plant and animal tissue culture have helped significantly in monitoring these cellular damages in successive cell cycles. Human lymphocyte culture is now a valuable tool for routine monitoring of persons exposed to occupational hazards of chemical substances.

Hazardous chemicals like venyl chloride, methyl-isocyanate (MIC) or phosgene of the 'Bhopal gas' fame can cause total disruption of cellular components leading to death. Thus monitoring of environmental toxicants through cell biological methods gives better insight into the problem and may help the development of suitable remedial measures. Moreover, long-term exposure (chronic) to very low concentrations of toxicants may often be revealed only through the detection of damage to the cellular components vis-a-vis the genetic components.

Molecular Monitoring

In the monitoring of environment, molecular probe is primarily based on small segment (oligonucleotide) of Nucleic acid (DNA or RNA) capable of recognizing complementary base sequence in the target DNA from the sample organism (DNA probe). It could also be through the sequence recognition of specific protein (Antigen-Antibody), as is done in *immunoassay*. DNA probe or DNA-gene probe as it is called, helps in the detection of the gene rather than its product. While immunoassay identifies the amplified gene product.

These recently developed molecular probes are utilized in various biotechnological studies. In the arena of environmental analysis, these are very useful in the diagnosis of infectious diseases, identification of waterborne pathogens; microbes in mixed cultures and food contaminants. They are very sensitive, accurate and faster too. While the conventional tests, based on morphology and physiology, may take a few (4-5) days, the molecular technique takes only a few hours.

Initially it requires time and effort to develop a particular assay. But once optimized, it offers tremendous advantage over the traditional analytical technique.

DNA-gene Probe

It is a gift of modern biology and is used variously in basic and applied aspects of biotechnological studies. The principle lies in the 'hybridization' of complementary base sequence of DNA strands, where a given strand can only pair with its complementary one.

The steps involved in the process are discussed in the following lines.

Step 1. Extraction, separation and isolation of DNA fragments.

Step 2. The double stranded DNA is then heated and dissociated into two single strands and these single stranded nucleic acid molecules of known genetic function constitute the probes.

Step 3. Labelling of the probe.

For easier identification of such a probe, segments of DNA are 'labelled.' These labelling could be achieved either with (i) radioactive isotopes (32_P or 35_S) or with (ii) non-radioactive methods using biotin (vitamin H) or fluorescent technique (light emitting) at a particular wave length.

Step 4. DNA hybridization.

If the target DNA in the test sample has the matching base sequence with the probe, then a double helix will be formed. Such a double strand constitute the 'hybrid' molecule and the process is known as DNA hybridization. The hybrid molecule can be identified easily due to the labelling of the probe. This will provide the genetic information of the microbe in question and can be conducted on mixed cultures as well.

Step 5 PCR technique for DNA amplification.

DNA probes mostly need 10^5 to 10^6 copies of the target gene to produce a reliable positive signal and thus need to be amplified.

This amplification process is done with the help of a thermostable enzyme DNA polymerase (Taq. polymerase isolated from the bacterium

Thermus aquaticus and is heat stable). It can create millions of copies of DNA from a single copy of the target DNA molecule. This process is known as *polymerase chain reaction* or simply PCR. This invention has now been undoubtedly established as one of the most far reaching developments in molecular biology and has become a handy tool in the hands of biotechnologists. The technique has been justifiably compared with 'finding a needle in a haystack and then producing a haystack of needles by way of amplification.'

The PCR method involves three steps, viz. denaturation, annealing and extension of DNA. These steps constitute a cycle and with 25-30 cycles, a massive amount of DNA can be obtained (2n PCR products). In fact, PCR machine (automated thermal cycler) has been developed, which allows the operation to be completed within a few hours. It requires the presence of the enzyme (DNA polymerase) and two synthetic *primers* (short DNA molecules), which are complementary and bind to two sites on either side of the target DNA to be amplified and then extend to give a new strand. When these two ingredients (enzyme and primers) are supplied, PCR can literally amplify almost any piece of DNA.

Using both DNA probe and PCR technique, it is now possible to detect bacteria and viruses for water quality monitoring upto 1/100 ml approximately. Bej could identify coliform bacteria (*E. coli*) and enteric pathogens like *Shigella* and *Salmonella* in water through the use of lac Z and lam B gene analysis.

It is thus possible to quickly assess the bacterial safety of potable water supplies in conjunction with the conventional techniques. It has also been developed for food borne pathogens like *Listera*, and *Vibrio cholerae*.

Immunoassay

Immunological techniques based on antigen-antibody (protein) reactions are now widely adopted in various environmental analysis including diverse pesticides/herbicides, and identification of microbial pathogens and their toxins in food and water. They are useful only in those cases where substances show immunological properties. Overview of these techniques have been made by Swaminathan and Konger, Vanderlon, and Notermans. Of these techniques, both enzyme immunoassay (EIA) and latex agglutination tests are widely applied.

Enzyme immunoassay relies upon an enzyme tag, where an enzyme is used as a marker, viz. Horse Radish peroxidase, Glucooxidase and Alkaline phosphatase. They are covalently bound to a ligand (antibody

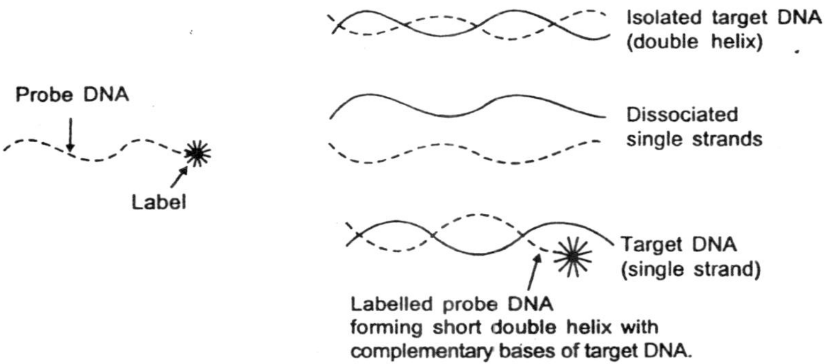

Fig. 7.2. DNA probe.

protein). In recent years the use of monoclonal antibody (MAb) which is a homogeneous antibody derived from single clone of cells, has made the test more specific, sensitive and time saving too.

Latex agglutination assay, on the other hand, is simpler where polysterene latex particles are coated with antibodies. Test samples are added to sensitized latex particles and after proper shaking they are incubated overnight. If antigen is present in the sample, sensitized particles agglutinate within 10 minutes.

Metabolic products formed due to microbial growth can also be detected. Quantitation of these metabolites may often indicate the number of microbes present. Assays have been developed for Cholera toxin, *Salmonella*, *Listera* and *Yersinia* species.

Assay techniques have also been developed (using MAb) for pesticide/herbicide contamination in water bodies. These agrochemicals may either be of synthetic or microbial origin. They can also be used in the analysis of phytosanitary quality of seed products for sale as disease-free ones. Some of the pesticides which have been measured by immunoassays are triazines, aldrin, 2,4,-D, DDT, paraquat,. glyphosate, etc. Moreover, these methods can detect pesticide concentrations in water much lower than the detection limits of conventional systems (viz. gas chromatography).

Immunoassays for environmental contaminants (both living and nonliving) are attractive for their cost-effectivity, sensitivity and accuracy. In approximately 80% of the cases the results obtained through them agree with the conventional techniques.

Bioluminescence

It is a completely new concept and is based on plasmid encoded certain gene sequences that produce assayable flurogenic signals

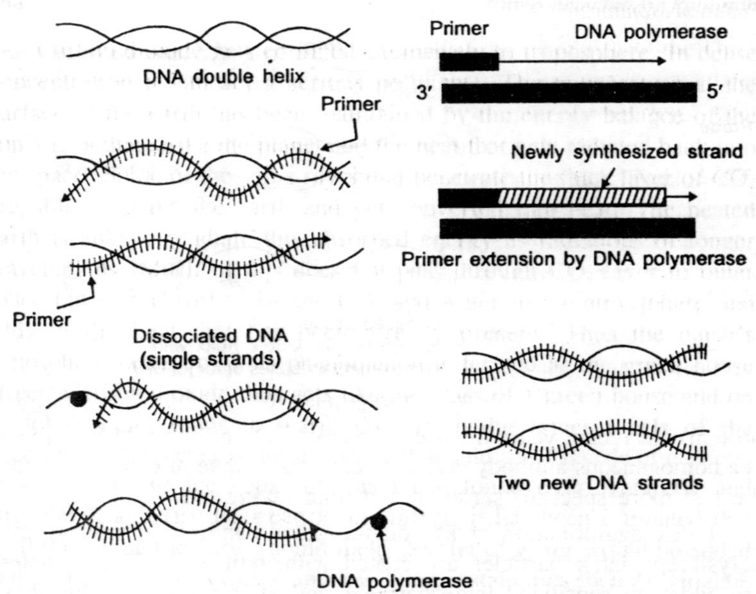

Fig. 7.3. PCR technique.

whenever the genes for catabolism are expressed in luminescent bacteria like *Vibrio* or *Photobacterium*.

It is a highly sensitive and attractive means of monitoring contamination of ground water and subsurface soil. The Lux Reporter genes produce visible light (blue-green) in host bacterium and some bacterial strains have been developed through gene-cloning in *Pseudomonas* for tracing the degradation of Napthalene, Salicylate, Toluene and Xylene. The changes in emission spectra occur due to changes in fluorescent protein and the enzyme luciferase.

In future, fibre-optic methods of remote light sensing and cell-immobilization technique would help in on-line monitoring system.

BIOSENSOR

Biosensor is an analytical device based on the sensing response of biological materials (immobilized) in combination with an electrochemical transducer to convert the biological reaction into a digital electronic signal which is proportional to the concentration of the target substance (analyte). It is highly specific and accurate in detection.

The concept of biosensor is usually attributed to Clark and Lyons. The 'enzyme electrode,' however, was christened by Updike and Hicks. Since then, it has gained popularity and a vast array of sensors have

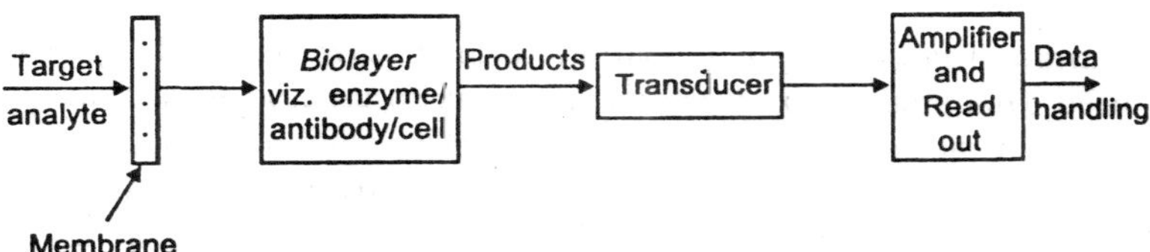

Fig. 7.4. Flow diagram of general biosensor.

been developed based on different biodetecting elements. Till recently, it has largely been used in monitoring the efficiency of industrial bioprocesses (fermentation tanks *in situ*), health care for detecting blood glucose level, urea in body fluid and in military purposes for monitoring toxic gases in warfare. They are, however, now finding more and more application in the realms of environmental monitoring and pollution detection.

A biosensor essentially comprises three components.

1. The biological component consists of immobilized biological sensing materials, viz. enzymes, immune-agents (antibody/antigen), lectin, DNA, whole microbial cell, and higher plant or animal tissue slices. The advantage being conferred by biological material is the ability to operate at ambient temperature.

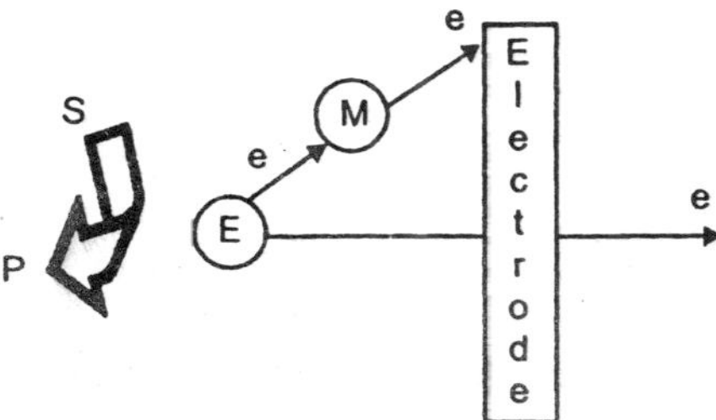

2. The physical component is a transducing element which converts biochemical interactions into electrical or optical signal and it could be made of platinum, gold or graphite.
3. While the interface is a polymeric film or membrane linking the biological component to the transducer.

Sensors could be of indirect or direct type. In the former two electrodes (sensing and reference) are used. Whereas in the latter, the biological component is directly placed on the electrode offering more sensitivity and accuracy as the electrons are transferred from the analyte to the enzyme or other sensing element, and then directly to the electrode. Sensors, whether enzyme or whole cell, mainly work on the principle of gas electrodes, viz. O_2, CO_2, H_2O, NH_3, H_2S, etc.

Categories

Enzyme electrode

Here purified enzymes are required. If immobilized, the electrode can be utilized repeatedly.

Immobilized cell biosensor

Mainly microbial cells or tissues are used. As multiple enzymes of the cell may come to play in this case, care should be taken about selectivity.

Optical biosensor

It uses optical principle to convert biological activity into electric signal. Some such sensors use optical fibres and fluorescent molecule-tagged antibody to detect antigen or vice-versa. Since these are non-electrical, they have advantages of *in vivo* applications and multiple analyte can be examined using different monitoring wave lengths. The fluorescence intensity is measured by a detector and then converted into electrical signal. They are of immense value particularly in medical science. They can also be used in environmental studies. Optical sensors are resistant to electrical disturbances, have a very short response time and wide range of materials can be used for their fabrication. Other advantage is that the signal remains unaffected even if 'fouling' occurs on the membrane surface from the bio-film. The main drawbacks of this sensor are its fragility, cost and bulkyness. However, recent development in fibre optics has helped the system in many ways.

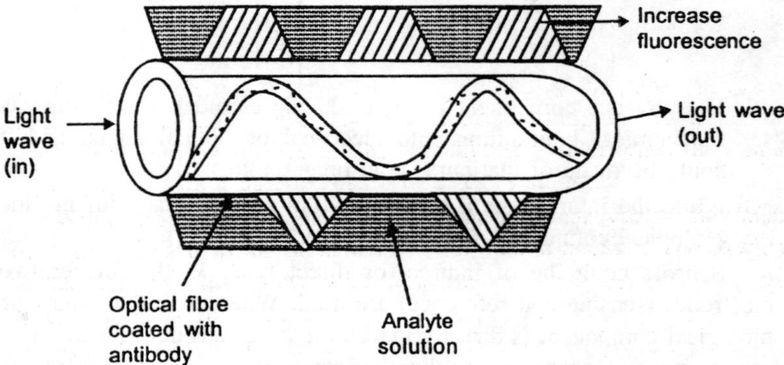

Fig. 7.5. Schematic diagram of optical sensor.

ISFET based devices (ion-sensitive field-effect transistor)

It is a semiconducting device for measuring extremely small changes in the analyte.

Biosensor for environmental application does not differ in principle from those used for other purposes. Kits have been developed to identify specific pollutants. Biochips (biocatalyst on silicon chip surface) can monitor change in the environment, viz. microbial response to the presence of heavy metals and organic toxins in soil, water and air.

H_2O_2 biosensor

It is based on oxidoreductase enzyme (viz. peroxidase), where O_2 is used as H_2 acceptor forming H_2O_2. The rate of production of H_2O_2 gives the measure of the analyte present in the sample.

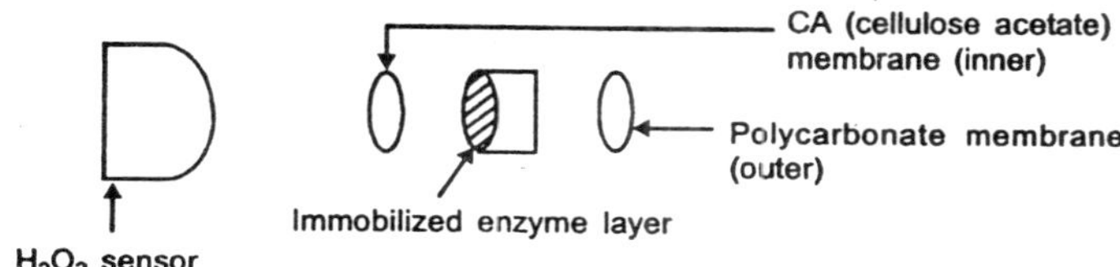

Fig. 7.6. Schematic diagram of H_2O_2 biosensor.

The membrane could be of cellulose acetate (CA) or collagen on which the enzyme is immobilized. The enzymatic membrane can be replaced as and when necessary. H_2O_2 sensors are used in continuous monitoring of blood glucose *in vivo*, different industrial process control and waste water treatment by placing the sensor in the flowing stream.

Microbial biosensor

They are composed of immobilized microbial cells and can be classified as either (i) respiratory activity measurement type, or (ii) electrochemically active metabolite measurement type.

Besides, there could be thermistors for measuring heat generated due to metabolic activities or photodetectors with luminescent bacteria where change in light intensity can be detected, viz. decrease in intensity due to metabolic' inhibition by heavy metals or other toxins. For microbial

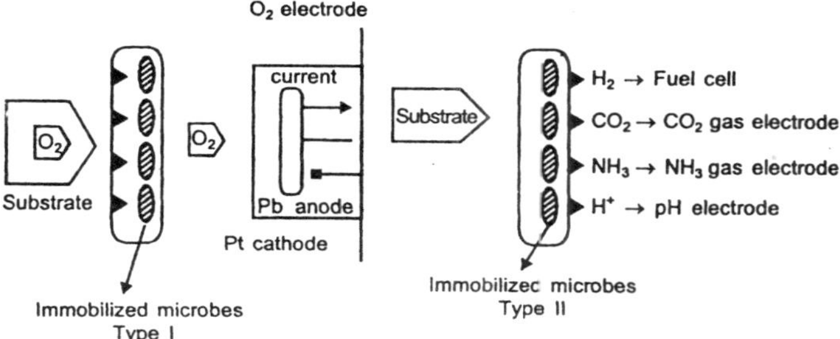

Fig. 7.7. Microbial sensors.

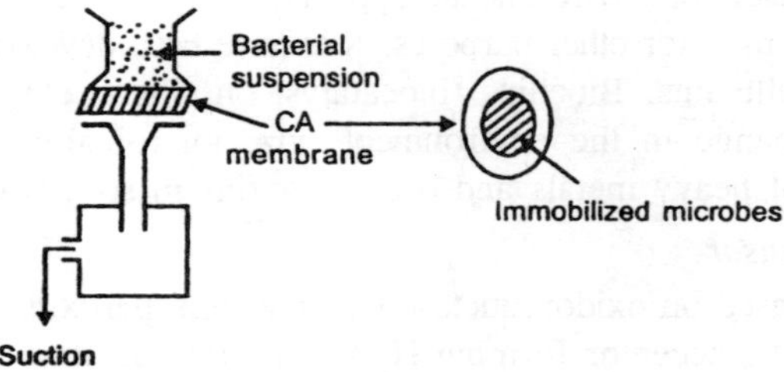

Fig. 7.8. Preparation of microbial membrane.

sensor, usually membrane entrapment of cells (cellulose acetate) technique is used these days, rather than the gel (polyacrylamide /collagen) type. After the membrane is prepared, it is stored in a buffer solution (pH 7) at 4°C.

The advantage of microbial-sensors are that they are more tolerant to pH and temperature than the enzyme electrodes. They are also comparatively cheaper and have longer life span. But the disadvantages include longer response time and at the cell level due to many types of enzymes selectivity in necessary. For this mutant bacterial strain deficient in a particular enzyme is more suitable.

Gas phase biosensor

The biosensors which are commercially available are used for assessing compounds particularly in the solution phase. However, recent finding of piezo-electric crystals (Quartz crystals) as immuno-chemical sensors in the gas phase hold promise and convenient in the area of environmental analysis. Formaldehyde can be assayed in the gas phase using formaldehyde dehydrogenase layered onto a Mh, piezo-electric crystal.

Applications

1. BOD_5 (biological oxygen demand) is a widely used test in organic pollution detection. Conventional test takes five days of incubation. While BOD sensor using *Trichosporon* (Yeast), as oxygen probe, takes only 15 minutes. Its selflife is 20 days if continuously used.
2. Microbial biosensor for detecting CH_4 and CO_2 gas (called gas sensor) has been developed. For methane, immobilized bacterium *Methylomonas* is used and it takes 2 minutes. While for carbon dioxide, *Pseudomonas* (a particular strain) is used. Its life time is more than a month. *Thiobacillus*based sensor can detect SO_2 in the environment. CO detector can help detecting carbonmonoxide in mines and many industries so that fire alarm could be given.

3. Pesticide-specific antibodies (immunoassay) have been utilized to detect the presence of herbicides like triazines and carbamates in ground water with the sensitivity of 0.13 to 0.7 mg/l within 16 minutes. For malathion the detection could be upto 16.5 ppm, for sevin 0.5 ppm and for parathion it is even up to 0.1 ppm. Immunoelectrodes are very useful when the analyte concentration is very low.

   Graphite electrode with the fixed cyanobacterium *Synechococcus*, can measure electron transport inhibition in the organism during photosynthesis by herbicide action. The sensitivity is found to be about 50 $\mu g/1$ and the total time taken is 10 mins.

   Use of acetylcholine esterase (Ac ChE) obtained from bovine erythrocytes may also help the detection of carbamate and organophosphate group of insecticides in water. Portable pesticide monitors are available in the markets of developed countries. Other biosensors against polychlorinated biphenyls (PCBs), chlorinated hydrocarbons and aromatic compounds can be used.

4. For the detection of phenols, phenol oxidase enzyme obtained from mushrooms and potatoes have been used.

   Maleic dehydrogenase (MDH) based fuel cell can detect methanol contamination in drinking water upto 10^{-3} ppm. This is much below the limits of the regular GLC (gas-liquid chromatography) or MS (mass spectrometry) analysis.

5. Heavy metals can be detected and estimated using enzymes with -SH group. Cu ^{2,} is detected using the enzyme tyrosinase.

Some of the biological and physical components used in biosensor for environmental purposes are presented in the following chart.

Biological component	*Physical component*	*Parameter measured*
Trichosporon cutaneum	O_2 electrode	BOD
Azotobacter vinelandi	NH_3 electrode	Nitrate
Methylomonas flagellae	O_2 electrode	CH_4
Bacillus subtilis	O_2 electrode	Mutagen screening
Mixed Nitrifying bacteria	O_2 electrode	NH_3 and NO_2
NADH and Dehydrogenase	Redox electrode	Ethanol
Antibody to Parathion	Piezo-electric crystal	Parathion (Pesticide)
Cholinesterase	Chem. F.E.T.	Nerve gas
ACH receptor	Conductimeter	Nerve gas

Thus the domain of biosensor technology is growing and basic research is concentrated on various application possibilities, selectivity, accuracy, rapidity and cost-effectivity. For detecting pesticide concentration by enzyme sensor it may now cost approximately $ 3.00 per test against $ 15.00 in conventional test.

Molecular film technology is being improved for a uniform planar coating of sensing material. While *Hybrid sensor* concept has also developed. It has a combination of immobilized cells and enzyme membrane to have improved sensitivity. Efforts are continuously being made to improve upon the sensing technology and the field has assumed such an importance that a separate journal on *biosensor* is solely devoted to it.

In USA, of the different agencies engaged in environmental biotechnology development, NASA (National Aeronautics and Space Administration) and NIST (National Institute of Standard and Technology) are trying to evolve better types of sensors for the accurate detection of carcinogens (cancer causing agents) and other hazardous toxins in soil and water. In such cases biosensors have been found to be superior in sensitivity than ordinary physical instruments.

8

Commercial Pollution

From a broad point of view, industry encompasses all human endeavors to provide a better material life. But every level of industry-obtaining raw material, manufacturing, using products, and ultimately disposing of products-produces wastes which are discharged into the environment. Pollution may be defined as the addition to air, water, or soil of any material (or heat) that is usually not found there, or that is in excess of normal amounts. Thus while the discharge of most wastes is synonymous with pollution, emissions from smokestacks and drains of factories are far from the only sources of industrial pollution. Consider oil, for example. Spillage and pollution may occur in the process of drilling and obtaining crude oil from wells. There may be further spillage and pollution in transporting oil. Refineries pollute as they make oil into gasoline and other fuels. Finally, exhaust pollution results from the burning of gasoline in individual automobiles.

Thus, industrial pollution cannot be blamed solely on manufacturers. The blame must be shared by the whole of industrial society which desires, produces, and uses the products. Conversely, cleaning up pollution and preventing new pollution problems will demand understanding and cooperation by everyone. We cannot all do as we please with material goods and still have a clean environment.

Attitudes, Assumptions, and Pollution Problems

Why Do Humans Polluted?

Unless we discover the answer to the question "Why do humans polute?" and make some basic changes, we are more than likely to clean up one mess only to find ourselves making another. By understanding the causes underlying our pollution habits, we stand some chance of changing basic attitudes and behavior in such a way as to find permanent solutions to pollution problems.

A basic problem is that we tend to concentrate on single goals. As industrialists or consumers, as individuals or groups, humans tend to pursue single narrow objectives and let other things drop where they may. In his book *The Naked Ape*, Desmond Morris describes this tendency as a legacy from our primate ancestors. The ape goes after a banana and drops the peel. We go after a candy bar or soft drink and usually drop the wrapper or container. Similarly, we drive our cars with little concern as to what or how much is coming out of the tailpipe and what damage it does. We wash cleaning fluids, paint thinners, oil, grease, and all manner of other unwanted material down drains and sewers with little thought of where it will come out and the effects that it may have when it does. Factories still are frequently located on rivers or lakes simply to have a convenient way of flushing away wastes. The smokestack is the simplest way of dumping wastes into the air, where wind will presumably carry them away.

Secondly, as individuals we have a generally casual attitude toward accepting pollution. For example, workers could use the power of a strike to demand that a factory or an industry stop polluting, but in fact they don't. Consumers could organize consumer boycotts of goods from a polluting factory, but in fact they don't. Not many consumers are inclined to use pollution by the manufacturer as a criterion in choosing whether or not to buy a particular item. We must seriously ask ourselves, "Is the polluter more guilty than the people who accept the pollution?" Certainly the former could not exist without the latter.

Assumptions Underlying the Casual Attitude toward Pollution

The casual attitude toward pollution, in turn, is underlain by one or more of the following assumptions:

1. *Threshold level.* It is assumed that below a certain level of concentration, pollutants will have no ill effect. This "certain level" is the *threshold level.*
2. *Dilution.* It is assumed that pollutants will mix freely in air and/or water and will thus be diluted below threshold levels.
3. *Assimilation.* It is assumed that wastes will re-enter the natural biological or geochemical cycles of the Earth.
4. *Immobility of solid wastes.* It is assumed that solid wastes will stay where they are put.
5. *Accidents won't happen:* In all our activities we tend to assume that accidents (oil spills, chemical leaks) won't happen.

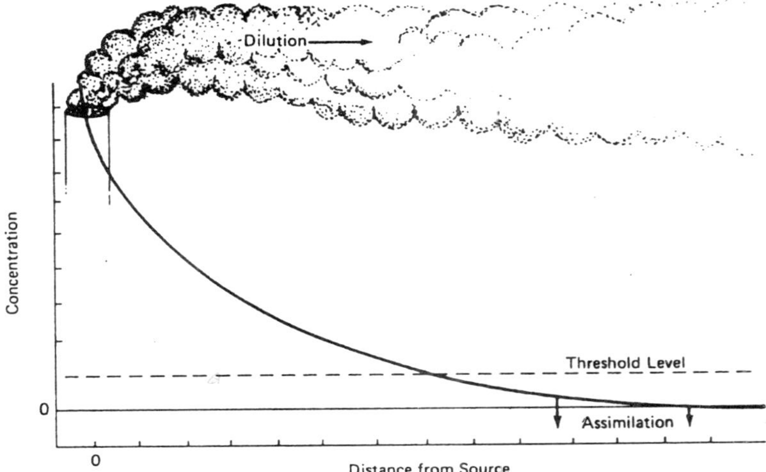

Fig. 8.1. By dilution, the concentration of a pollutant diminishes with distance from the source. The threshold level is that level below which it is assumed there is no ill effect. After dilution, it is assumed that assimilation will reduce pollution levels to zero. With modern chemical pollutants, both assumptions may be invalid.

These assumptions do have some validity. The first three involve the means which natural ecosystems use to dispose of their own pollutants of both physical and biological origin. For example, volcanoes vent large amounts of sulfur dioxide (SO_2), a gas highly poisonous to both plants and animals. Forest fires produce carbon monoxide (CO), a poisonous gas, as well as the nonpoisonous carbon dioxide (CO_2). Natural vegetation gives off a hydrocarbon gas, ethylene (C_2H_2), which acts as a plant hormone and in higher concentrations is extremely toxic to plants. However, in the amounts produced by nature these gases are readily diluted to threshold levels and then totally removed by assimilatory processes. For example, sulfur dioxide, ethylene, and carbon monoxide are readily absorbed and metabolized by soil microorganisms.

Likewise, animals produce urine and fecal wastes which in large concentrated amounts are very serious pollutants. However, in natural ecosystems, populations are small or mobile enough that undesirable amounts of these wastes do not accumulate in one place. Also, these natural organic and inorganic wastes are readily metabolized by organisms and assimilated into the nutrient cycles.

Sediments may be thought of in a similar way. In runoff from most naturally vegetated land, sediments are dilute enough that they do not harm aquatic life as they wash downstream. Their natural rate of deposition is slow enough that they are assimilated in the natural course of succession without causing disturbance. Further, such natural deposits do not tend to migrate; they tend to stay where they land. These processes work so admirably in natural systems that it is not surprising we should assume that they would work as well for us and our wastes. The question addressed in the next section is why they do not.

Limits of Assumption

The question of why pollution problems exist despite the natural processes of dilution and assimilation brings us back to the theme of balances. Wastes do not accumulate to undesirable levels if the production of pollutants is balanced by dilution and assimilation; in natural ecosystems, this is generally the case. Humanity's problem is not that the natural processes don't operate, but rather that the critical balance is exceeded. This comes about in three basic ways: (1) overproduction of wastes, (2) introduction of unique chemicals, and (3) reduction of assimilative capacity.

As a result of both growing population and increasing affluence, we produce wastes in much greater quantities than are found in natural ecosystems. In 1973 it was estimated that burning coal and oil contaminated with sulfur released 10 times more sulfur dioxide into the atmosphere than comes from all natural sources. Ethylene production from auto exhaust was estimated at 1000 times nature's production. Such overproduction of wastes occurs with countless other compounds.

Unique chemicals

Modern chemical technology now produces and markets some 70,000 organic chemicals for use in insecticides, herbicides, synthetic fibers, plastics, and so forth, and about 10,000 new chemicals are added each year. Many of these chemicals are completely unique to nature, that is, they do not occur in nature even in small amounts as do sulfur dioxide, ethylene, and carbon monoxide. Therefore, in many cases, nature has not evolved any way of assimilating them and consequently they accumulate.

More importantly, some of these new compounds do not seem to have threshold levels-that is, no minimum exposure can be considered safe. Any level above zero may have harmful effects, particularly when periods of exposure are prolonged. As air, water, and soil become generally polluted with these compounds, exposures may be lifelong.

Reduction of assimilative capacity

Alteration of the environment in many cases reduces its assimilative capacity. As we noted, soil microorganisms are highly effective in assimilating sulfur dioxide, carbon monoxide, and ethylene. Vegetation is effective in removing other air pollutants. However, how much vegetation and unpaved soil is left in our cities? We also noted that sediment, through destroying the aquatic life in streams and rivers, reduces the capacity of the streams to assimilate organic wastes. Dredging and filling wetlands destroys the enormous potential of these systems for assimilating nutrient wastes and hence preventing eutrophication or other undesirable effects.

Finally, it is interesting to note that nature does not oblige organisms to live in the center of natural pollution sources. Volcanic vents and hot sulfur springs, for example, have few, if any, inhabitants. By contrast, the structure of an industrial technological society obliges most of its members to live and work in cities, the very heart of pollution centers. Thus, we tend to maximize rather than minimize our exposure to pollutants. Put another way, we create a pollution soup in which we oblige ourselves to live.

To free ourselves from the ill effects of pollution, it is necessary to understand the relationship between particular pollutants and natural balances and processes in more detail. We will then have the basis for understanding how human activities must be adjusted to fit within the limits of natural balances.

Assumptions Applied to Pollution Problems

Air Pollution

Major air pollutants

A wide range of inorganic gases, organic compounds, inorganic metallic substances, and soot particles is discharged into the atmosphere by motor vehicles, factories, power plants, home furnaces, and waste incineration plants. Many of these compounds are known to have injurious effects on human health, and may cause death of both animals and plants. Principal compounds, their major sources, and their important health effects.

In large part, wastes are discharged into the atmosphere through exhaust pipes, chimneys, and vents with the simple assumptions that they will dilute to threshold levels and then disappear. Unfortunately, these assumptions are invalid for several reasons.

City air-limited dilution

When the outpouring of pollutants is concentrated in a limited area, as it is in a city, undesirable levels of air pollution are inevitably created at times. Wind and rising air currents flush the pollutants away, and mix and dilute them with large volumes of surrounding air, thus reducing problems. However, such air currents are not always present. In still air, dilution is limited to the rate of diffusion, that is, the natural movement of molecules from an area of high concentration to one of lesser concentration. Since particles such as soot diffuse rather slowly, remarkably high concentrations can build up in surrounding air.

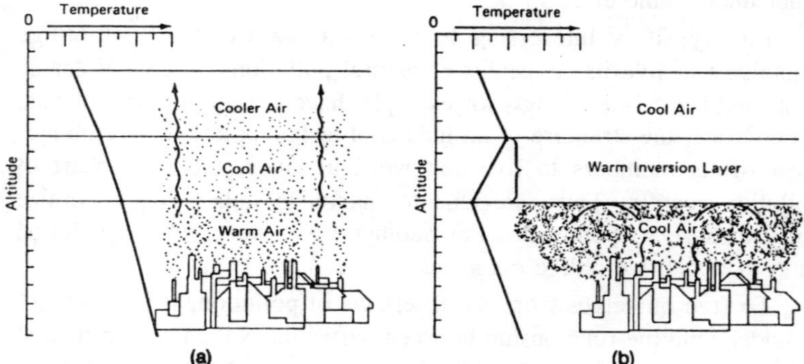

Fig. 8.2. Temperature inversion. (a) Warm air rises, dispersing pollutants. (b) With a temperature inversion, a warm air layer overlying the cool air prevents pollutants from rising and being dispersed.

Aggravating the still-air condition is a weather phenomenon called a *temperature inversion*. Normally, air temperature decreases with increasing height above the ground. In this situation, the warm air near the ground rises (because warm air is lighter than cold air), carrying pollutants upward and dispersing them at higher altitudes. In a temperature inversion, the cold air is at the ground and warm air is above. This situation develops with the influx of a cold front during which the more dense cold air moves in under the warm air. With a temperature inversion, the upward currents of warm air are blocked and pollutants stay in the cold air near the ground. The effects of a temperature inversion may be intensified by local topography, as in Mexico City and Los Angeles, where the surrounding hills or mountains prevent pollutants from moving horizontally.

Weather conditions which inhibit the dispersion of pollutants and hence result in their building up to high levels are referred to as air pollution *episodes*. Air pollution disasters which have resulted from such episodes include the following: London, 1150 deaths; London, 4,000 deaths; Donora, Pennsylvania, 20 deaths; New York, 400 deaths.

While such episodes are commonly cited to emphasize the seriousness of air pollution, they may actually distract as from the real issues. By associating air pollution and weather we tend to blame the pollution on the "terrible weather." This is a mistake. The weather patterns that produce episodes are quite normal. The tragedy lies in our failure to balance the volume of our pollutants with the air space available to receive them.

The citing of particular episodes and tragedies also tends to obscure the fact that average levels of pollutants in city air are manyfold higher than in clean air. Countless cases of eye and nasal irritation, coughing, fatigue, and asthma attacks are known to be associated with air pollution. Lungs are especially affected by pollutants in the air. In order to allow exchange of carbon dioxide and oxygen, they have a very large surface area of delicate body tissue. This tissue is intimately exposed to and affected by air pollutants. The most significant factor in lung diseases such as chronic bronchitis, emphysema, and lung cancer has been shown to be "personalized air pollution" cigarette smoking. However, more generalized air pollution certainly aggravates these conditions. Overall health costs resulting from generalized air pollution in the United States have been estimated as high as $10 billion per year. When all this is considered, the loss in human health due to air pollution is much greater than particular episodes would suggest.

Air pollution also has severe effects on plants. It has killed countless trees and shrubs in cities. Many species can no longer be grown in cities and others are severely stunted.

City air pollution contributes to increased erosion of buildings and monuments, corrosion of metals, weakening of textiles and other fibers, and deterioration of paint. Also, the general dirt from air pollution demands increased washing of cars, windows, clothing, and so forth, and still it is difficult, perhaps impossible, to escape a perpetual dingy look.

Clearly, the volumes of pollutants we produce in cities, even given average dilution conditions, still accumulate to levels above the minimum thresholds for assuring human health, growing plants, and maintaining materials.

Another reason why we cannot assume that pollutants will simply dilute to threshold levels is the phenomenon of *synergistic interactions*.

A synergistic interaction is that which occurs when two or more substances interact and cause an effect much greater than one would anticipate from the addition of their separate effects. You have probably heard of synergistic effects in connection with certain drugs and alcohol. Small doses of certain tranquilizers have a relatively mild effect, as do modest amounts of alcohol. However, when taking these drugs is combined with drinking alcohol, the effect may be fatal-tragically greater than would be anticipated on the basis of their separate effects.

Similarly, individual pollutants at existing concentrations might seem relatively harmless. However, in real life we are invariably exposed to many pollutants simultaneously and the potential for synergistic effects is virtually infinite. As time passes, scientists are discovering more and more synergistic effects involving pollutants. Three well-known effects are those relating, respectively, to photochemical smog, fine particles, and smoking.

Photochemical smog

In the early period of the Industrial Revolution, the commonest pollutants in most cities were particulate matter (smoke particles) and sulfur dioxide from burning coal. Most coal is contaminated with sulfur and, when burned, produces sulfur dioxide. As the use of coal gave way to cleaner-burning oil and natural gas during the first half of this century, air pollution was vastly lessened. However, in the 1950's and 1960's, virtually every city found itself increasingly enveloped by a brownish haze commonly called *smog*. It is more correctly referred to as *photochemical smog* because sunlight plays a role in its formation.

The worst culprit in producing photochemical smog is the automobile. Ideally, gasoline, which is a hydrocarbon (molecules made of hydrogen and carbon), should burn to carbon dioxide and water as the only waste products:

$$C_xH_x + O_2 \rightarrow H_2O + CO_2$$

Unfortunately, gasoline burned in the cylinder of the internal combustion engine does not reach this ideal. Gasoline molecules are incompletely burned, leaving various hydrocarbon molecules in the exhaust. Also, under conditions of combustion, some of the nitrogen of the atmosphere combines with oxygen to form various nitrogen oxides (NO, NO_2, NO_3). Further, carbon monoxide (CO) also results from incomplete burning, as does some sulfur dioxide from sulfur contamination in the fuel, and lead, if present as an antiknock additive. All these wastes which leave the exhaust pipe along with carbon dioxide and water are to a greater or lesser extent toxic compounds and even by themselves are hardly desirable. However, their toxic effects are intensified by reactions between them, particularly between nitrogen oxides and hydrocarbons. Rather than being diluted further and gradually assimilated in the environment, these two compounds undergo a complex series of chemical reactions with each other, and with oxygen and water vapor in air to form ozone (O_3) and a wide variety of organic compounds consisting of various combinations of hydrocarbons with oxygen and nitrogen atoms. Sunlight provides the energy for these reactions; hence the resulting haze of this pollution is called *photochemical* smog. Ozone and many of the carbon-containing compounds, particularly one called *PAN* (for peroxyacetyl-nitrate), are extremely poisonous to both plants and animals. They are known to be responsible for eye, nose, and throat irritation and it is likely that they contribute to more serious disorders that develop over the long term. Thus, the interactions between nitrogen oxides and hydrocarbons are synergistic. Their end effect is a level of toxicity much greater than the effects of these compounds by themselves would suggest.

Fine particles

Synergistic reactions may also involve fine particles (less than 0.002 mm) of soot or smoke from burning any fuel or incinerating wastes. Such particles consist basically of nonreactive carbon. However, these particles, which are so small that they escape through most filters and remain suspended in the air for long periods, are potent adsorbers of metal atoms such as lead, hydrocarbons, sulfur, and nitrogen oxides. In other words, the fine particle collects and carries virtually every other pollutant. Many, perhaps most, of the chemical reactions resulting in the formation of more toxic compounds (as described in the formation of photochemical smog) may take place on the surface of fine particles. Then, when inhaled, these fine particles are drawn deep into the lungs where they may remain indefinitely. The lungs are equipped to filter out only relatively coarse particles; they are not adapted to filter out these fine particles. Some authorities feel that the increasing frequency of lung cancer, emphysema, and other chronic respiratory diseases in urban areas may be partly attributed to the synergistic effect of metal atoms, hydrocarbon compounds, and so forth, being carried into and lodged in the lungs by fine particles.

Smoking

Cigarette smoking has been clearly associated with increased risk of lung cancer, heart disease, emphysema, and many other health problems. On top of this, there appears to be a synergistic interaction

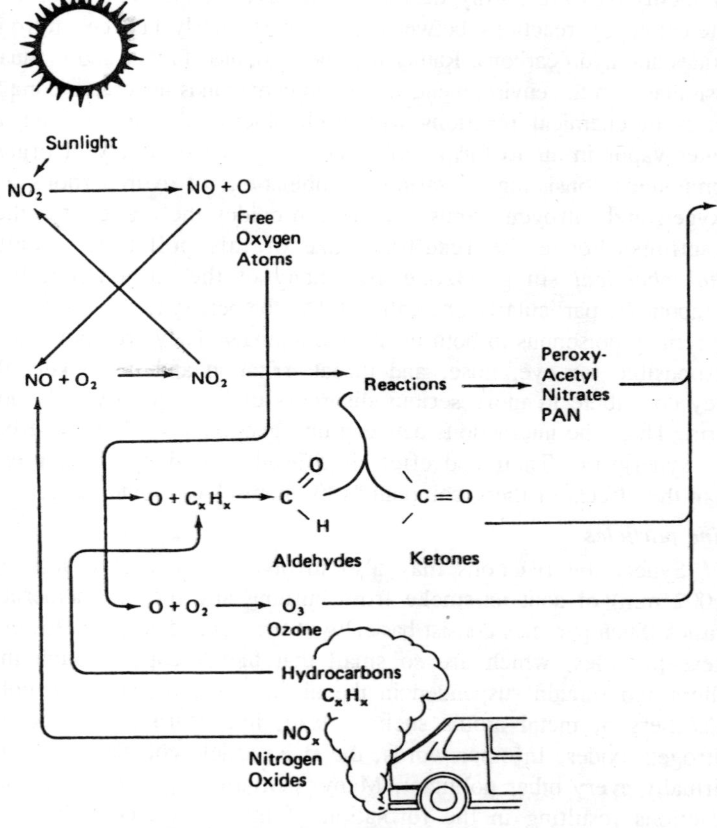

Fig. 8.3. Formation of photochemical smog.

between smoking and general air pollution which increases the risk even more. For example, General air pollution has little significant effect on the incidence of chronic bronchitis among nonsmokers. However, among smokers, pollution results in a marked increase in the incidence of chronic bronchitis. It is fortunate that the prime contributing factor in this case, smoking, is one that we can choose to avoid.

Widespread effects

In the past, as described above, air pollution was generally considered basically an urban phenomenon. Consequently, the reasoning followed (and still persists among many people) that if urban pollutants could be diluted into the atmosphere at large, the final concentrations

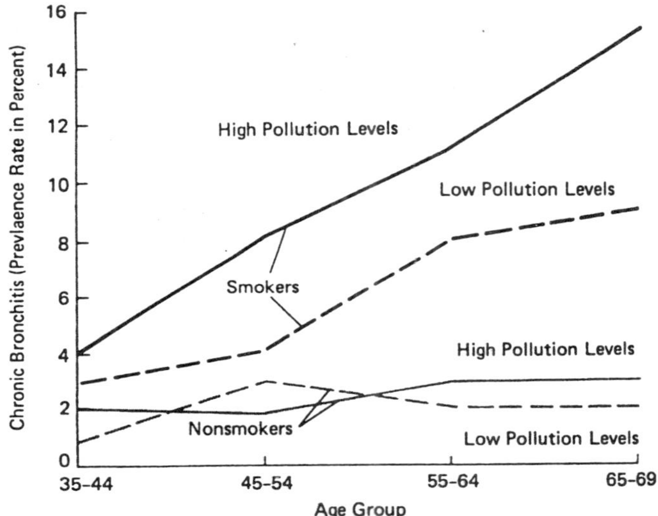

Fig. 8.4. Synergistic effect between smoking and other air pollution.

would be so low that they would cause no problems. This is the old assumption that "dilution is the solution to pollution." Therefore, taller smokestacks-up to 300 meters (1000 feet)-were constructed for many industries and power plants in order to disperse pollutants more widely. Also, power plants have been constructed near coal fields in remote areas to remove their polluting effects from the concentrated areas of cities and instead to disperse them in areas of low pollution. However, much evidence has accumulated that this practice simply results in spreading harmful effects more widely. This is illustrated by sulfur dioxides leading to the formation of acid rain and the widespread effect of air pollution on plants.

Sulfur dioxide and acid rain

Sulfur dioxide (SO_2) is a gas that is poisonous to both plants and animals. Sulfur dioxide is produced mostly by power plants which burn coal to generate electricity. A large power plant may burn 10,000 tons of coal a day; if this coal is contaminated with 3 percent sulfur, some 900 tons of sulfur dioxide per day will be discharged.

As was noted earlier, in the natural cycle sulfur dioxide may be removed from the air through assimilation by soil microorganisms. However, to avoid the toxic effects in the meantime, industries have attempted to dilute the sulfur dioxide by building taller smokestacks to disperse the gas. Ironically, this effort has largely circumvented the natural process of assimilation and created a new pollution problem. For the natural process to work, sulfur dioxide must come in contact with the soil and its microorganisms. Tall smokestacks erected to promote dilution largely *prevent* this. But everything must go somewhere eventually. Airborne for long periods, sulfur dioxide gradually reacts with oxygen and water vapor in the air to form sulfuric acid (H_2SO_4). Thus 900 tons of sulfur dioxide from one day's operation of a single large power plant become some 1500 tons of sulfuric acid by the addition of oxygen and hydrogen to the molecule. The sulfuric acid is diluted by rainfall but even then the rain is commonly 10 to 100 times more acid than normal; in some cases it is even 1000 times more acid than normal. Nitrogen oxides contribute in a similar way by forming nitric acid (HNO_3). Rainwater containing such acids is called *acid rain*.

The effects of acid rain are numerous. Perhaps most striking is the dissolving of limestone and marble. Many statues and monuments have been eroded more in the last 50 years than they did in the previous 200. It also increases the corrosion rate of all metal structures, such as bridges. However, the most insidious long-term effect of acid rain is a gradual lowering of the pH of water and soil. This can lead to gross alteration of aquatic ecosystems and a greatly increased rate of leaching. For example, Cornell University biologist Carl Schofield has observed that more than half the lakes in the Adirondack Mountains (northern New York State) above 600 meters (1800 feet) have become highly acidic and 90 percent of these are devoid of fish. The death of the fish is due to both the acidity and the leaching effect of acid rain. In addition to decreasing pH, the acid precipitation leaches from the soil aluminum compounds which are toxic to fish. In another study, the water draining from a forest area in New Hampshire was monitored; it was found that leaching of nutrients had increased three- to tenfold because of acid rain. This constitutes a serious loss of fertility, which ultimately must be reflected in a decline in productivity.

Diabolically, the effects of acid rain are observed in what are generally considered unpolluted areas, hundreds of miles from pollution sources. The emissions which cause acid rain in the Adirondacks come from industries along the Great Lakes. The acid rain in New Hampshire comes from New York City. Similarly, sulfur dioxide originating in England has caused extensive acid rain damage to lake and stream ecosystems in Sweden. Almost everywhere that the pH of rainwater is measured, observers note some increase in acidity over that of pure rainwater. Therefore lesser effects can be presumed to extend even more widely. A United Nations conference in the fall of 1977 recognized acid rain as a global pollution problem.

Federal air pollution laws restrict the sulfur dioxide emissions somewhat, but to prevent the impact of acid rain, regulations need to be much more stringent. Unfortunately, because of shortages of high-quality (low-sulfur) oil and natural gas, some leaders in industry and government are asking that air pollution regulations be relaxed to allow the burning of more coal and low-grade oil, which have high sulfur contents. If this occurs, acid rain problems can only become more severe. Obviously dilution is not the solution to pollution in the case of sulfur dioxide.

Air pollution and plant growth

There have been countless cases of vegetation-agricultural crops, ornamental plants, and forest species-being severely damaged or killed by air pollution. However, even more insidious than the outright visible damage, air pollution is also responsible for a general reduction in plant growth which can occur without other conspicuous signs of damage or abnormality. For example, a recent study in Yonkers, New York, showed that photochemical smog reduced sweet corn and alfalfa yields by 15 percent. Field experiments at Riverside, California, showed that yields of sweet corn were reduced by 72 percent, alfalfa 38 percent, radishes 38 percent, grapes 60 percent, navel oranges 50 percent, and lemons 30 percent as compared to similar plants grown in clean, filtered air. Another study in the San Bernardino Mountains of California showed that timber production had been reduced by 75 percent. Many other studies show similar results. Air pollution has forced the complete abandonment of citrus growing in certain areas of California and vegetable growing in certain areas of New Jersey-areas that were formerly among the most productive regions in the country.

The effects in most areas of the country are not this severe, for many important agricultural areas receive relatively little pollution, but nationwide the average loss of agricultural and forest production is estimated to be between 1 and 2 percent. This apparently small percentage is far from insignificant. With an annual corn production in the United States of about 6 billion bushels, a 2-percent loss amounts to about 120 million bushels.

Most importantly, the situation threatens to get worse. Air pollution control efforts of recent years have markedly reduced some pollutants in cities and undoubtedly the situation is better than if no pollution control had been exercised. However, more people driving more miles, and industry burning more coal in place of cleanerburning oil and natural gas, as well as urban and industrial expansion in general, have been offsetting factors. Airline pilots report seeing the telltale haze of photochemical smog over wider and wider areas. For example, at times the smog extends continuously from Chicago to Washington, D.C., and continuously down the East Coast from Boston to Miami. The great concern is that if widespread air pollution gets gradually worse, reductions in crop production could occur with unanticipated, disastrous suddenness. The effect may be sudden, because reduction in growth (or any other pollution damage) is not necessarily a linear function of the pollution level. That is, one unit of pollutant does not produce one increment of damage, two units, two increments, and so on. Instead, plants will tolerate a given level of pollution with very little, if any, noticeable effect. But with a small increment in pollution above that level, the plant is pushed beyond its capacity to cope with the pollution insult and the damaging effect may increase drastically.

Walter W. Heck of the U.S. Department of Agriculture and North Carolina State University has stated, "An educated guess suggests that a doubling of present pollution concentrations on the East Coast could, under otherwise favorable environmental conditions, produce from 25 to 100 percent loss of many agronomic and horticultural crops and severe injury to many native species. We are not far from pollution levels which could cause precipitous effects on agricultural production in the more humid areas of the United States." There are proposals to alleviate city air pollution by moving industries into rural areas, thereby aiding dilution of the pollution into the countryside. You can see that this could result in an unwitting and catastrophic sacrifice of important agricultural areas.

Global effects

Some waste products discharged into the air may affect the entire Earth. Pollutants that affect the ozone shield, and carbon dioxide and other pollutants affecting climate are two examples.

Ozone shield

Earlier, we noted that ozone (O_3) produced in the lower atmosphere is a serious pollutant in that it is poisonous to both plants and animals. At the same time, paradoxically, ozone is absolutely essential in the stratosphere (upper atmosphere) in that it acts as a shield against ultraviolet radiation (UV). Ultraviolet is a part of the natural radiation from the sun; the wavelengths are just slightly shorter and have higher energy content than those of visible light. However, when UV penetrates living tissues, it is preferentially absorbed by proteins or nucleic acids such as DNA, and its high energy enables it to actually break the chemical bonds of these molecules. Consequently, UV is extremely destructive to biological tissues and is capable of causing mutations.

Some UV does penetrate to the surface of Earth; it is responsible for sunburns and is involved in some 200,000 to 600,000 cases of skin cancer per year in the U.S. However, we are spared the worst effects of UV because most of it is absorbed and hence screened out by the ozone in the stratosphere. Without this ozone "shield," the biological damage to both plants and animals would be disastrous. Indeed it is doubtful whether life could even exist on land without the protection of the ozone layer. Interestingly, UV creates this shield itself by causing some oxygen molecules to split into separate oxygen atoms, some of which, in turn, combine with oxygen molecules to become ozone. Simultaneously, free oxygen atoms may combine with ozone, breaking it down to oxygen gas. Thus, a balance of ozone H oxygen is maintained in the stratosphere.

Certain pollutants diffusing gradually into the stratosphere from the lower atmosphere have damaging effects on the ozone layer. In particular, chlorine atoms catalyze the breakdown of ozone. By *catalyze* it is meant that a single chlorine atom can participate in the reaction repeatedly without itself being changed. Therefore a single chlorine atom can break down millions of molecules of ozone, upsetting the natural ozone balance.

A major potential source of chlorine reaching the stratosphere is the chlorofluorocarbons such as freon ($CFC1_3$) used as the propellant in aerosol cans. Chlorofluorocarbons liquefy under modest pressure and are relatively nontoxic and nonreactive. Thus, a small amount of liquid chlorofluorocarbon in an aerosol container can act as an inert ingredient that provides an even pressure over the life of the can. By 1974, the United States alone was spraying chlorofluorocarbons into the air at the rate of about 230 million kilograms (500 million pounds) per year.

Since the chlorofluorocarbons appeared relatively harmless no real concern existed about their being discharged into the atmosphere. It was assumed that they would be diluted and assimilated. However, in the mid-1970's a number of scientists reported that far from being assimilated, chlorofluorocarbons were diffusing into the stratosphere where they were breaking down and releasing free chlorine atoms.

The chlorine is eventually removed from the stratosphere by combining with hydrogen to form hydrochloric acid (HC1), which finally

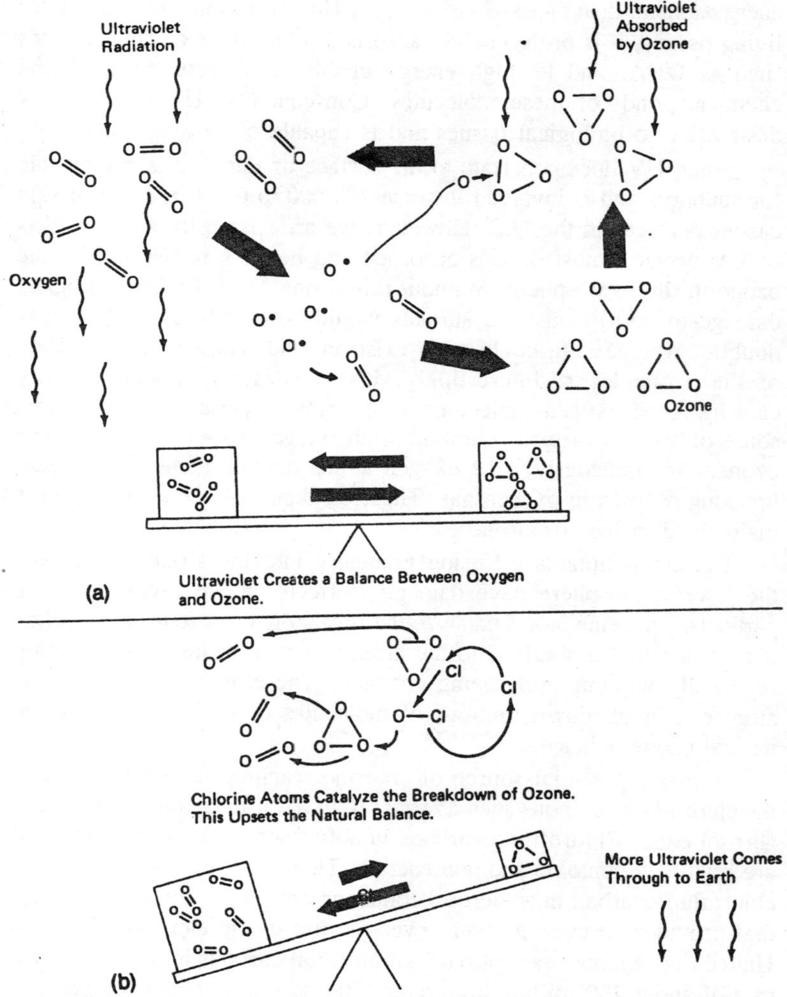

Fig. 8.5. Ultraviolet radiation and the oxygen-ozone balance in the stratosphere. (a) Ultraviolet light causes the formation of ozone, which absorbs ultraviolet light. (b) Chlorine atoms catalyze the breakdown of ozone; that is, a single chlorine atom may function over and over as shown to break down an infinite number of ozone molecules.

returns to Earth by way of rainfall. However, this process is very slow; therefore a relatively small amount of chlorine in the stratosphere can have a very large and prolonged effect. A report from the National Research Council concludes that a continuing release of chlorofluorocarbons at the 1973 rate would cause a reduction in the ozone layer of between 2 and 20 percent. Although the exact degree of the effects cannot yet be predicted, such a reduction in the ozone layer would produce substantial increases in human skin cancer and would have deleterious effects on plants and animals. While the extent of the damage to the ozone layer and the exact consequences of such damage are somewhat controversial, it is not wise to take a "wait-and-see" attitude. For one thing, it will take about 10 years for the chlorofluorocarbons released today to reach the stratosphere. Then, because of the catalytic nature of chlorine, the effects may endure for several hundred years.

The United States, in this instance, acted quickly by phasing out the use of chlorofluorocarbons in aerosol cans and is working on control of other uses of chlorofluorocarbons. Unfortunately, a number of other countries are still using chlorofluorocarbons in aerosol cans.

Additionally, chlorofluorocarbon compounds are not the only threat to the ozone layer. Carbon tetrachloride (CCl_4) is another substantial and perhaps even more significant source of free chlorine. In addition, nitric oxide (NO) can break down ozone in a manner similar to chlorine; high altitude aircraft, such as the supersonic transports (SST's), nitrogen fertilizers, and automobile exhaust are all direct or indirect sources of nitric oxide.

The lesson here is that when we do not definitely know what will happen to things dispersed into the environment, it is not safe to assume that they will be assimilated, that nature will take care of them. By so doing, we may be planting highly destructive time bombs which, once the fuses are lit, may be quite beyond our ability to control or stop.

Pollution and climate

So far we have stressed toxic or chemical effects of pollutants. However, such effects cannot be our only concern. Remember that the world ecosystem depends on subtle balances involving abiotic factors such as temperature and moisture, as well as biological factors. Disturbing the abiotic factors can be as destructive as direct poisoning of ourselves or agricultural crops. In this regard carbon dioxide and suspended particles have special significance.

Both carbon dioxide (CO_2) and suspended particles are natural constituents of the atmosphere. We have already discussed the indispensable role of CO_2 in the carbon cycle between photosynthesis and respiration. Suspended particles include ash and soot from volcanoes and natural fires, dust (clay particles) blown from deserts, and water droplets from condensation of water vapor (clouds and mist). Therefore, it might appear that additions by humans of carbon dioxide, suspended particles from burning fuel, and other materials would not change anything. However, both suspended particles and CO_2 have marked effects on energy radiated to and from the Earth. Hence they are critical factors in determining overall temperature and thus climate. There is much evidence that our contribution of suspended particles and CO_2 to the atmosphere is already affecting climate and that the effects may become much more severe in the future.

As the sun's radiation strikes the atmosphere, it may simply be reflected into space or it may penetrate down to the Earth itself. Only the energy that penetrates the atmosphere actually adds to the energy balance of the Earth; what is reflected does not. The more reflection, the less energy received by Earth. This is where suspended particles play an important role. Light is reflected from the upper surface of clouds, haze layers, dust particles, and so forth. Therefore, the more suspended particles, the more reflection and the less energy penetrating to the Earth, with resulting cooler temperatures. Climatologist Reid Bryson states, "An increase of one percent in the normal reflectivity of the Earth from perhaps 37 to 38 percent would lower the mean temperature of the Earth about 1.7°C, or 3.1°F." There is some direct evidence of this phenomenon: Times when exceptional volcanic activity increased the dust in the atmosphere have been correlated with periods of cooler temperatures.

Carbon dioxide affects the opposite side of the Earth's energy balance, namely, the radiation of heat. Energy reaching the Earth is largely in the form of light. Upon striking the Earth, most of the light is absorbed and in one way or another converted to heat. The heat is eventually reradiated from the Earth in the form of infrared (heat) radiation. Carbon dioxide in the atmosphere is transparent to light radiation but it tends to absorb and thus impede the passage of infrared radiation. This means that energy can get in but has trouble getting out. Therefore, atmospheric and surface temperature increases until there is enough heat "pressure" to overcome the resistance. The more CO_2 in the atmosphere, the more blockage of heat outflow and hence the greater the increase in temperature. This phenomenon is called the *greenhouse effect*, because of its similarity to what occurs in a greenhouse or in a car left sitting in the sun. Light energy enters through the glass and is absorbed and converted to heat. The glass impedes the exit of infrared radiation; hence the interior temperature increases. Carbon dioxide is not the only molecule that works in this way: Water vapor, ozone, and certain organic molecules have a similar effect.

Humans seem bent on altering both sides of the Earth's heat balance. Since the beginning of the Industrial Revolution, ever-increasing quantities of CO_2 have been added to the air through the burning of fossil fuels (coal, oil, and natural gas). It is estimated that an equal quantity of CO_2 has been added by the cutting and burning of forests to make way for agriculture and the oxidation of organic matter in the soil due to agriculture. At least half the CO_2 has been assimilated in oceans or in other ways, but the other half has simply remained in the air, gradually raising the CO_2 concentration of the atmosphere. Since 1860 the concentration has increased about 13 percent, from about 290 to 331 parts per million (from 0.029 to 0.033 percent).

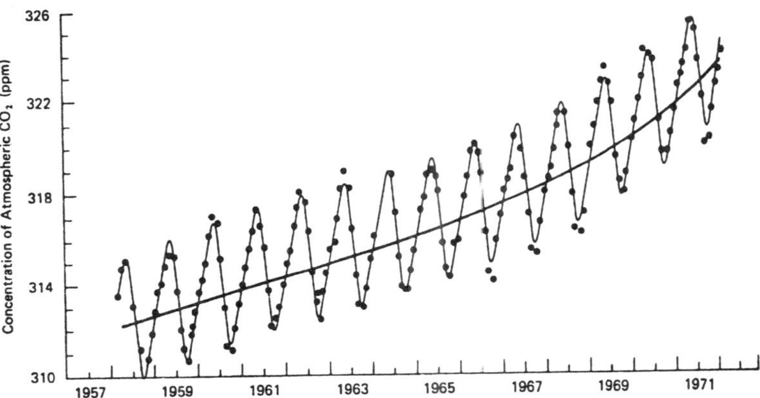

Fig. 8.6. Carbon dioxide concentration in the atmosphere fluctuates between winter and summer due to seasonal variation in photosynthesis.

Paralleling this increase in CO_2 from the 1880's to the 1940's was a gradual increase in the average world temperature of about 0.4°C (0.7°F).

However, since 1940 and continuing into the 1960's and 1970's, average temperatures have declined, largely reversing the previous increase. This has occurred in spite of the continued increase in CO_2. Bryson believes that this decrease in temperature is due to an increase in suspended particles since World War 11, overshadowing the CO_2 effect. You will recall that suspended particles tend to cool the atmosphere, while CO_2 tends to warm it. The increase in suspended particles is the result of human activities. Important sources are dispersed photochemical smog and other pollutants from cities and industry, aircraft exhaust, smoke from "slash and burn" agriculture (burning forests to clear land for agriculture, a common practice in the tropics), and increased wind erosion of soil because of desertification. It is estimated that the total quantity of suspended particles traceable to human activities approximately equals that produced by natural sources. Further, man's potential to pollute could increase the suspended particle concentration so greatly over the next 50 years that global temperatures could drop by as much as 3.5°C (4.3°F)enough to trigger another ice age.

However, another ice age in the near future is considered unlikely, because the CO_2 greenhouse effect is still operating. In this regard it is interesting to contrast the Northern and Southern hemispheres. The increase in suspended particles is largely a phenomenon of the Northern Hemisphere. They are mostly produced in the Northern Hemisphere and tend to settle out of the atmosphere before they reach the Southern Hemisphere. Carbon dioxide, on the other hand, diffuses evenly through the atmosphere of the entire globe. In keeping with their respective effects, it is found that the recent cooling trend is a phenomenon observed only in the Northern Hemisphere. Measurements in the Southern Hemisphere show that the warming trend observed prior to 1940 has continued unabated. It is predicted that the CO2 effect will soon counterbalance the suspended particle effect in the north as well, and general warming will resume.

A 1977 report from the National Academy of Science also stresses that the CO2 greenhouse effect has the most dire implications for the future. According to the report, unconstrained use of fossil fuels over the next 200 years would cause a four- to eightfold increase in atmospheric CO_2. In turn, this could increase average world temperatures by 6°C (10.8°F) or more. According to the report, this temperature increase would probably not lead to a massive melting of the polar ice caps and subsequent flooding of all coastal and lowland areas, a fear that has often been stated. However, the temperature change, in the words of the report, "would exceed by far the temperature fluctuations of the past several thousand years and would very likely, along the way, have a highly significant impact on global precipitation."

The connection between temperature and precipitation is most important. Bryson points out that very modest shifts in temperature, whether toward warmer or cooler, dramatically alter the pathways of major air currents. In turn, this drastically alters patterns of precipitation: Some regions receive more; others receive less. Agricultural crops and practices the world over are intricately attuned to average local moisture conditions. Therefore any change in precipitation is more than likely to have severe disruptive effects on agricultural production. While scientists may debate the direction, extent, and timing of temperature changes, there is little doubt that they are occurring, and the implications should be clear. Thus, even given virtually perfect dilution and pathways of assimilation, the Earth is not large enough to handle carbon dioxide in the volumes that we are producing, without upsetting fundamental balances. Again it points to a desperate need for us to recognize limits and attune our activities to what the Earth can sustain.

Water Pollution

Natural waters receive numerous pollutants from a wide variety of sources: nutrients from sewage outlets and fertilizer runoff; pesticides and herbicides from agricultural runoff; oil, grease, and numerous chemicals from street and highway runoff; chemicals from the fallout of air pollutants; chemicals leached from landfills and other dumps; chemicals from industrial processing; and waste heat. Historically, we have tended to hold the same assumptions about dilution, threshold levels, and assimilation of these pollutants by water as by air. As with air pollution, we have found that these assumptions are not fully valid and we are therefore confronted with many pollution problems. We shall discuss only a few of the areas that present significant problems.

Nutrients and eutrophication

The *eutrophication* is the series of events caused by additions of nutrients and leading to excessive growth of algae, then to depletion of dissolved oxygen by bacteria decomposing the algae, and finally to kills of fish and other aquatic organisms because of lack of oxygen. Eutrophication is one of the critically important forms of water pollution and, in many areas, it threatens to become worse. It is a classic example of humans exceeding the assimilative capacity of the natural system. Even though the nutrients are natural substances, the ecosystem balance is upset in such a way that a chain reaction which disrupts the entire system is initiated.

Thermal pollution

Waste heat is a byproduct of many industrial processes. Waste heat must be dissipated into the environment, where it may raise temperatures to an undesirable extent; hence waste heat is referred to as *thermal (heat) pollution*. Particularly troublesome are electric power plants in which fuel is used to produce steam to drive turbogenerators. In such plants about two-thirds of the heat released from the fuel is dissipated into the environment in the process of recondensing the steam. The most convenient and economical way to dissipate the waste heat is to pump water from a lake, river, or other natural body of water over the cooling coils and return the warmed water to the natural body.

The water going through the cooling system itself gets hot enough to kill most organisms. However, intake pipes are screened to prevent the entrance of fish and dilution factors are calculated so that the overall temperature increase in the receiving body will not be enough to harm organisms. So much for the theory! There are many cases of fish being killed by being drawn against intake screens. Also, planktonic organisms (microscopic free-floating organisms) which are critical in many food chains are not screened out but go through the system and are killed. Finally, experience and experiments have shown that even modest changes in temperature can have farreaching repercussions on an ecosystem. Some of the possible effects include:

1. Increasing temperature may promote or intensify the latter phases of eutrophication in which oxygen depletion leads to fishkills. This occurs because warmer water holds less dissolved oxygen than cooler water. At the same time, increased temperature raises the metabolic rate and hence the rate of oxygen consumption by both bacteria and fish. Thus, more oxygen is being consumed by these organisms at the same time that less is available. The result may be large numbers of fish killed by oxygen deprivation.
2. Increasing temperature may affect the species composition of the producer level and hence the entire food chain. Many valuable species, namely green algae and diatoms, have lower optimum temperatures for growth than do noxious blue-green algae. Thus, thermal pollution can lead to a replacement of desirable algae by the undesirable blue-greens.
3. Increased temperatures may disrupt critical predator-prey relationships. For example, trout have a lower optimum temperature than the minnows they feed on. Consequently, increased temperatures enable the minnows to escape from the trout more easily. Hence the minnow population proliferates, while the trout population starves.

4. Many synergistic effects come into play as a result of increased temperatures. Fish that are resistant to diseases at lower temperatures may become highly susceptible at increased temperatures. Also, increased temperatures may render fish more sensitive to other pollutants such as heavy metals and pesticides.
5. Fish may be attracted to the warmer temperatures of a thermal discharge, but then may be killed by the sudden drop in temperature when the discharge is turned off, as it must be for periodic maintenance of a power plant.

Since our consumption of electrical energy continues to increase, we must be exceedingly wary about increasing the impact of thermal pollution. Heat cannot be dissipated into natural bodies of water without potentially wide-ranging effects. An alternative is to dissipate waste heat into the air by means of cooling towers. While discharging heat into the atmosphere may have some local climatic effects, so far these have not been shown to be significant. Curtailing our profligate use of energy is also an alternative which deserves more consideration.

Chlorinated hydrocarbons, heavy metals, and bioaccumulation

Many chemicals discharged into water are diluted and assimilated; however, in some cases quite the reverse occurs. Instead of becoming ever more diluted and finally disappearing, some chemicals "reappear" in organisms at much *higher* concentrations. This phenomenon of chemical buildup or accumulation to higher concentrations in a biological system is known as *bioaccumulation*, or *biomagnification*.

Bioaccumulation occurs when a substance is taken in by an organism but cannot be metabolized or excreted. Therefore the organism accumulates the substance. The effect of bioaccumulation becomes magnified when several steps of a food chain are involved. The first organisms in the food chain accumulate a modest level of the substance. However, the second-level organisms accumulate much more, because in the course of its life an animal must eat many times its own weight in food to compensate for energy use.

All the polluting substance contained in the ingested food is concentrated in the bodies of the feeders. Since their biomass is only about one tenth the biomass of what they eat, the concentration of the polluting substance is increased tenfold. This concentrating effect is repeated throughout the food chain, each step increasing the bioaccumulation tenfold or more. A four-step food chain, thus, may produce a biomagnification of ten-thousandfold. Chlorinated hydrocarbons

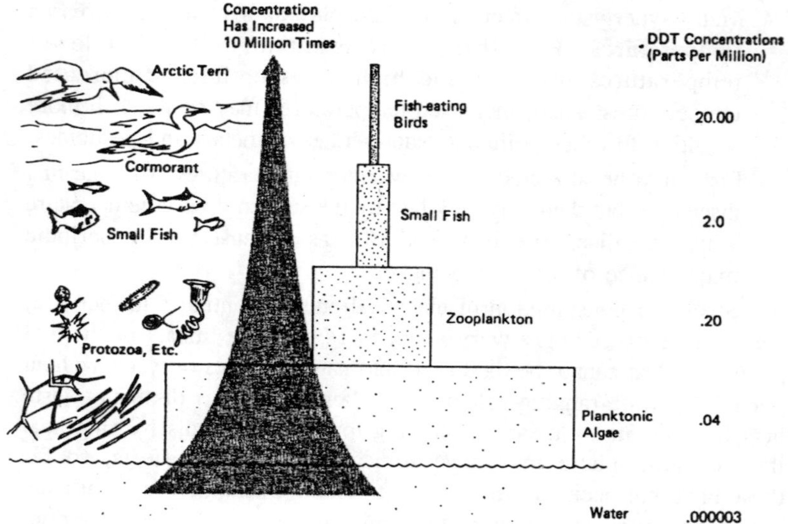

Fig. 8.7. Biomagnification.

and heavy metals are two classes of compounds that have proven particularly susceptible to bioaccumulation and hence are particularly dangerous as pollutants.

Chlorinated hydrocarbons

Chlorinated hydrocarbons, also called *organochlorides*, are synthetic organic compounds in which one or more hydrogen atoms have been replaced by chlorine atoms. Bromine and fluorine atoms, which are chemically similar to chlorine, may also be substituted, giving rise to brominated or fluorinated hydrocarbons, respectively. Chlorine, bromine, and fluorine all belong to a chemical group known as *halogens*. Therefore this entire group of substituted hydrocarbons is known as *halogenated hydrocarbons*. Such compounds are widely used in plastics, electrical insulation, pesticides, flame retardants, wood preservatives, and many other products.

Many chlorinated hydrocarbons have two features which render them particularly susceptible to bioaccumulation: extreme chemical stability and high solubility in fat but relatively low solubility in water. Extreme chemical stability means that these chemicals persist almost indefinitely. They do not break down in the environment nor can they be metabolized by organisms. The high fat-solubility but low water-solubility means that they are readily absorbed by organisms because organisms contain virtually the only fat in the environment. Once in organisms they tend not to be excreted because excretion again demands solubility in water. The result is bioaccumulation.

A classic case of bioaccumulation of a chlorinated hydrocarbon involves the pesticide DDT (dichlorodiphenyltrichloroethane). The insecticidal (insectkilling) properties of DDT were discovered shortly before World War II and it was subsequently used in huge quantities through the late 1960's for the control of virtually all kinds of insect pests, particularly disease-carrying insects such as malaria mosquitoes and fleas which carry typhus. It was assumed that any excess DDT would simply be diluted by the environment and thus disappear. It was therefore a great shock when it was discovered that, far from disappearing, DDT was accumulating through food chains and was responsible for the reproductive failure and/or death of countless birds, including our bald eagle, which held positions at the tops of food chains. DDT was also found to be accumulating in humans; however, no specific harmful effects have been identified.

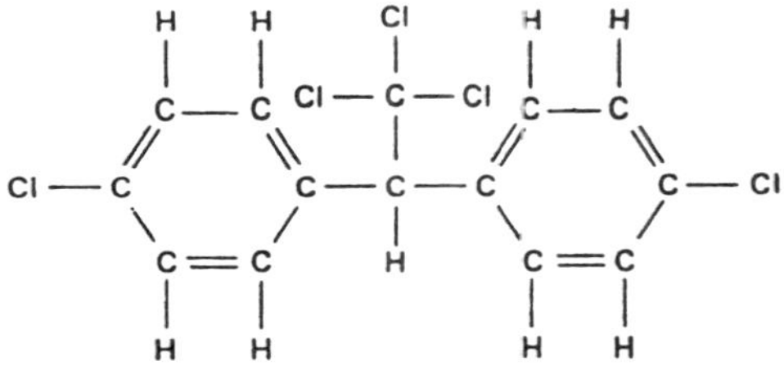

```
          H     H        Cl        H     H
          |     |        |         |     |
          C --- C   Cl - C - Cl    C --- C
        //       \\      |       //       \\
Cl -- C            C --- C --- C            C -- Cl
        \         /      |       \         /
          C === C        H         C === C
          |     |                  |     |
          H     H                  H     H
```

DDT (DICHLORODIPHENYLTRICHLOROETHANE)

Fig. 8.8. DDT. This pesticide is a classic example of a chlorinated hydrocarbon that is subject to bioaccumulation.

For these and other reasons, DDT has been banned for most uses in the United States and some other countries. However, DDT continues to be exported for use in a number of other areas of the world. And, just as significantly, the DDT story is repeated by numerous chlorinated hydrocarbon chemicals and other halogenated hydrocarbon compounds as well.

For example, PCB's (polychlorinatedbiphenyls) are widely used in plastics, electrical insulation, and carbonless printing paper, and escape into the environment from these and other sources. Like DDT, PCB's have been found to be accumulating in many species, and are present in many human food sources. Even more ominous, PCB's are much more toxic to humans than DDT. Even low doses have caused reproductive failure in monkeys and higher doses are conspicuously carcinogenic in rats. With the discovery of PCB's in many species of fish in the Great Lakes and in the Hudson and Mississippi rivers, these waters have been declared hazardous and as a result commercial fisheries have been closed. PCB's are now being phased out of certain uses.

In 1976, an episode occurred involving yet a third kind of chlorinated hydrocarbon. Kepone, an insecticide, had been allowed to escape into the James River from a manufacturing plant located in Hopewell, Virginia. Potentially toxic amounts of kepone accumulated in fish, forced the closing of all commercial fisheries on the James River, and threatened fishing in Chesapeake Bay. A study concluded that the exceedingly high stability of kepone and the supply of it in the river sediments will force commercial fisheries on the James River to remain closed for at least several decades and perhaps for as long as 100 years.

Many other such episodes might be cited and new episodes seem almost certain to occur in the future, because literally thousands of halogenated hydrocarbons are in use and new ones are continually being introduced. Many have the basic characteristics of chemical stability and fat solubility which lead to bioaccumulation.

Heavy Metals

As the name implies, heavy metals include that group of metallic elements with relatively high atomic weights, such as lead, mercury, copper, cadmium, and zinc. These particular heavy metals have received the most attention as pollutants but many others may yet be added to the list. In general, heavy metals tend to bind strongly with protein molecules which in many cases are enzymes. You may recall that the functioning of many enzymes actually depends upon a specific protein-metal ion combination, thus giving rise to nutritional requirements for certain trace minerals. However, the wrong kinds of metals, such as mercury or lead, or even too much of an essential trace element, such as zinc or copper, can upset this critical protein-metal ion balance, thus impairing or even stopping the action of certain proteins. Frequently the wrong protein-metal bonding is quite specific. Mercury and lead, for example, have a strong tendency to combine with certain enzymes in the central nervous system. Hence, they readily lead to nervous disorders including insanity, mental retardation, coma, and death. Mercury, in addition, has been shown to combine specifically with a protein that functions closely with the genetic material, DNA. This may explain why mercury poisoning often leads to severe birth defects. Tragically, once these effects occur, they are in most cases irreversible.

This protein binding capacity of heavy metals leads to bioaccumulation as well as toxicity. Bound to a protein, the metal atom cannot be excreted. Hence very small doses over a period of time can gradually accumulate in the body to reach damaging, if not lethal, levels. A classic instance of this phenomenon is the "Minamata" disease, named for a small fishing village in Japan.

In the mid 1950's, cats in Minamata began to show spastic movements followed by partial paralysis and later coma and death. At first this was thought to be a peculiar disease of cats and little attention was paid to it. However, concern escalated quickly when the same symptoms began to occur in people; such additional symptoms as mental retardation, insanity, and birth defects also were observed. Scientists and medical experts diagnosed the problem as acute mercury poisoning. But what was the source of the mercury? It was found that a chemical company near Minamata was discharging waste containing mercury into the river that drained into the bay where the Minamata villagers fished. Mercury deposited in the sediments was absorbed by bacteria and biomagnified through the food chain to the fish. Then, villagers who subsisted on a diet high in fish accumulated toxic, and even lethal, levels of mercury. By the time the situation was brought under control, some 50 people had died and 150 had suffered serious bone and nerve damage. Even now, the tragedy lives on in crippled bodies, retarded minds, and children with severe birth defects.

A worldwide search for mercury prompted by the Minamata tragedy revealed dangerous levels of mercury in fish of many other areas, including our own Great Lakes. Subsequent investigations revealed another aspect of the problem. Previously, mercury was not considered to be a threat because the metallic form of mercury is not particularly poisonous. Most mercury goes through the digestive tract without ever being absorbed. However, bacteria living in bottom sediments not only absorb mercury, they put it through a chemical reaction in which mercury atoms become attached to organic compounds, giving rise to what is called "organic mercury." Of particular importance is a reaction known as *biomethylation*, in which the mercury is attached to a methyl ($-CH_3$) group to yield a compound called methyl mercury ($Hg-CH_3$). Unlike mercury itself, methyl mercury is absorbed nearly 100 percent; then it is nearly 100 times more toxic than metallic mercury and is not readily excreted.

With these discoveries, efforts have been made to sharply reduce discharges of waste mercury. Thus the hazard of future episodes of poisoning from environmental mercury has been greatly reduced.

However, mercury remaining in sediments from past discharges continues to be a problem in some areas. For example; it was discovered in 1977 that fish from two Virginia rivers contained dangerously high levels of mercury. The source of the mercury was past industrial discharges. Although the factories and the discharges themselves had been shut down 27 years previously, the mercury was still leaching from sediments and accumulating in food chains.

Having recognized and corrected for the hazards of mercury should not make us complacent. It should make us much more wary of the danger inherent in heavy metals. For example, tin and other heavy metals also undergo biomethylation reactions that increase their toxic potential. Tin has been shown to have a very specific and negative effect on a particular kidney enzyme. Such specific effects mean that very low doses can be quite damaging because all the atoms are accumulated in a single system. Furthermore, as with air pollutants, synergisms may occur between heavy metals. For example, copper and zinc in combination have been shown to be more than 10 times as toxic to fish as either element alone.

Thus, as our industry and technology use greater and greater amounts of metals (tin use has doubled in the last 10 years), the potential for future Minamata-type disasters on perhaps an even larger scale is distressingly high. This potential can be offset if we get over the idea that these metals will simply dilute and disappear in the environment and instead take precautions to limit their escape.

It should also be noted that water and food are not the only sources of human exposure to heavy metals. The air is another major source of exposure because these metals are also discharged into the air as we incinerate trash which contains such things as mercury batteries, as we burn coal which contains various heavy metals as contaminants, and as we bum gasoline containing lead additives. Regarding the latter, studies show that strikingly high percentages of urban children have elevated levels of lead in their blood, much more than can be explained by ingestion of paint chips which contain lead and which have been a prime source of lead poisoning in the past.

Solid Wastes and Accidents

The assumption of dilution obviously holds only for gaseous or liquid wastes discharged, respectively, into air or water. For solid wastes disposed of in or on the ground, we tend to hold the converse assumption-they will stay where they are put. Many cases prove that this assumption is equally invalid.

Leaching from municipal and industrial landfills

The leaching from municipal landfills may pollute ground water. A similar but even more serious threat exists with respect to dumps of industrial wastes. Most notorious are wastes from the chemical industry. In the course of manufacturing synthetic organic chemicals for plastics, pesticides, solvents, and other uses, extraneous chemicals are also produced in reaction vessels. Many of these chemical wastes are halogenated hydrocarbons, which, we have observed, are often highly stable, toxic, carcinogenic, and subject to bioaccumulation. Indeed, they are frequently referred to as *hazardous wastes*. Unfortunately, they have not been treated with the respect that they deserve. In large part chemical companies have simply put such wastes in steel drums and buried them in landfills. What happens twenty or thirty years later as the drums rust through? The potential for tragedy is vividly illustrated by what happened at Love Canal.

Love Canal was an abandoned canal bed near Niagara Falls, New York. Years ago it served as a convenient burial site for thousands of drums of waste chemicals. When the canal was filled, homes were subsequently built along the old banks and life went on normally-until 1978. In 1978, residents in the Love Canal area observed that they were experiencing an unusually high rate of miscarriages, birth defects, liver disease, and other health problems. They also observed that after rains, strange black chemicals oozed out of the ground and through their basement walls. They called in health authorities to ask if there was any connection, and indeed there was. The chemicals were identified as various toxic chlorinated hydrocarbons. The "time bomb" in Love Canal had gone off.

Insidiously, there are many similar time bombs ticking away in various parts of the country. In the last 30 years the use of synthetic organic chemicals has increased manyfold, and the volume of hazardous wastes has increased likewise. Much of this waste has been and still is disposed of in the ground. The Environmental Protection Agency estimated in 1978 that close to 90 percent of such disposal was inadequate and that 1200 to 2000 dumps were leaking hazardous chemicals into soil and ground water. This is not an encouraging thought when we recall that ground water is directly or indirectly the source of water for nearly all of us. Indeed, there are already hundreds of reports of well water contaminated with at least traces of hazardous chemicals, and more such reports are coming in all the time. In 1979 the Environmental Protection Agency estimated that the cost of cleaning

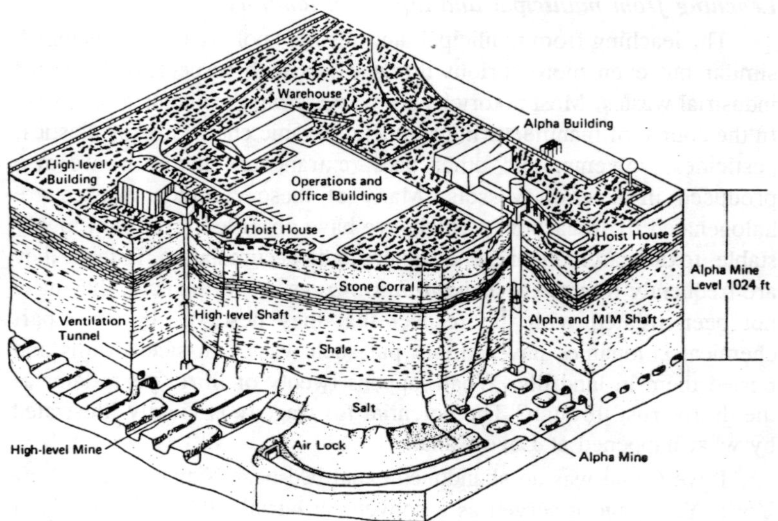

Fig. 8.9. Disposal of radioactive wastes from nuclear power plants.

up dumps of hazardous chemical wastes-action imperative to prevent further contamination of ground water-could be as high as 50 billion dollars. Even this expenditure would not purify the ground water that is already contaminated; we can only wait for the ground water system to gradually flush itself out-which, in some cases, may take hundreds of years. Clearly, burying hazardous wastes in the ground, with the tacit assumption that they will stay put, has been a tragic and costly mistake. Safe alternatives must be put into effect.

Nuclear wastes

As we proceed to generate more 'and more of our electricity by means of nuclear power, there is a corresponding increase in the production of nuclear wastes. These nuclear wastes consist of highly radioactive elements which are extremely potent in causing mutations which may lead to birth defects and/or cancer. Some of the wastes may retain their radioactivity for periods up to 100,000 years. Therefore, the safety of nuclear power depends not only on the safe operation of the power plants themselves, but also on isolating these wastes from the biosphere for very long periods.

The nuclear industry and various government experts are confident that suitable techniques are available to keep nuclear wastes where they are put. However, the public is quite well aware that elaborate waste containment facilities and plans for monitoring do not, in fact, give assurance that this is the case. There is still the possibility, indeed the probability, of human failure. In 1973 a leak occurred in a tank at the Hanford nuclear waste storage facility in the State of Washington. The leak went unnoticed for six weeks despite the fact that both the loss and the increasing radioactivity in the ground were being recorded on automatic monitors over the entire period. The problem of safe disposal of nuclear wastes is the basis for much of the public reaction against nuclear power plants.

Accidents

The fallacy of the assumption that things stay where they are put may be extended to include the general tendency to assume that things will go as planned, or said another way, that accidents won't happen. The shortcoming of such an assumption is self evident: people will make mistakes and accidents will happen. As technology uses increasingly toxic compounds and greater and greater amounts of almost everything, the stage is set for very simple mistakes or accidents to result in widescale disasters.

As an example of such an event, in 1973 a few sacks of a fire retardant chemical got mixed up with an animal feed additive by a distributor in Michigan. If the chemical had been of low toxicity the amounts that were fed to the animals would have had little, if any, effect. However, the fire retardant chemical was PBB, a highly stable, bioaccumulating halogenated hydrocarbon closely related to PCB but some five times more toxic. The results of this accident: Numerous people, mostly farm families, became sick, suffering varying degrees of nervous disorders; some 500 farms had to be quarantined; 30,000 cattle, 1.5 million chickens, thousands of sheep and hogs, and tons of cheese, milk, and eggs had to be destroyed because of the contamination, resulting in economic ruin to many farmers. The damage was estimated on the order of 100 million dollars, not including any compensation for individual human suffering. Moreover, the chemical is remaining and recycling in the Michigan ecosystem. Several years after the initial incident, reaccumulation from "unknown" sources was still causing sporadic occurrences of PBB poisoning.

In another incident, this one in the town of Seveso, Italy, in 1976, a safety valve in a chemical plant malfunctioned, and about a kilogram (2.2 pounds) of material was released into the air-a seemingly minor mishap. But in this case the material was dioxin, a chlorinated hydrocarbon and one of the most toxic substances known. The entire town of 100,000 residents had to be evacuated; hundreds of people suffered severe skin ailments; animals died by the thousands; and consumption of all local food was banned. A year later an area around the factory was still uninhabitable and there is much concern that birth defects may occur in the next generation.

Even relatively nontoxic materials take on disaster potential if the volume is large. Oil is a case in point. Crude oil is a mixture of natural organic compounds and in modest quantities is broken down by organisms and assimilated. However, the huge amounts which may come from an accident involving a supertanker can result in enormous ecological disasters. In March 1978, the supertanker *Amoco Cadiz* went aground off the French coast, spilling 220,000 tons of crude oil. Some of the results: 200 miles of one of Europe's most picturesque coastlines affected; over 20,000 birds, including a whole colony of rare puffins, wiped out; 9,000 tons of oysters made inedible and their culturing grounds ruined; marine worms which are essential in the food chain for commercial fish obliterated; tourism of the region cancelled out, affecting the economic lives of thousands. The longer-term effects are not yet known, but scientists believe they will be severe and last for many years.

Unfortunately the *Amoco Cadiz* was not the first such disaster, nor is it likely to be the last. With more and more oil being shipped in supertankers, more and even worse such disasters become increasingly probable in the future.

Coping with Pollution

Given all the problems and potential problems of pollution, it is tempting to call for an immediate moratorium on all further polluting. However, a moment's thought reveals that this is hopelessly simplistic. In manufacturing anything, only a fraction of the raw material consumed ends up in the product; the remainder becomes waste. In turn, the use of any consumable product is invariably synonomous with the release or discharge of waste products into the environment. Thus, stopping the output of wastes cannot be done short of closing out all human activity on Earth.

But pollution is not to be passively accepted, either. Somewhere between "closing out" humanity and accepting all pollution as inevitable, there is a long and laborious pathway of developing and implementing both technological and behavioral changes which will lead to controlling or managing wastes. With such control, the polluting impact of wastes can be reduced even if they can't be eliminated altogether. Then perhaps we can enjoy the benefits of both technology and a clean environment.

But, as mentioned, the pathway is laborious and ultimately it involves not just "they" who make laws or manufacture products. Ultimately it must involve all of society. The overall process can be divided into three steps: (1) recognizing threats of pollution, (2) devising methods of control, and (3) implementing controls.

Recognizing Threats of Pollution

The threats of pollution to human health, plant life, and global ecology in general should be clear from the preceding discussion. However, a few points deserve emphasis.

First, it should be apparent that we can no longer assume that pollutants will simply dilute to threshold (safe) levels and then disappear by assimilation. This is particularly true of synthetic organic chemicals and heavy metals that are subject to bioaccumulation.

Second, we need to revise our thinking as to what threshold levels are or even if they exist at all. Historically we have tended to think of threshold levels in terms of short-term exposures and assume that if it doesn't hurt today, it won't hurt tomorrow. But now we face lifelong exposures to various pollutants. More and more, scientists are finding that long-term exposure to low levels of pollutants may be just as disastrous, or more so, than short-term, high doses. The carcinogenic potentials of cigarette smoking and asbestos fibers are prime examples. Whether or not there is a safe level for long-term exposures is difficult to determine experimentally. To learn the effect of a given exposure over a period of 40 years could require 40 years. However, based on general genetic theory, most scientists now concede that any substance that is mutagenic or carcinogenic in experimental organisms has no threshold level. According to this view, any exposure above zero produces some risk of inducing cancer and the risk simply increases with increasing exposure.

Compounding the problem of determining the threshold levels for a given compound may be an almost infinite number of possibilities for synergistic interactions among and between various pollutants and environmental factors. Many maladies of "unknown cause" from which we presently suffer may in time be shown to be due to such synergisms and/or long-term exposures to what we thought were harmless compounds.

Finally, it should be emphasized that some pollution effects may have worldwide impact and be irreversible once we have allowed them to occur. The only choice will be to suffer the long-term consequences.

Potential destruction of the ozone shield and altering the climate by means of the CO_2 greenhouse effect are included in this category.

In conclusion, we need to develop a new point of view, one in which we evaluate pollutants against the background of natural nutrient cycles and balances. Unless our pollutants in kind and amount clearly fit into this background of natural processes and balances, we should assume that the biosphere will not take care of them. Sooner or later they will build up or accumulate in one or another part of the cycle, upsetting the overall balance and producing far-reaching consequences of indeterminable magnitude.

Methods of Control

Approaches toward reducing pollution can be divided into four general areas: (1) trap the wastes and manage where they go; (2) chemically change objectionable wastes to nonobjectionable compounds; (3) modify or change the production method so that undesirable wastes do not result; and (4) discontinue the use of the product or operation that causes undesirable amounts of pollution.

Trapping wastes

Exhausts from furnaces, incinerators, smelters, and so forth can be passed through various types of filters or electronic precipitators which trap and remove particulates, such as smoke particles. Such devices do not remove polluting gases, such as sulfur dioxide (SO_2), which exist as individual molecules, or very fine particles. However, "chemical filters" can be used to remove specific compounds. For example, sulfur dioxide may be removed by "scrubbers," devices in which the exhaust is passed through a spray of lime which chemically combines with the sulfur dioxide and causes it to precipitate as a sludge of calcium sulfite/calcium sulfate ($CaSO_3$/ $CaSO_4$). Similarly, organic compounds can be removed by passing the air or water through activated carbon (charcoal) filters. Additional types of filters may be designed to remove other specific compounds. More than one device may be required to remove all the contaminants from the waste stream.

Trapping the pollutants, however, is only half the problem. They still must go somewhere. Little is really solved if trapped pollutants from one source are dumped somewhere else; this only trades one pollution problem for another. For example, disposal of sludges from sulfur dioxide scrubbers can present problems. Materials collected from air filters and preciptators are frequently washed down the drain, resulting in water pollution problems, and we noted the problems resulting from disposal of waste chemicals in landfills. However,

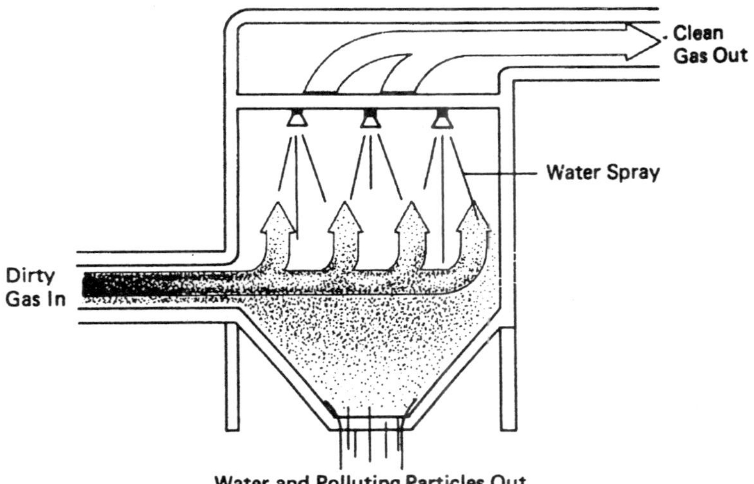

Fig. 8.10. Scrubber. Exhaust gases may be passed through a chemical and/or water spray to remove certain gases such as sulfur dioxide.

trapping wastes at least provides the potential for an acceptable, nonpolluting means of disposal. In addition, some wastes may be recycled or made into another useful product. For example, captured waste mercury can be reused. Trapped sulfur dioxide (SO_2) can be made into sulfuric acid (H_2SO_4), a widely used industrial chemical. Particulate ash may be made into building materials. However, such recycling or reuse won't tend to take place unless it is cost competitive. That is, sulfuric acid will not be made from waste sulfur dioxide unless it can be done at least as cheaply as obtaining sulfuric acid from other sources.

Chemical change

In many cases noxious chemical wastes can be chemically changed to innocuous compounds. This is the function of the catalytic converter used to control pollution from cars. As exhaust passes through the converter, a catalyst causes more oxygen to react with the carbon monoxide and unburned hydrocarbons, thus oxidizing them to carbon dioxide and water vapor. (Lead destroys the catalyst. Can you see why leaded gasoline should not be used in cars equipped with such converters?) The principle of chemical change can also be applied to all the hazardous chemical wastes in the halogenated hydrocarbon category. By use of high-temperature incinerators such wastes can be oxidized to carbon dioxide, water, and other harmless compounds.

Change the process or operation

Instead of adding filters, converters, or other devices, it may be possible to change the operation itself so that the same product is obtained without the noxious byproducts. For example, a Japanese auto manufacturer (Honda) introduced what is commonly called a *stratified combustion engine*. The engine has a modified combustion chamber which provides for more complete burning of fuel and hence produces relatively little carbon monoxide and hydrocarbon fragments. Several techniques exist for removing sulfur from coal before it is burned. Although mercury is used in the production of most chlorine today, methods do exist for producing chlorine without using it, thus eliminating discharges of waste mercury. Increasing safety standards to minimize the chance of accidents may also be put in this category.

Discontinue use

The ultimate way to eliminate pollution by an offending product or substance is to discontinue its production, or use. However, this assumes that suitable substitutes exist or that society is willing to forego whatever advantages the product offers. There are a number of examples of this approach. Sale of high-phosphate detergents has been banned in some areas where eutrophication is a problem and low- or zero-phosphate detergents have been substituted in their place. DDT and some other chlorinated hydrocarbon pesticides have been banned from general use and other pesticides have been substituted. In the United States, chlorofluorocarbons have been discontinued from use in aerosol cans, and other propellants have been substituted. Although substitutes for a particular product may be possible, they need to be regarded with caution since it is quite possible for the substitute to create pollution problems just as bad or worse than those of the original. For example, one proposed substitute for phosphate in detergents was found to be highly carcinogenic.

An example of society choosing to forego the advantages of a product was seen in the decision of the American people through Congress to abandon development of the supersonic transport (SST), although we did end up with the British-French Concorde anyway. The widespread public attack on nuclear power is another example of this approach in progress although the final decision here is not yet made. Additionally, it is not entirely clear that people who object to nuclear power really appreciate or have accepted the alternatives.

There are many proposals for decreasing air pollution in various cities by reducing traffic. These proposals range from such techniques as increasing city parking fees through the outright banning of all private vehicles from certain areas. The generally low acceptance or outright rejection of such proposals shows that the public may be unwilling to make the tradeoff in many cases.

Implementing Controls

We have discussed the threats of pollution and we have seen that there are methods for controlling pollution. Next is the need to choose and implement the controls to do the job.

The need for laws

Many people feel that industry should control its own pollutants on the basis of good conscience. However, good conscience or not, the following argument shows why it is effectively impossible for an industry to clean up its pollution unilaterally. Whatever method of pollution control is used costs money. In trapping wastes or chemically changing them to less toxic compounds, the cost of filters, precipitators, catalytic converters, and so forth may be considerable. Then there is additional expense in operating and maintaining such devices. In producing a product by a new method to avoid a polluting byproduct, a company must write off the capital invested in the old production equipment, make a substantial investment in new production equipment, and perhaps face a more expensive production procedure. In discontinuing a product, a company again must abandon its investment in production equipment as well as sacrifice all income from the product. Only in rare and exceptional cases does pollution control lead to cheaper methods or valuable byproducts that create an overall cost savings.

Suppose a company were to undertake pollution control unilaterally. It has basically two choices: It can pass the costs on to its customers in the form of higher prices for its products, or it can pay for the costs itself and hence sacrifice some of its profits. In a competitive system, both choices are basically untenable. If the costs are passed to the customer, the higher-priced products lose out to competing products because, other factors being equal, consumers will choose the lower-priced product. Alternatively, if costs are taken out of earnings there is less money available to replace equipment, develop new products, expand marketing, and so on. Here again, the company will lose out to competitors. Therefore, by virtuously undertaking pollution control, the company succeeds only in sacrificing itself to its competitors who don't adopt similar controls. Simply dropping a product because it pollutes, particularly if it is a major source of revenue, is an even more conspicuous economic loss for the company and its investors.

These economic realities dictate that industrial interests will vigorously attempt to avoid pollution control as far as possible because it is a cost that does not contribute to production or sales. They will fight even more vigorously against the banning of any product from which they derive significant profit. Examples of such actions abound. Therefore laws and means of enforcing compliance with the laws are necessary. Interestingly, when companies are finally forced into taking pollution control measures, they frequently make the best of it by extensively advertising whatever steps they have taken. Such advertising presents a virtuous public image and hides the fact that the industry vigorously opposed and may still be opposing the regulations on the legal level.

Laws and compliance

People often comment, "Why don't they pass a law..?" It is important to recognize that in a democracy laws are not passed by edicts of the President or anyone else. They are passed by Congress, state legislatures, city councils, and other governing bodies. In turn legislators respond to their constituents, who are individuals like you and me. If we want laws, we need to make our voices heard.

Public interest can be brought to bear on government in various ways. In the elective process one can support those candidates who share one's views. Representatives can be written or called to support or not support particular legislation. Through membership in environmental interest groups, one can support professional lobbyists, lawyers, and others who work to pass and enforce environmental legislation. These avenues of participation exist at local, state, and federal levels.

Through the 1960's and early 1970's a wave of ecological public interest and awareness did result in the formation of politically active environmental organizations and many environmental laws were passed. Most significant was the National Environmental Policy Act of 1969 (NEPA), which set the stage for many laws which followed. Most significant in the area of pollution are the Clean Water Act of 1972, the Clean Air Act of 1970, the Safe Drinking Water Act of 1974, and the Toxic Substances Control Act of 1976. Additionally, many states and local governments have laws which extend or expand upon the provisions of federal laws. Under these laws billions of dollars have been spent by both industry and government to control various pollutants and significant progress has been made in many areas. Certainly the situation is much better than it would have been if no action had been taken.

However, the existence of these laws and the fact that some progress has been made should not make us complacent concerning the future. First, these laws, as all laws, are subject to change by amendment or outright repeal. For example, in 1977 under mounting industrial pressure and with environmental zeal fading, important provisions of the Clean Air Act, which prevents further deterioration of air quality in many regions, were nearly lost. The granting of delays in the time by which the auto industry must meet certain standards on auto emissions has become almost routine.

Second, the process of reaching compliance (actually meeting the standards and requirements set forth by the laws) will continue well into the 1980's and probably far beyond. Here again, progress toward compliance will proceed only as far and as fast as public pressure demands. Without continuous public pressure there is plenty of continuing pressure from industrial interests to delay compliance indefinitely.

Finally, scientific investigations are really just beginning to reveal the magnitude and seriousness of the more subtle pollution problems such as those involving bioaccumulation and long-term exposures, various synergistic interactions, acid rain, the CO_2 greenhouse effect, and the ozone shield.

To prevent backsliding where progress has been made, to continue toward compliance of existing laws, and to meet new challenges, there will be a continuing need for public interest and involvement.

Benefit-cost ratio

As environmentalists promote higher degrees of pollution control, industry counters by pointing out the high costs involved. There is no question but that pollution control does cost money and that these costs are passed on to consumers in the form of more expensive products, higher utility bills, and so on. Thus it appears that we might save money by tolerating the pollution and not having controls. This is not necessarily so. Industries would save money, because they do not pay many of the hidden costs of pollution; however, the public does. The hidden costs of pollution include: higher health insurance premiums to cover the costs of pollution-related illnesses; higher product costs to pay for absenteeism because of pollution-related illnesses; higher maintenance and cleaning costs because of increased corrosion and dirt from pollution; higher food and wood-product costs because of crop and timber losses caused by pollution; higher fish and shellfish costs because of reduction of populations as a consequence of pollution;

higher transportation costs for traveling to more distant recreational areas because nearby areas are polluted. Therefore, as citizens, our choice is not between paying for pollution control and not paying for pollution control; the real alternative is between paying the costs of pollution control or paying the many hidden costs that result from pollution. The question is: What are the relative costs in the two areas?

In attempting to arrive at concrete answers regarding relative costs, professionals perform *cost-benefit* analyses. In such analyses, professionals estimate as accurately as possible the *costs* of controlling or eliminating various pollutants. These costs are compared with the monetary *benefits* that may be achieved, such as reductions in health-care costs, maintenance and cleaning costs, food and wood-product costs, and so on. The result is a *benefit-cost ratio.* If benefits are greater than the costs, pollution control is economically justified. On the other hand, if costs are estimated to be greater than benefits, the effort is not worthwhile.

The problem in determining a benefit-cost ratio is that values assigned to many factors that enter into costs and/or benefits are crude estimates at best. Depending on one's point of view, one may come to quite different conclusions. For instance, industry is prone to maximize cost factors and minimize benefit factors, at least for controlling its own particular pollutants. On the other hand, environmentalists are likely to underestimate costs and place high values on potential benefits. Workers who stand to lose their jobs if a polluting factory is closed will undoubtedly perceive relative costs and benefits differently than residents who are only affected by the pollution and have no vested interest in the factory. Further, certain benefits may be purely aesthetic-for example, the pleasure of having clear air and distant views. What monetary value should be placed on these? Here again, viewpoints will differ greatly.

Decisions, therefore, will be based not only on scientific data regarding the effects of pollution, but also on how individuals like you and me perceive and express our values. For example, the environmental movement of the late 1960's and early 1970's took place because enough people valued its benefits more than they feared its costs. The result was the passage of the aforementioned and many other environmental laws and the progress in pollution control that has been made to date. Indeed, costbenefit analyses performed by the Environmental Protection Agency show that benefits derived from pollution cleanup have outweighed the costs. However, in spite of such analyses, it appears that the values of our society may now be shifting and that people are seeing the costs of pollution control as greater than the benefits. The result has been a decline in movement toward environmental goals, if not some backsliding.

It is necessary to reemphasize the hidden costs of pollution-costs which we all pay, whether or not we suffer direct health effects or other inconveniences from pollution. Also, much more emphasis should be placed on *deferred costs* which result from not controlling pollution or not implementing proper methods of waste disposal. For example, disposal of chemical wastes in landfills may have been the least expensive alternative in the short run. However, inherent in such decisions was the deferred cost of billions of dollars which we must spend to take care of those dumps, since they now are threatening our water supplies. Proper disposal of the materials in the first place would have been much cheaper. The same may be said regarding today's pollution. Improving pollution control may seem too expensive and not worth the cost. However, by not exercising better pollution control, we may well be deferring incalculable expenses into the future. Consider, for example, the cost that may come from reducing productivity of both natural and artificial ecosystems through the effect of acid rain that leaches nutrients, or the enormous medical expenses that may come from the bioaccumulation of more and more halogenated hydrocarbons, heavy metals, and so on. Until we recognize and respond to the basic limits of what the biosphere can dilute and assimilate, and keep our output of pollutants within these limits, it is inevitable that we will be setting the stage for future tragedies.

Pollution and Lifestyle

Once decisions have been made to reduce pollution, there remains some choice in the methods to be used. We tend to consider pollution control in terms of add-on devices or processes such as filters or converters. However, do such devices really solve the problem? Recall that pollution is the inevitable result of excessive material and energy flow demanded by present lifestyles. Whenever there is a one-direction flow of materials, as opposed to recycling, materials will inevitably accumulate at certain points and present pollution problems. Add-on pollution control devices may redirect the flow and make it more tolerable for a time, but they don't get at the underlying problem, the flow itself. In fact, they may actually increase it. Filters, converters, and so on themselves must be manufactured and hence represent a

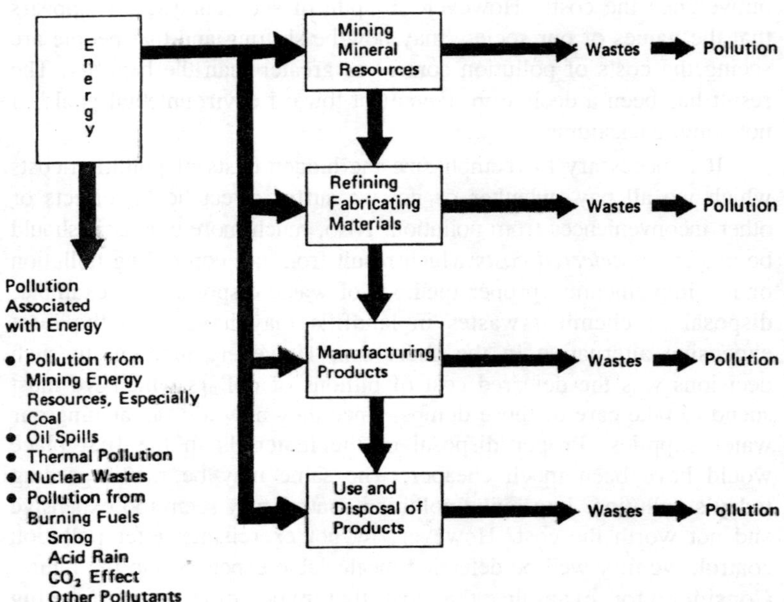

Fig. 8.11. Use and disposal of products is the end of a long series of events with pollution occurring at every step. Reducing consumption at the end would reduce pollution at all the intervening levels.

further flow of materials. In addition, they require more energy to operate, which requires more flow of fuel and waste products of combustion and, in turn, more pollution control; and so the vicious cycle goes on.

Action which can be exercised by individuals and which should be given more serious consideration in national planning and policy-making is the development of lifestyles which use fewer materials and less energy, thereby lessening the flow and the fundamental output of pollutants. Actions such as product reuse, extending product lifetimes, and reducing consumption which were discussed at the end of Chapter 6 are just as or even more important in connection with reducing industrial pollution.

9

APPLICATION OF BIOSOLIDS

Human waste excreted by all of the world's 6.8 billion population must be disposed of by some means. In the United States and many other countries of the world, municipal wastes are treated and subsequently land applied as a method of disposal or recycling. Most methods of municipal sewage treatment produce large amounts of bacteria as the soluble organic matter is converted to bacterial biomass. This material is known as biosolids. Animal wastes result in manures (solids) or liquid effluents that can also be land applied. All of these wastes are routinely applied to soils to provide plant nutrients or as a source of water for plant growth or groundwater recharge.

In the United States, the re-use of treated municipal wastewater effluent provides an opportunity to conserve water resources. Land application of liquid wastes can also provide an alternative to disposal in areas where surface waters have a limited capacity to assimilate elements such as nitrogen or phosphorus, which in excess can result in pollution. The solids that result from municipal wastewater treatment processes contain organic material that, when properly treated and applied to land as "biosolids," can improve the productivity of soils or enhance revegetation of disturbed ecosystems. Animal manures can also be land applied beneficially to agricultural land. However, besides the documented benefits of land application, there are also potential hazards, which have caused the public response to the practice to be mixed.

BIOSOLIDS AND ANIMAL WASTES

Use of animal wastes and manures as a fertilizer source for agricultural crop production has been practiced since the days of the

Roman Empire. During the 20th century in both the U.S. and Europe, small agricultural farms frequently consisted of both crop and animal production. Consequently, animal wastes were naturally land applied to enhance crop production. Although fossil-fuel based fertilizers replaced much of the use of manures, following World War II, the practice continues today, particularly in developing countries.

In the U.S., land application of municipal wastewater and biosolids has been practiced for its beneficial effects and for disposal purposes since the advent of modern wastewater treatment about 160 years ago. In Britain in the 1850s, "*sewage farms*" were established to dispose of untreated sewage. By 1875, about 50 farms were utilizing land treatment in England, as were many others close to other major cities in Europe. In the U.S., sewage farms were established by about 1900. At this same time, primary sedimentation and secondary biological treatment was introduced as a rudimentary form of wastewater treatment, and land application of "*sludges*" began. It is interesting to note that prior to wastewater treatment, sludge *per se* did not exist. Municipal sludge in Ohio was used as a fertilizer as early as 1907. Early on land application was carried out with little regard to potential pollution.

Since the early 1970s, more emphasis has been placed on applying sludge to cropland at rates to supply adequate nutrients for crop growth. In the 1970s and 80s, many studies were undertaken to investigate the potential benefits and hazards on land application, in both the U.S. and Europe. Ultimately in 1993, Federal regulations were established via the "Part 503 Sludge Rule." This document—"The Standards for the Use and Disposal of sewage Sludge"—was designed to "adequately protect human health and the environment from any reasonably anticipated adverse effect of pollutants." As part of these regulations, two classes of treatment were defined as "Class A and Class B" biosolids, with different restrictions for land applications, base don the level of treatment.

Land application increased when restrictions were placed on ocean dumping. By the year 2000, 60% of all biosolids were land applied in the U.S. Currently most land application in the U.S. utilizes Class B biosolids. However, due to public concerns over potential hazards, in some areas of the U.S., land application of Class B biosolids has been banned.

Nature of Wastewater (Sewage)

Sewage sludge is defined in the part 503 rule as the solid, semi-solid, or liquid residue generated during the treatment of domestic sewage in a wastewater treatment plant. The term biosolids is not used in the Part 503 rule, but EPA (1995) defines biosolids as "the primarily organic solid product yielded by municipal wastewater treatment processes that can be beneficially recycled" as soil amendments. The term biosolids has been controversial because of the perception that it was created to improve the image of sewage sludge in a public-relations campaign by the sewage industry. For our purpose, the term biosolids implies treatment of sewage sludge to meet the land-application standards in the Part 503 rule.

It is estimated that approximately 5.6 million dry tons sewage sludge were used or disposed of annually in the United States in 2000, of which approximately 60% were used for land application. However, EPA estimates that only approximately 0.1% available agricultural land in the U.S. is treated with biosolids.

Biosolids are applied to agricultural and nonagricultural lands as a soil amendment because they can improve the chemical and physical properties of soils, and because they contain nutrients for plant growth. Land application on agricultural land is utilized to grow food crops such as corn or wheat, and nonfood crops such as cotton. Nonagricultural land application includes forests, rangelands, public parks, golf courses, and cemeteries. Biosolids are also used to revegetate severely disturbed lands such as mine tailings or strip mine areas.

Wastewater (Sewage) Treatment

Class A versus Class B Biosolids

Biosolids are divided into two classes on the basis of pathogen content: Class A and Class B. Class A biosolids are treated to reduce the presence of pathogens to below detectable levels and can be used without any pathogen-related restrictions at the application site. Class Biosolids can also be bagged and sold to the public. Class B biosolids are also treated to reduce pathogens, but still contain detectable levels of them. Class B biosolids have site restrictions to minimize the potential for human exposure until environmental factors such as heat, sunlight, or desiccation have further reduced pathogen numbers. Class B biosolids cannot be sold or given away in bags or other containers or used at sites with public use.

Methods of Land Application of Biosolids

The method of land application of biosolids essentially depends on the percent solids contained within them, which determines whether the biosolids are liquid in nature or a "cake".

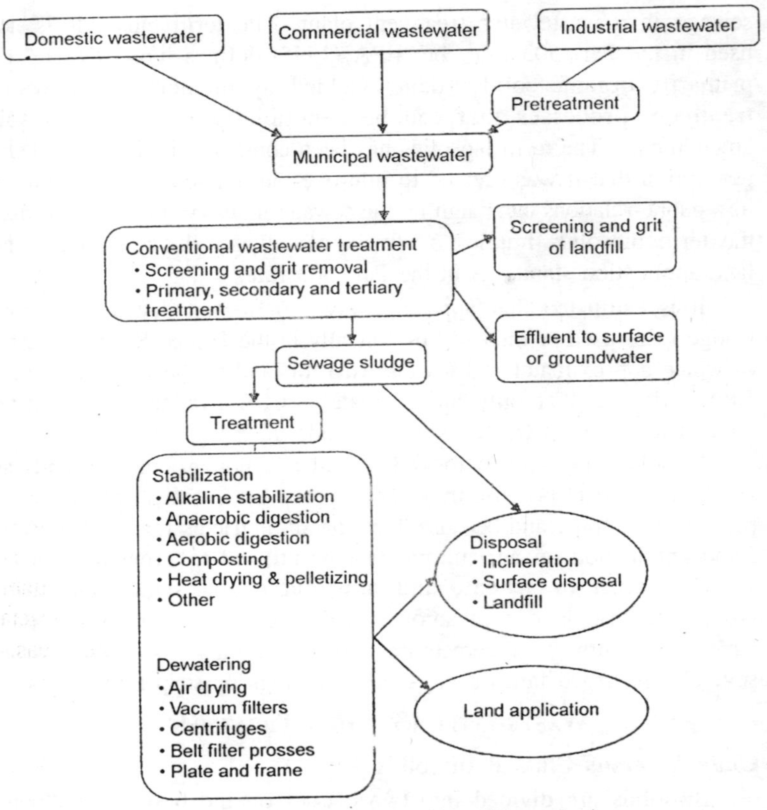

Fig. 9.1. Simplified scheme of biosolids production.

1. *Injection*. Liquid biosolids are injected to a soil depth of 6-9 inches. Injection vehicles simultaneously disc the field. Injection processes reduce odors and bioaerosols, as well as the risk of runoff to surface waters.
2. *Surface Application*. Here, liquid or cake biosolids are surface applied and subsequently tilled into the soil.

Benefits of Land Application of Biosolids

Biosolids as a Source of Plant Nutrients

Biosolids contain all the elements essential for the growth of higher plants. Nitrogen and phosphorus in particular are abundant, making biosolids attractive as a fertilizer source. Nitrogen and phosphorus are typically present at concentrations of 1-6% on a dry weight basis. Because plants need more nitrogen for growth than phosphorus, when biosolids are applied at a rate to supply sufficient nitrogen, this means that excess phosphorus is applied, which over time can accumulate in the soil.

In addition to nitrogen and phosphorus, biosolids provide other nutrients such as Ca, Fe, Mg, K, Na and Zn, in amount adequate for crop needs. Finally, note that some liquid biosolids ($<18\%$ solids) provide an additional input of water, which can be important in arid regions where crop irrigation is necessary.

Table 9.1 Analysis of anaerobically digested sludge

Element	*Concentration (Dry weight basis)*
Metals	(mg/kg^{-1})
Copper	520
Nickel	13
Lead	59
Chromium	29
Cadmium	3.5
Zinc	1900
Silver	4.7
Arsenic	ND
Mercury	0.51
Molybdenum	12
Selenium	ND
Other Elements	(G 100 g^{-1})
Phosphorus	3.3
Calcium	3.6
Magnesium	0.45
Sodium	0.4
Organic carbon	16.6
Nitrogen	
Total Kjeldahl N	3.4
inorganic N	0.16
Total solids	2.8

Biosolid Impact on Soil Physical and Chemical Properties

Soil organic matter enhances soil structure, through the formation of secondary aggregates. This results increased soil pores, which facilitate air and water movement through the soil. Continuous cropping of soils leads to degradation of both soil organic matter and hence soil structure. Applications of biosolids to soils increases the soil organic content, improving soil structure. Land application improves soil physical properties such as water infiltration and retention, and reduces the soil's susceptibility to erosion. Chemically, land application of biosolids can be beneficial by increasing soil cation exchange capacity (CEC).

Reduced Pollution

In most instances, broad-scale land application of municipal wastes at appropriate loading rates results in far less pollution than if the material had been concentrated by disposal at a single site. When loading rates are controlled, the soil has a chance to transform many waste components into plant-available nutrients. Thus, plants are able to take up these nutrients and complete their natural cycle. These include carbon, nitrogen, sulfur, and phosphorus. Other important sludge components that are recycled include micronutrients such as zinc, iron, and copper. However, when found in high concentrations, these metals can be toxic to plants. Additionally, the soil environment helps stabilize other potential pollutants found in biosolids, such as lead, cadmium, zinc, and arsenic, by trapping them into their solid phases. When this happens, the pollutants do not leach into groundwater and are much less likely to be taken up by plants. However, it is important to note that the metal contaminant itself is still retained in the soil and remains a potential source of pollution.

Hazards of Land Application of Biosolids

Site Restrictions

The federal regulations for managing a biosolid land application site include several restrictions.

Some states have much more stringent site criteria than those of the Part 503 rule.

In addition to site restrictions, EPA imposed limitations regarding minimum time durations between applications of Class B biosolids and the harvesting of certain crops, the grouping of animals, and public access to the site.

If the limitations are followed, EPA concluded that the level of protection from pathogens in Class B biosolids is equal to the level of protection provided by the unregulated use of Class A biosolids.

Nitrates and Phosphates

Biosolids almost always contain large amounts of nitrogen (N) and nitrate (NO_3^-) and ammonium (NH_4^+). In addition, they contain organic forms of nitrogen that are readily transformed to NO_3^- via ammonification and subsequent nitrification. Nitrate ions are very soluble in water and ionic in nature (negatively charged). Therefore excess nitrates leach easily through soils and can reach aquifers. Nitrates are of public concern due to the potential for methemoglobinemia. This disease, also known as blue baby syndrome, can occur in young infants due to the drinking water high in nitrates (> 10 ppm). Because of this potential hazard, biosolid and land application rates should be matched with crop N requirements. In addition, for irrigated agriculture, irrigation rates should be managed to reduce excess surface runoff or excess sub-surface leaching of NO_3^-.

Biosolids also contain large amounts of phosphate (P) as HPO_4^{2-} or $H_2PO_4^-$. Since plants require more N than P, when biosolids loading rates are based on potential plant N uptake, excess P can accumulate in soil. During many years of continuous land application, soil P concentrations become excessive and can lead to eutrophication of estuaries via surface runoff. Interestingly, in the future, biosolid land application rates may have to be matched to crop P requirements and thus additional N will need to be applied to crops as fertilizer.

Metals and Organics

All sludges have small amounts of essential trace metals needed for plant growth, but they also contain variable amount of potentially toxic heavy metals. Moreover, even essential trace elements can be present in such high concentrations that they induce toxicities to plants or microorganisms. Metal of particular concern include Zn, Cu, Cd, Ni, Pb, Hg, Mo, and As. The amount of metal contaminants in a particular sludge depends on the amount of industrial inputs into the municipal sewage system. It is therefore illegal to discharge excessive amounts of metal into municipal wastewater lines, and such wastes must often be treated on site prior to disposal. The soil environment also influences the toxicity of the metals associated with any particular sludge. Sludge-amended soils with high pH have lower plant-available metal concentrations than do sludge-amended low-pH soils. This is because the water solubility of most metals increases as pH decreases. Thus, one management strategy to reduce metal mobility and toxicity towards plants is to lime soils to a neutral or alkaline pH. The organic matter content of soils also affects metal availability. In general, soils with high organic matter content (>5%) exhibit relatively low metal uptake by plants, as metals are sorbed and complexed by the polymer-like organic carbon structure of organic matter. However, when low-molecular-weight organic molecules (usually present in the early stages of plant tissue decay) form complexes with metals, their mobility and plant availability can be dramatically increased in the soil environment. Once metals are introduced into soil, their bioavailability and mobility can be manipulated by changing the valence state of the metal or by altering soil factors that influence their solubilities. While short-term effects of metal additions to soil can be beneficial, the long-term fate of these metals is more difficult to predict. This is because metal pollutants do not biodegrade and therefore continue to accumulate in the soil environment.

Biosolids can also contain organic compounds that can adversely affect public health. These include trace amounts of pesticides, polyaromatic hydrocarbons (PAHs), plasticizers, volatile organics, and solvents. Many of these compounds are degraded during wastewater treatment. However, the more refractory and insoluble compounds such as chlorinated hydrocarbons do not degrade during treatment, particularly if they are sorbed to biosolids. As in the case of metals, it is bioavailability and mobility of these compounds that determines their ultimate fate and also the potential public health hazard. Biodegradation and mobility are affected by soil type, in particular, soil texture, organic-matter content, pH, and soil moisture content. The complexity of each site and the interactions of the above factors determine whether or not these organic compounds degrade or accumulate in soil, and whether or not they have the potential to contaminate aquifers.

Chemicals were subjected to a formal risk assessment utilizing several exposure pathways. The risk assessment conducted to support the part 503 rule was then utilized to develop risk-based standards.

Overall, concern over the potential public health hazard with regard to metals has decreased in the United States, for two major reasons. First, a large amount of research has been conducted on crop uptake of metals, including both food and nonfood crops, as well as the fate of metals in soil. Contrary to the dire predictions of some scientists, the "time bomb theory" with respect to metals has not come to pass. Essentially, this theory held that since organic matter in soils is known to complex and accumulates metals, a "flood" of metals would be released when the organic material eventually degraded. In fact, an "aging" effect has been observed for metals, in which bioavailability is observed to decrease with time. The second factor that has reduced fears with respect to metals is enhanced pretreatment technologies that reduce metal inputs into sewage and hence biosolids. Thus biosolid metals contents have decreased dramatically form the 1980s to the present. Despite this, some scientists still have concerns about the effects of metals on the ecosystem, due to the fact that metals do not degrade. This concern is particularly true in Europe.

Emerging Chemicals of Concern

Dioxin-like chemicals

Dioxin and dioxin-like chemicals have been the target of EPA investigation and are considered a group for risk assessment. These compounds are chlorinated hydrocarbons within the family known as polychlorinated biphenyls (PCBs). EPA recently conducted a survey of dioxin concentrations in biosolids, and the results have shown that dioxin is not frequently present in biosolids at levels that would cause concern.

Pharmaceuticals

These compounds are routinely found in biosolids, since they are present in a variety of personal care and skin products, and hence enter wastewater from homes. Some of these compounds are known to be endocrine disruptors.

Flame retardants

Polybrominated diphenyl ethers (PBDEs) are flame retardants and hence enter the food chain through use in fire extinguisher and flame-retardant materials. The use of the these compounds is banned in many European countries, and California will become the first U.S. State to ban some PBDEs. The fate and transport of PBDEs is currently unknown.

Pathogens

EPA established two categories of biosolid: Class A biosolids, which have no detectable concentrations of pathogens, and Class B biosolids, which have detectable concentrations of pathogens. In terms of land application, a combination of treatment and site restrictions are intended to result in a reduction of pathogenic and indicator microorganisms to undetectable concentrations prior to potential public contact.

Class B biosolids routinely contain human pathogen. The pathogens found in a particular source of biosolids reflect the incidence of pathogenic disease in the community from which the biosolids are derived.

Also of concern are emerging pathogens such as the SARS virus (severe acute respiratory syndrome). However, regardless of the pathogen of concern, the major routes of potential human exposure to pathogens in biosolids remains the same, specifically via air, soil, and water. Exposure can also occur via vectors, such as flies, and to prevent this, "vector-attraction" reduction requirements are enforced. These involves specific biosolid treatment and rapid incorporation of land applied biosolids ($<$ 6 hours).

Exposure via air

Human exposure to pathogens via air results from the formation of aerosolized biological particles that are referred to as bioaerosols. Until recently, little was known of the risk of infection from bioaerosols generated during land application of biosolids, and this topic was utilized by environmental activists to challenge the efficacy of land application.

Characteristics of biological aerosols

The term biological aerosol is used to describe biological particles which have been aerosolized. These particles may contain microorganisms (bacteria, fungi, and viruses) or biological remnants such as endotoxin and cell wall constituents such as peptidoglycan. Bioaerosol sizes range typically from 0.5 to 30 μm in diameter and are typically surrounded by a thin layer of water. In other instances, the biological particles can be associated with particulate matter such as soil or biosolids, depending on the place of origin. Bioaerosol particles in the lower spectrum of sizes (0.5 to 5 μm) are typically of most concern, since these particles are more readily inhaled or swallowed.

Bioaerosols generated from the land application of biosolids may be associated with soil or vegetation, depending on the type of land application. For example, if a front-end loader is used to load a biosolids spreader, it is possible that soil will be in contact with the biosolids and therefore be associated with any aerosol generated by it. In this situation the soil particle or vegetation is known as a "raft" for the biological particles contained with the aerosol. However, for soil particles to be aerosolized, the particles need to be fairly dry, and low soil moisture contents are known to promote microbial inactivation.

Exposure via groundwater

In principle, pathogens originally present in biosolids applied to land can contaminate surface or groundwater. However, most soils limit the movement of microbes to groundwater. Normally, significant migration will only occur in coarse textured soils or karst topography, with a shallow depth to groundwater. Viruses have the greater possibility to migrate through soil; however, they have been found to tightly bind to biosolids, and little leaching appears to occur. No direct cause and effect has been identified in surface or groundwater near land where biosolids has been applied.

Exposure via soil

Soil

Pathogen survival in and transport through soil are considered together in this section. Human pathogens that are routinely found in domestic sewage sludge include viruses, bacteria, protozoan parasites, and helminths. Of those pathogens, viruses are the smallest and least complex, generally have a short survival period in soil, and have the greatest potential for transport in soil. Survival of viruses has been shown to be temperature-dependent and decreases as temperature increases. Soil type affects virus survival, with longer survival occurring on clay loam biosolids-amended soils than on sandy loam biosolids-amended soils. Rapid loss of soil moisture also limits virus survival.

Like virus survival, bacteria survival in soil is affected by temperature, pH, and moisture. Soil nutrients availability also plays a role in bacteria survival. Lower temperatures usually increases survival, as do a neutral soil pH and soil at field capacity. Of the pathogenic bacteria, *Salmonella* and *Escherichia coli* can survive for a long time in biosolids-amended soil—up to 16 months for *Salmonella*. In contrast, *shigella* has a shorter survival time than either *Salmonella* or *E. coli*. Studies on indictor organisms have shown that total and fecal coliforms as well as fecal streptococci can all survive for weeks to several months, depending on soil moisture and temperature conditions.

Regrowth is also important when evaluating the survival of pathogenic and indicator bacteria in soil and biosolids compost. *Salmonella*, *E. coli*, and fecal coliforms are all capable of regrowth. Following land application of biosolids, regrowth of actual pathogens is negligible. However, regrowth of pathogens can occur in Class A biosolids if they are stored prior to land application and exposed to reinoculation via bird excrement. Regrowth has also occurred during composting processes. Regrowth of fecal coliforms is more common than pathogen and has been documented even following land application of Class B biosolids.

The protozoan parasites often associated with biosolids include *Giardia* and *Cryptosporidium* spp. However, little research has been conducted on the survival of these parasites in biosolids-amended soil. Helminths are perhaps the most persistent of enteric pathogens. *Ascaris* eggs can survive several years in solids.

The transport of microorganisms through soils or the vadose zone is affected by a complex array of abiotic and biotic factors, including adhesion processes, filtration effects, physiological state of the cells, soil characteristics, water flow rates, predation, and intrinsic mobility of the cells, as well as the presence of biosolids. For viruses, the potential for transport is large, although viruses can adsorb to soil colloidal particles and to the biosolids themselves, thus limiting transport. Virus sorption is controlled by the soil pH. Most viruses are negatively charged (isoelectric point 3–6), so that at a neutral soil pH, soil sorption is reduced, whereas at mor acidic soil pH values, the viruses are positively charged, increasing sorption.

The larger size of bacteria means that soil acts as a filter, limiting bacterial transport. Soil would also limit the transport of the even larger protozoa and helminths. However, microorganisms may be transported through soil cracks and macrochannels via preferential flow.

Pathogens survival and transport in soil should be evaluated from a public-health perspective. Pathogens are routinely present in Class B biosolids and are capable of surviving for days, weeks, or even months, depending on the organism and environment. Therefore, site restrictions with durations based on subsequent land use are necessary following land application. For many soils, contamination of aquifers due to vertical migration of pathogens from land-applied biosolids is unlikely because of the sorption of viruses and the soil filtration potential for large pathogens. However, in coarse textured, sandy soil or high-permeability karst topography, groundwater contamination events are possible.

Sources of Animal Wastes

Animal wastes predominantly include manures from cows, pigs, and chickens. Animal wastes are pollutants of increasing concern both to the public and to regulatory bodies because they have the potential to contaminate both surface and groundwater. Consequently, animal wastes must now be included as part of the agricultural production cycle and figured into the cost of operating a farm or livestock facility. Animal agricultural wastes can be divided into two production types;

range and pasture production, and confined or concentrated animal production.

In range and pasture systems, the concentration of wastes is generally much more diffuse or dispersed than it is when large numbers of animals are confined to relatively small areas. Range and pasture systems have two principal effects on surface water quality: (1) increased turbidity through the movement of soil particles into streams, rivers, and lakes; (2) increased fecal coliform counts in areas of heavy animal use. Although we know that grazing systems may adversely affect some measures of water quality, we will focus here on the highly concentrated animal production units and the methods of preventing and controlling pollution form these concentrated units.

In the past, animals were concentrated only intermittently. The period of confinement was a transitory phase followed by a return to pasture, after such management activities as milking or shearing. However, animal production is occurring in increasingly controlled environments owing to the success of efforts to raise productivity and diminish climatic, feeding, and mortality variables. Larger numbers of animals are being raised in *concentrated animal feeding operations* or CAFROs—principally, feedlots, dairies, swine operations, poultry houses, and intensive aquaculture. The number of CAFO operations more than doubled form 1982 to 1997, increasing from 5,000 to 11,200. Almost every country in the United States has a CAFO with more than 10,000 animals. This shift in production methods has changed the age-old method of reincorporation of animal wastes as manure on the farm where it was produced. Specialization has largely divorced animal production form the production of crops: a concentrated animal facility may be located far from crop production, and the same family (or the same corporation) may not purse the two types of production.

The production of large numbers of animals on a small land base has resulted in the stockpiling of wastes at specific locations, the construction of large waste-storage ponds, and, often times, waste applications to land in excess of agronomic crop needs.

Nonpoint versus Point Source Pollution

In discussing sources of animal wastes, it is important to understand the terms point and nonpoint contaminant sources. The term "nonpoint pollution" is misleading and is often misuses. In animal agricultural systems, true *nonpoint sources* are those in which potential contaminants are not concentrated during production and do not pass through a single or small number of conduits for disposal. These nonpoint sources include corrals, feedlots, and extensive and intensive pasture systems.

Point sources are those facilities that concentrate pollutants of contaminants to a significant degree and pass these contaminants through a pipe, ditch, or canal for disposal.

According to EPA regulations, however, some concentrated animal feeding operations may be designated as point sources requiring an individual National Pollution Discharge Elimination System (NPDES) permit. In this case, a CAFO is defined as a lot or facility without vegetation, where animals are confined for 45 or more days per year. The number of animals needed to meet this definition as a CAFO depends on several factors; however, the key determinant is whether or not the facility discharges into navigate waters, as determined by the method of discharge. The method of discharge is judged by the 25-year, 24-year storm event, which is the required event that a facility must be designed to meet. This design criterion is a storm of 24 hours duration whose probability of occurrence is once every 25 years. If a facility does not discharge form storms smaller than the 25-year, 24-hour storm event, it may be treated as a point source. This "double standard" recognizes the fact that what appear to be agricultural point sources can safely be treated as nonpoint sources because the pollutants being discharged are either not concentrated enough to warrant specific controls at the pipe or are not laden with hazardous materials.

The 25-year, 24-hour storm criterion does not mean that it is certain that once every 25 years a storm of a certain size and duration will occur. Another, possibly clearer, way of looking at this standard is what within 100 years it is likely that four storms that meet the 25-year, 24-hour storm size and length will occur. However, these four storms may occur back-to-back or be spread out over a period longer than 25 years. Therefore, given the hydrologic record, 25 years is the average return period for a storm of this size and duration.

Benefits of Land Application of Animal Wastes

Land-applied animal wastes provide nutrients for plant growth, similar to land application of biosolids. Land application is one the best methods for disposal of excess manure or manure slurry. While supplying some of the essential nutrients for crop production, manure is also a beneficial soil amendment for increasing tilth, aeration, and water-holding capacity. Land application does have some disadvantages, however, including the distribution of weed seeds, the possible accumulation of salts, and the application of excess nutrients that may leach and again become pollutants. Before large quantities of manure and/or slurries can be applied, it is necessary to know: (1) the relative nutrient content; (2) the rate of mineralization (decay rate); (3) the salt load; (4) the concentration and type of toxic elements; (5) the proper time and method of application; and (6) the amount and type of weed seed.

The nutrient content of manure can vary greatly, depending upon the age of the livestock in question, the rate of feed consumption, the feed ration, and the manure handling and storage practices prior to land application. Two facts are especially important when deciding upon the application rate for manure; (1) the moisture content of the manure directly affects the nutrient percentage; and (2) manure loses N as NH_3 when it dries.

The rate of mineralization of manure is the percentage available for plant uptake each year. This rate is given as a decay series at three levels of nitrogen at the time of application. The amount applied each year is the quantity of manure that should be added to maintain an annual mineralization rate of 220 kg of nitrogen per hectare per year for a given N% and decay rate. Local climatic conditions such as extreme heat or resistance may cause the decay rate to change considerably, thereby affecting the application rate as well. Note that the amount of manure that needs to be applied decreases each year; this decrease is due to residual N from the previous applications. Note also that the decay rate is maximal during the first year of application, but decreases dramatically in subsequent years.

The most effective means of maintaining the nutrient value of manure depends on the form in which it is applied to cropland. If it is being applied as a slurry, it should be injected below the surface; but if the manure is applied as a solid to the surface, the treated soil should be tilled immediately. This reduces nuisance odors, nutrient losses by volatilization, and the potential for groundwater pollution caused by runoff.

Hazards of Land Application of Animal Wastes

Concentrated animal agriculture produced the following specific pollutants in the wastes resulting from animal metabolic activity:

1. Nitrates and phosphates with the hazards similar to those from biosolids.
2. Pesticides that are used in CAFOs can be a concern for both surface and groundwater contamination. For example, coumaphos, an organophosphate, is commonly used in dips for animals crossing

the southern borders of the Unites States. While relatively immobile, coumaphos is known to be persistent and has been found at some depths when it has not been disposed of properly. Other pesticides, such as toxaphene, are no longer used in animal dips.

3. Biochemical oxygen demand (or BOD) is a measure of the quantity of oxygen (often measured in kilograms of O_2) needed to satisfy biochemical oxidation of organic matter in a waste sample in five days at 20°C. While not a specific pollutant, the BOD is one of the important general indicator of a substance's potential for environmental pollution of surface waters. This measure of pollution capability is important because animal wastes typically contain a high level of BODs, on the order of 0.45–3.6 kg per 454 kg of excreted material.
4. Specific microbial pathogens. Animal manures can be a source of specific microbial pathogens that are not found in biosolids. These include *E. coli* O157:H7, which is an enterohemorrhagic *E. coli* excreted by cows. Cows are also a source of *Cryptosporidium parvum*. Chickens are frequently inhabited with *Campylobacter* spp. Thus, although they do not contain human viruses, animal manures to contain pathogens capable of human infection.

Public Perceptions of Land Application

Public perceptions of land application of organic wastes are highly variable. First, land application of animal manures is and has been considered a "natural country way of life", with few criticism from the general public. This is despite the fact that cow manures, for example, contain pathogens at least as hazardous as those found in biosolids and despite the fact that such wastes were in part responsible for the Milwaukee *Cryptosporidium* outbreaks in 1993. It is also noteworthy that foods raised on land amended with manures are technically classified as "organic," which is not the case when land is amended with biosolids. Public perception of land application of biosolids in part is a function of land availability and population density. For example, in the desert Southwest, agricultural areas are often located far from urban centers, so that there are fewer surrounding residents who come into contact with the process. In contrast, in the Northeast, the potential impact of land application is much greater, because of less land and larger populations.

Soil and Land Pollution

Mining, agriculture, and deforestation are important energy-intensive activities that impact economies and at the same time directly and indirectly cause soil and land pollution. Mining produces vast quantities of almost sterile and structureless geologic materials, such as crushed rock that often contain significant amounts of toxic metals, such as lead and cadmium, and salts. Mine overburden and tailings are often stockpiled next to large open pit excavations. Modern agricultural production requires the use of large quantities of commercial fertilizers and pesticides, and produces animal wastes, all of which can pollute land and water.

Land deforestation indirectly affects the quality of land and water by increasing the rates of soil erosion and sediment transport, and accelerating the loss of the nutrient-rich soil surface. Invasive exotic plant species also have a significant impact on the quality of our lands by crating soil conditions that may be toxic to other plants and by increasing fire hazards. All of these activities in turn can affect soil salinity and acidity of surrounding land areas by releasing or concentrating unwanted metals, salts, and acid or acid-forming minerals. These materials can also be released into air or water sources.

Because these activities have played a traditional key role in the growth and development of our modern society, to date their impacts on the environment of our modern society, to date their impacts on the environment have not been closely monitored or regulated. It is important to recognize the impacts that these activities have on our environment and there is a need to achieve a balance between their social benefits and the need for the preservation of our environment.

Surface Mining

Mining of coal and metal ores was one of the earliest contributors to the industrial revolution. When transformed, these ores became both the fuel and the building blocks of industrialization. Although carbon-based plastic materials, together with such organic chemicals as pesticides and solvents, have dominated industrial production since the early 1950s, metal-based goods remain fundamental to modern industry. Numerous modern goods—from cars to paints—require the use of such common metals as iron, aluminum, and copper. In addition to these three metals, other less common metals and metalloids, such as lead, cadmium, nickel, mercury, arsenic, and selenium, are essential for the manufacture of these and other goods. Metallic elements are therefore commonly found in industrial wastes, where they have complex and still poorly understood effects on the environment. What is known is that uncontrolled and concentrated releases of metals into the environment present both short and long-term hazards to human health and adversely affect the environment. Industries that mine and process ores, drill for oil and gas, and/or burn coal also generate large volumes of salt-containing wastes. For these industries, the predominant chemical species include sodium (Na^+), calcium (Ca^{++}), sulfate ($SO_4^=$), and chloride (Cl^-), and carbonate ($CO_3^=$) ions, which are also very abundant in the natural environment. Because these wastes are not intrinsically hazardous or acutely toxic, they do not pose an immediate risk to health and the environment. Nonetheless, the volumes of these wastes that are generated each year are massive enough to be of concern.

Mine Tailings

Mining activities and, in particular, strip mining of metal ores produce vast quantities of residues called *mine spoils* and *mine tailings* that may contain significant concentrations of metals. Mine spoils or *overburden* consist of surface materials that do not contain the metal of interest and that are therefore stockpiled at surface, often resembling large "mesas." Mine tailings, in contrast, are the crushed mineral rock that has been processed to release the metal of interest. These are often pumped as a slurry in "lifts" of 3-m dimension into valleys or depressions. Mine tailings can be 35 m deep due to successive depositions of lifts. Thus, these residues, which are usually composed of unweathered primary minerals, can alter the environment physically and chemically. Strip mining for copper, for example, produces large quantities of tailings that often contain concentrations of 100-10,000 mg kg^{-1} of such metals as cadmium and lead. Similarly, iron pyrites (FeS_2), which are often associated with copper, silver, and lead ores, can have a devastating impact on the aquatic environment because their oxidation releases sulfuric acid and into the environment. The overall reaction is described as follows:

$$FeS_2 \text{ (pyrite mineral)} + 3.75O_2 + 3.5\,H_2O \rightarrow Fe(OH)_3 \text{ (solid)} + 2SO_4^{2-} + 4H^+ \quad ...(1)$$

In an acid stream (pH <3), fresh pyrite can react in a cascading effect with soluble ferric iron in (Fe^{3+}), creating even more acidity. The reaction rate is controlled by the oxidation of Fe^{2+} to Fe^{3+} in the presence of O_2, and results in lowering the pH of the environment. This process can also occur biologically via autotrophic bacteria which thrive at pH 2-3).

Mining operations that threat or leach ores and/or store acid chemicals for the extraction of metals can generate large volumes of acidic metal-containing wastewaters and/or leachates. For example, low-grade Cu ore is often extracted by means of sulfuric acid heap leaching. In this process crushed Cu ore is continuously leached with sulfuric acid until most of the Cu is solubilized due to both the high acidity and formation of Cu-sulfate complexes. Spent acid solutions, usually contaminated with other metals, must be neutralized and stored in lagoons or impoundments. Gold mining also produces vast quantities of spent ores and liquid process streams that usually contain residual levels of cyanide (CN^-) complexes. Metal-cyanide complexes are usually either stable in the soil environment or biologically degraded into nontoxic forms of N. However, when released into aquatic systems, these residues can be extremely toxic to fish if free cyanide is released into the water.

Air Emissions

Metal smelting and refining processes generate wastes that may contain multiple hazardous metals, such lead, zinc, nickel, copper, cadmium, chromium, mercury, selenium, arsenic, and cobalt. These elements may be found in the ores uses or they may be added as mixed metals into the melts to produce metal alloys. Thus, metal-containing smelter wastes have to be treated and disposed of as hazardous wastes. Smelting and refining require very high temperatures to reduce the metal ores (such as pyrite and bauxite for iron and aluminum production) into pure metal and to refine metals and alloys. For example, iron melts at 1536°C, Copper melts at 1083°C, and aluminum melts at 660°C. At these temperatures, many other metals and metal compounds volatilize; for example, the boiling points of mercury, cadmium, zinc and arsenic are 357°C, 765°C, 906°C and 613°C, respectively. Therefore, smelter and metal refining stacks that do not have gas scrubbers can release significant amounts of relatively volatile toxic metals into the atmosphere that eventually deposit onto the land.

DEFORESTATION

Deforestation is simply the conversion of forested tracts of barren lands. This is usually done by clear-cutting tress and removing the wood. Forested areas are typically cleared to make room for agricultural operations or to harvest wood as a fuel source or for lumber products. Much of the deforestation cccurring globally is due to slash-and-burn operations that make room for agricultural operations.

The process of deforestation results in many undesirable environmental impacts at multiple scales. Local impacts include decreasing soil stability, increasing erosion and sediment transport into streams, reduction in biodiversity through loss of habitat, and alterations to microclimates that typically increase local temperatures because of loss of vegetation and increased numbers of heat islands. Degradation of air quality is often at the regional scale if deforestation is being driven by burning downed slash. This promotes episodes of high levels of atmospheric particular matter and carbon monoxide gas that are harmful to the health of both humans and wildlife. Deforestation can also produce impacts on a global scale. Research over the past decade has shown that the cutting and burning of large forest tracts is quickly liberating large amounts of carbon and increasing levels of the greenhouse gas, carbon dioxide, in the atmosphere. Removing forest vegetation further disrupts the global carbon balance by eliminating the living trees that served as a sink for carbon dioxide. Photosynthesis in trees converts atmospheric carbon dioxide into plant cellulose, drawing carbon out of the atmosphere and storing it as biomass.

Local Land Pollution Impacts of Deforestation

Removal of forest vegetation increases the potential of soils to become eroded by wind and/or rainfall. Runoff during precipitation events can produce both the erosion of soils and the transport of sediments into river systems. These sediments will degrade water quality by increasing turbidity and levels of dissolved nutrients (e.g., phosphorus and nitrates). Experiments to document the effects of deforestation on watershed dynamics and stream water quality have been conducted in several experimental watersheds throughout the U.S. Results form the Hubbard Brook Experimental Forest in New Hampshire show large increases in dissolved nutrient levels and sediment loads in-stream for a deforested watershed area, as compared to a control forested area watershed.

A more serious form of land-based pollution has been tied to deforestation in areas of South America. High-levels of mercury have been found in the blood of people in many rural communities in Brazil where fish is a staple food. The high mercury levels were initially attributed to gold mining operations found throughout these areas. Further study has shown that naturally occurring pools of mercury found in soil and organic matter were being readily transported into streams through runoff following deforestation. The removal of forest vegetation allowed mercury that was initially stabilized in soil organic matter to become mobile and the transported into streams.

Regional Air Quality Impacts of Deforestation

Deforestation is often accompanied by the burning of biomass. Sometimes the burning is done to clear slashed vegetation, and at other times harvested forest vegetation is burned as a fuel source for heating and cooking. In either case the burning of forest biomass on large scales can cause serious air quality problems. Particulate mater, ozone, and carbon monoxide are all produced when forest biomass is burned, and all pose health risks to humans.

Soil Acidity-Salinity

Acid Soils

Acid soils occur naturally or develop as the result of continuous additions of acid-forming fertilizers. Natural acid soils are usually found in the tropics, the result of thousands of years of excessive weathering of soil minerals. High rainfall and year-around high temperatures leaches all basic cations (such as Na, Ca, Mg, and K) and pH buffering minerals (such as carbonates). Also, this climate promotes the transformation and subsequent leaching of Si form Si-based minerals, leaving acidic iron and aluminum oxides minerals. For example, soluble aluminum can release protons into the soil environment by the following general reaction:

$$Al^{3+} + H_2O \rightarrow Al(OH)_3 \text{ (solid)} + 3H^+ \qquad \ldots(2)$$

Similarly, the presence of pyrite minerals in some soils can lead to the formation of acidic soil conditions, in a reaction similar to Equation (2) above.

Agricultural soils can also become acidic due to the continuous additions of large amounts of acid-forming fertilizers such as ammonia and urea. For example, one mole-equivalent weight of ammonium (NH_4^+) can produce two mole-equivalent of H^+ after it is fully oxidized to nitrate (NO_3^-) in the soil environment.

Other sources of acid-forming chemicals that impact the soil environment include coal-burning air emissions (SO_2, NO_x) that are hydrolyzed and scrubbed out of the atmosphere by rain.

Salinity

Soil salinity is a measure of the minerals and salts that can be dissolved in water. In most cases, the following mineral ions are found in soil-water extract listed in order of importance:

Na^+, Cl^-, Ca^{++}, $SO_4^=$, HCO_3^-, K^+, Mg^{++}, NO_3^-

Increased soil salinity has progressive and often profound effects on the structure, microbial diversity, and plant activity of soils. Soil salinity is measured by using electrical conductivity (EC) measurements of a water-saturated soil paste extract.

An excessive concentration of Na ions in soils produces an imbalance in the ratio of monovalent cations to divalent cations. This is measured by the exchangeable sodium percent (ESP). Salt-affected soils are thus also classified by their EPS.

There are numerous sources of soil salinity. Natural soil salinity occurs in hot arid and semi-arid climates with ≤27 cm annual rainfall. Soils and lands that have shallow water tables can develop saline soils due to excessive water evaporation and the concentration of salts. Poor water quality and irrigation practices also contribute to the salinization of thousands of acres of farmland each year around the world. Salt-affected soils occupy, on a global basis, 952.2 million ha of land. These soils constitute nearly 7% of the total land area or nearly 33% of the potential agricultural land area of the world.

Soil Erosion

Soil particles can act as carriers of other contaminants that are sorbed to particulate surfaces. For example, phosphorus is often associated with soil particles and sediments. When soil particles are eroded and discharged into an aquatic environment, the resulting sediments increases the P nutrient levels of the water and can cause excessive growth of algae and other aquatic plants. This process, together the concomitant reduction in oxygen, is known as eutrophication.

Organic chemicals including herbicides, insecticides, fuels, solvents, preservatives, and other industrial and agricultural chemicals, can be similarly adsorbed and desorbed form waterborne soil particulates.

Naturally occurring particulate contaminants come from many sources, including agricultural operations, logging, construction-related activities, mining and quarrying, and unpaved roads, and from wind erosion. Soil erosion is a natural process that occurs continuously, but is often accelerated by human activities. Several factors are required for soil material to become dislodged and transported into air or water. Soil must be susceptible to erosional processes, which generally requires that the soil erosion, soil particles become dislodged. Energy inputs must be adequate to dislodge particles. In the second phase, the particles are transported. Various soil properties, which we will examine, determine the susceptibility of soil particles to dislodgement.

Soil Water Erosion and Control

We will first consider particle movement caused by water. Soil particles are used formed into aggregates, which vary considerably in size, shape, and stability. Organic and inorganic materials and certain soil cations are the primary aggregating and inter-particle cementing agents. In the detachment phase, individual particles are dispersed or separated from aggregates or cemented particles. The source of the energy responsible for detaching soil particles is either raindrop impact or the flow of runoff water. When raindrops, which travel at approximately 900 cm s^{-1}, hit bare soil, the kinetic energy of the raindrops is transferred to the soil particles, breaking apart, aggregates and dislodging particles. Dislodged particles can be moved over 1 m in the splash from raindrop impact. They are moved larger distances by runoff water, which can dislodge additional particles through sourcing action. Smaller particles are transported more easily than large ones, and faster flowing water can carry a heavier particulate load than slow-moving water. When uniform shallow layers of soil are eroded off areas of land, this is called *sheet erosion*. Directed water flow cuts channels into the soil. Small channels are called *rills*; large channels are *gullies*.

The process of water erosion has been described by the United States Department of Agriculture (USDA) Universal Soil Loss Equation (USLE), later modified to the Revised Universal Soil Loss Equation (RUSLE).

$$A = 2.24R \times K \times LS \times CP \times P \qquad \ldots(3)$$

where:

A = the estimated average annual soil loss (metric tons/hectare)

R = the rainfall and runoff erosivity index. This describes intensity and duration of rainfall in a given geographical area. It is the product of the kinetic energy of raindrop and the maximum 30-minute intensity.

K = the soil erodibility factor. K is the related to soil physical and chemical properties that determine how easily soil particles can be dislodged. It is related to soil texture, aggregate stability, and soil permeability or ability to absorb water. It ranges from (very easily eroded) to 0.01 (very stable soil).

LS = a dimensionless topography factor determined by length and steepness of a slope. The LS factor is related to the velocity of runoff water. Water moves faster on a steep slope than a more level one, and it picks up speed and longer the slope, the faster runoff water will flow. The faster water flows, the more kinetic energy it can impact to the soil surface (kinetic energy = mass × velocity^2).

C = the cover and management factor. Cover of any kind can help protect the soil surface from raindrop impact and can force runoff water to take a longer, more tortuous path as it moves downslope, slowing the water and reducing its kinetic energy.

P = the factor for supporting practices. This factor takes into account specific erosion control measures. Erosion control practices reduce the P factor.

In the past few decades, farmer have tried to reduce tillage that leaves soil bare and to minimize the amount of time that the soil surface is exposed to raindrops. These new agricultural practices are collectively known as *Reduced Tillage* or *Minimum Tillage* systems. On highly erodible lands, specific erosion control practices include contour planting strip cropping or terracing, all of which can effectively reduce erosion.

Bare soil construction sites and along road cuts is often covered with synthetic fabrics called geotextiles. These coarse woven materials provide immediate protection and may be used in conjunction with seeding of cover corps that can provide long-term cover. Grass or other plants can be seeded with a hydroseeder that sprays a mixture of seed, fertilizer, mulch, and polymers that cement the mixture into a cohesive soil covering that gives temporary protection to the soil surface until the seeds can geminate and plants cover the soil. Permeable barriers made of straw bales or woven fabrics can be used to slow water and reduce its ability to carry sediments. Runoff water can be trapped in settling ponds in which water velocity is eliminated or greatly reduced, allowing suspended particles to settle out, and reducing sediment loads before overflow water is released. If suspended colloids are in a dispersed condition, flocculating agents may be added to aggregate particles into larger assemblages that rapidly settle out of suspension. *Gabions* or wire mesh containers filled with rocks can also be used to control water erosion.

Soil Wind Erosion and Control

Like water erosion, wind erosion has two phases: detachment and movement. As the wind blows, soil particles are dislodged and begin to roll or bounce along the soil surface in a process called *saltation*. Large soil particles can move relatively short distances in this way, but more importantly, as the large particles bounce and strike smaller particles and aggregates, they provide the energy necessary to break aggregates apart and suspend smaller particles in the air. Smaller particles remain suspended in air for longer periods of time and are therefore more likely to travel much longer distances. As in the case of water erosion, models that examine the factors important in wind erosion are useful in predicting wind erosion.

It should be noted that finer textured soils (those with more silt and clay sized particles) are less erodible than sandy soils. This reflects the ability of soil aggregates to hold the soil in place during high wind events. On the other hand, PM_{10} consists largely of silt-sized particles, and $PM_{2.5}$ is mainly clay. Therefore, soil wind erosion and particulate matter production are not directly related.

Wind velocity, a major factor in soil wind erosion, can be decreased with windbreaks. These may be living wind-breaks of planted trees, shrubs, or grasses, or they can be constructed material such as fences or screens. Windbreaks are most effective when placed perpendicular to the direction of the prevailing wind. Effects of windbreaks extend to as much as 40 to 50 times the height of the windbreak; however, the area adequately protected by the windbreak is usually smaller. Effective control is usually considered to extend to about 10 times the height of the windbreak. Wind erosion is reduced by a rough soil surface.

Surface roughness can be controlled by creating ridges or a rough surface with tillage implements. Ridges 5 to 10 cm in height are most effective for controlling wind erosion. Soil surface can also be protected by providing vegetative or other surface cover, such as straw, hay, animal manure, or biosolids. The soil water erosion control measures discussed earlier also provide effective wind erosion control.

Various amendments that bind soil particles together, including calcium chloride ($CaCl_2$), soybean feedstock processing by-products, calcium lignosulfate, polyvinyl acrylic polymer emulsion, polyacrylamide, and emulsified petroleum resin are applied to unpaved roads to reduce particulate emissions. Unpaved roads can also be covered in gravel or similar nonerodible surfacing materials. However, most of these treatments generally offer only temporary dust control and must be periodically repeated.

Agricultural Activity

Fertilizers

Plants need numerous chemicals in order to complete their life cycles. There are at least 16 *essential elements* required for the growth of all plants: C, H, O, N, P, K, Ca, Mg, S, Fe, Mn, Zn, Cu, Mo, B, and Cl in various ionic forms. Interestingly, soil microbes require these same elements. In undisturbed ecosystems, plants obtain these nutrients from the soil solution via mineral weathering, atmospheric inputs, inputs from stream deposition, and nutrient recycling due to death and decomposition of vegetation. The availability of the nutrients depends on abiotic soil factors and chemical and biological properties. Agricultural crop production has always relied on soil components for nutrient sources. However, excessive cropping and in particular dense monoculture practices deplete soil plant nutrients, especially N, P, K, and Ca. Thus, over years of continuous crop production, large amounts of nutrients are removed, with a concomitant decline in productivity. Therefore, N, P, K, and other plant nutrients must be periodically augmented by the use of fertilizers, including animal or human wastes. Fertilizers may contain any of the essential nutrients, but the majority of fertilizers applied to agricultural soils contain nitrogen (N), phosphorus (P), potassium (K), or some combination thereof. These are so-called *macronutrients* because plants take them up in larger amounts than the other essential nutrients.

Fertilizer use dramatically increased around the time of World War II, as improved crop varieties and management practices, together with increased mechanization, made fertilizer use both practicable and profitable. In the 1980s, however, fertilizer use began to level off, reflecting both lower agricultural profitability and increased environmental concerns related to fertilizer use. Nonetheless, the combined annual per capita use in the U.S. of NPK fertilizers is about more than 150 lbs ($\sim$70 kg). The aforementioned concerns associated with the use of NPK fertilizers and wastes include excessive surface and groundwater pollution by water-soluble nitrates and colloid-bound phosphates due to poor agricultural fertilizer and waste management practices.

Pesticides

Extensive use of synthetic pesticides began in the 1940s with DDT used to control mosquitoes. This was quickly followed by the adoption of pesticides in large scale monocultural agricultural production. Initially pesticide use was credited with significant increases in food production. However, the negative aspects of their indiscriminate use also became evident. For example, extensive use of insecticides and herbicides has created new generations of pesticide resistant insects and plants.

In 1962, Rachel Carson's book *Silent Spring* brought public attention to the fact that chlorinated pesticides were very persistent in the environment. These chemicals can accumulate in animal fatty tissue and produce fish kills when released into waterways. DDT, associated with the rapid decline of some birds of pray, was banned for agricultural use in the United States in 1973. Other chlorinated pesticides were also banned, but have been replaced by much less persistent, but more acutely toxic, pesticides. In addition, in recently years new links have been discovered between some types of cancer and low-level exposure to some pesticides like 2,4-dichlorophenoxyacetic acid (2,4-D), 2,4,5-trichlorophenoxyacetic acid (2,4,5-T), and other pesticides.

Less persistent pesticides are usually much more soluble in water than chlorinated hydrocarbons. Unfortunately, these new pesticides are more like to leach to groundwater or be found in the agricultural runoff if they are not degraded fast enough in the soil environment. Today, pesticides continue to be used extensively in modern farming, urban lawns, parks, and golf courses primarily to control weeds, fungi, and insect infestations. Unfortunately, even less persistent pesticides have their problems. In 2003, the U.S. EPA concluded that atrazine, the second most widely pesticide (herbicide) in the U.S., could cause sexual abnormalities in frogs. In addition, atrazines, the most common family of herbicide chemicals found in groundwater are also potential endocrine disruptors.

Types of pesticides

The technical definition, stated in the amended *Federal insecticide, Fungicide*, and *Rodenticide act* (FIFRA), is that a pesticide is any substance or mixture of substances intended for destroying, preventing, or mixture of substances intended for destroying, preventing, or mitigating insects, rodents, nematodes, fungi, weeds, or any other undesirable pests. This also includes plant or insect growth regulators as well as defoliants that are used to cause leaves to drop form plants to facilitate harvest, and desiccants that dry up unwanted plant tissue. Under this definition, many chemicals, both newly developed and familiar, may be considered as pesticides and be regulated as such. For example, insect pheromones (sex attractants) may be used to attract certain insect populations, to confuse mating patterns, and thereby control insect population. In addition, ordinary dish detergent may be used to kill whiteflies or bees. Common tale salt (sodium chloride) is used to control weeds in beet fields in humid regions.

Insecticides are formulated to control particular insects. Two common insecticides are chlorpyrifos and malathion. Herbicides are formulated to control weeds. Glyphosate and atrazine are the two most common herbicides, accounting for 70-90% of the total herbicide use in the U.S. (US EPA, 2004). Fungicides are formulated to control fungi including molds and mushrooms. Chloropicrin, metam-sodium and 1,3-dichloropropene are the three commonly used fumigants applied to soil to control the nematodes and soil fungi in the U.S.

Pesticides may also be classified according to their mode of entry into the target pest. Contact pesticides enter the target pest upon direct application, while systemic pesticides must pass through a host organism before they enter their targets. For example, a contact insecticide, or its residue, kills target plants or insects on direct application, while a systemic insecticide kills insects only after moving through the system of the plant hosting the target insect. Thus, if a particular insect does not feed on the plant, it will not be harmed.

Finally, pesticides can be classified by the forms in which they are used. Fumigants, for example, are pesticides applied as gases. Fumigants may be used selectively to control dry-wood termites in houses or to control the pest population in stored products such as fruits, vegetables, and grains. They may also be released over large areas to remove many pests from soil.

Extent of pesticide use

Pesticides are sold or distributed by intra- or interstate commerce in the united States, and they must be registered by the U.S. EPA. The EPA has compiled substantial lists of pesticide ingredients whose applications must be reported. The EPA is also authorized, by the Federal Food, Drug, and Cosmetic Act (FFDCS), to establish tolerances for pesticide residues in raw and processed foods. The Food and Drug Administration (FDA) of the Department of Health and Human Services monitors and enforces the established tolerances.

In addition many individuals states in the United States have established other regulatory agencies to control pesticide applications in order to protect wildlife and water supplies. For example, Arizona has compiles as list of chemicals—the Groundwater Protection List—whose use must be reported. Similar requirements exists for the sales of these pesticides, so that significant under reporting of applications cannot occur without altering the regulatory agency.

According to the U.S EPA, in 2001 the use of conventional pesticides in the U.S. was estimated to be about 1.2 billion lbs (545 million kg), reflecting a slightly declining trend in use since the mid-1980s. These figures places the annual per capita use of pesticides at about 4 lbs ($\sim$1.9 kg). The U.S. EPA estimates that in 2001 about 78% of the products were used in agricultural production; 12% in home and garden settings; and the remaining 10% in forestry, industry, and government programs. Therefore, most of these chemicals were applied directly onto plants and animals on agricultural lands and water systems. In addition, industry and water utilities also use chemicals with pesticide-like properties. For example, according to U.S. EPA estimates in 2001, about 790 million lbs (360 million kg) of wood preservative chemicals and 2.6 billion lbs (1.19 billion kg) of chlorine and hypochlorite chemicals were used in the U.S. These highly toxic chemicals include creosote, pentachlorophenol, and CCA (chromate copper arsenate). Presently, pesticide product labeling must list their active ingredients and the EPA's registration number, as well as safe use instructions to minimize personal exposure and damage to soil and water environments.

It is interesting to note that despite the public awareness about numerous links between pesticide residues, their adverse health and environmental effects, and the increasing public demands for pesticide-free food, the largest growth sector for pesticides is in home and garden applications. Since 1995, the use of pesticides by the private sector (home and garden) has nearly doubled (From 7% to 12% in 2001).

Fate of pesticides

Depending upon their physiochemical properties, patterns of use, and local conditions, some pesticides may leach through the crop root zone and eventually contaminate groundwater at certain locations. The two most important properties of a chemical that determine whether a pesticide represents a threat to groundwater are its *persistence* and *mobility* in soil. During the registration of new pesticides, computer programs are used to estimate the potential for groundwater to be contaminated by the specific use of a particular chemical at various locations in the United States. Several states, including Arizona and California, consider the capacity of a compound to leach through the soil into groundwater as a criterion for inclusion in their lists of controlled chemicals.

After a pesticide is applied to a field, it may meet a variety of fates. Some may be lost to the atmosphere through volatilization, carried away to surface waters by runoff and erosion, or photodegraded by sunlight. Pesticides that have entered into soil may be taken up by plants (and subsequently removed), degraded into other chemical forms, or leached downward with water below the crop root zone. The amount of any particular chemical that ends up volatilized, leached, degraded, or in surface runoff depends upon site conditions, weather conditions, management practices, soil properties, and pesticide properties.

In evaluating the contamination potential of a particular pesticide, it is essential to consider its sorption (retardation) and transformation half-life behavior jointly. For example, a pesticide with low retardation and a long half-life (e.g., more than 100 days) poses a considerable threat to groundwater through leaching, particularly in soils having low organic matter. Conversely, a pesticide with large retardation and a long-life is more likely to remain on or near the surface of soils with moderate levels of organic carbon content, thereby increasing its chances of being carried to a lake or stream in runoff water. In terms of water quality protection, pesticides with intermediate retardation and short half-lives may be considered the "safest." Although they are not readily leached, they move into the soil with water, thereby reducing their potential for loss from erosion, and they degrade fairly rapidly, thereby reducing the chance for losses below the root zone. It was assumed that the rainfall and irrigation amounts exceeded the crop water use by twice the amount of water contained in the root zone at an optimum water content that moved the chemicals downward.

Glyphosate would be concentrated in the root zone to a depth of about 25 cm, atrazine would be concentrated near the bottom of the root zone (about 125 cm), and aldicarb would be concentrated at a depth of about 250 cm. A slightly higher percentage of the applied atrazine would exist in the system, compared with the other two pesticides, because it has a slightly larger half life. For a growing season of about 120 days, about 6% of the applied aldicarb and glyphosate would remain, while about 20% of the atrazine would remain. This example does not account for numerous differences in management practices that would influence the persistence and soil distribution of these pesticides.

Animal Wastes

Animal wastes contain several types of land pollutants that are of increasing concern both to the public and regulators. Besides traditional pollutants, discussed below, increasing evidence suggests that excessive use of animals waste on land releases measurable amounts of antibiotics, growth hormones, and pesticides containing toxic metals like arsenic. Animal agricultural wastes can be divided by two production types: range and pasture production, and confined or concentrated animal production.

In range and pasture systems, the concentration of wastes is generally much more diffuse or dispersed than it is when large numbers of animals are confined to relatively small areas. Range and pasture systems have two principal measurable effects on surface water quality: (1) increased turbidity through the movement of soil particles into streams, rivers, and lakes; and (2) increased fecal coliform counts in areas of heavy animal use. Although we know that grazing systems may adversely affect some measures of water quality, we will focus here on the highly concentrated animal production units and the methods of preventing and controlling pollution from these concentrated units. Concentrated animal production is very common and is occurring in increasingly controlled environments to raise productivity and diminish climatic, feeding, and mortality variables. Larger number of animals are being raised in *concentrated animal feeding operations* or CAFOs—principally, feedlots, dairies, swine operations, poultry houses, and intensive aquaculture.

Following World War II, manure was displaced as the primary fertilizer by fossil-fuel-based fertilizers as farms became increasingly specialized.

With the breakdown of the traditional cycle of reincorporation of wastes back in to the land, what was once an essential source of nutrients has now become a potential pollutant. Thus, the production of large numbers of animals on a small land base has resulted in the stockpilling of wastes, the construction of large waste-storage ponds, and, often-times, waste applications to land in excess of agronomic crop needs. To date, few states regulate the land application of animal wastes to the degree that biosolids are regulated.

Nonpoint versus Point Source Pollution

The term "nonpoint is misleading and is often misused in the context of animal wastes. In animal agricultural systems, true *nonpoint sources* are those in which potential contaminants are not concentrated during production and do not pass through a single or small number of conduits for disposal. These nonpoint sources include corrals, feedlots, and extensive and intensive pasture systems.

Point sources are those facilities that concentrate pollutants or contaminants to a significant degree and pass these contaminants through a pipe, ditch, or canal for disposal. The most common point sources are milksheds and barns, dairy and other food-processing plants, intensive indoor swine facilities, anaerobic and aerobic lagoons, and evaporative storage ponds. In addition, certain types of intensive aquaculture may also be point source of contaminants, with return flows highly nutrient-laden with fish excreta. According to EPA regulations, however, some concentrated animal feeding operations may be designated as point sources requiring an individual National Pollution Discharge Elimination System (NPDES) permit, In this case, a concentrated animal feeding operation is defined as a lot or facility without vegetation where animals are confined for 45 or more days per year. The number of animals needed to meet this definition as a CAFO depends on several factors; the key determinant is whether or not the facility discharges into navigable waters, as determined by the method of discharge. The method of discharge is judged by the 25-year, 24-hour storm event, which is the required event that a facility must be designed to meet.

Nonpoint sources, such as nondischarging concentrated animal feeding operations, require a different approach to prevention and mitigation of pollutants than do point source emissions from a pipe or conduit. At present, the nonpoint source approach to mitigation employs *Best Management Practices* (BMPs), as defined by the 1987 Amendments to the Federal Water Pollution Control Act. In contrast, point source methods employ methods termed Best Available Demonstrated Control Technology or Best Available control Technology. In 2003, the U.S. EPA (2003) published a Final Rule on CAFOs that is now used to permit animal feeding operations by establishing requirements that are more protective of the environment. Large amounts of animal wastes are land applied.

Specific Pollutants

Concentrated animal agriculture produces specific pollutants in the wastes resulting from animal metabolic activity.

INDUSTRIAL WASTES WITH HIGH SALS AND ORGANICS

Oil Drilling

The process of drilling for crude oil requires powerful drill rigs that use large quantities of drilling fluids. These fluids contain high-density weighing agents such as barium sulfate (barite). Other drilling fluids are composed of sodium chloride solutions, which are used to force crude oil up to the surface. These fluids must be disposed of once they are "spent", or no longer useful. Prior to 1985, these spend fluids were stored in ponds near the drill sites and often simply bulldozed over when the well was completed. Consequently, many older oilfields have large tracts of land contaminated with spent drilling wastes. These wastes are not considered hazardous because they do not contain significant amounts of metals. Although free barium is very toxic, the mineral barites ($BaSO_4$) is quite inert in the environment. On the other hand, NaCl is very soluble in water and can increase the salinity of surface waters, rendering them nonpotable.

Coal-Burning Electric Power Plants

Electric power plants produce millions of tons of *fly ash* and *flue gas desulfurization wastes* every year. Because these residues are not considered hazardous, they may be stored either in ponds or landfills, or, in the case of fly ash, they may be used as fill material. Fly ash is recovered from electrostatic precipitators that scrub out silt-size particulate matter from the flue gases generated from coal combustion. These particles generally arise from the incombustible silt and clay found in coal deposits. Upon exposure to high temperatures, silt and clay (which consists mostly of silica and alumina) combine to yield amorphous Si–Al-based spheres onto which other elements may condense. Typically, fly ash spheres also include Ca, Na, Fe, Mg, K, and Ti, with small amounts of other elements sorbed onto them, such as As, B, Ba, Cd, Cr, Cu, F, Mo, NI, Pb, S, and Zn. The concentration of these elements in fly ash vary widely, depending on the source of the coal. A typical empirical composition of fly ash is

$$10\ \text{Si} + 5\ \text{Al} + 0.5\ \text{Ca} + 0.5\ \text{Na} + 0.4\ \text{Fe}$$
$$+ 0.2\ \text{Mg} + 0.2\ \text{Mg} + 0.2\ \text{K} + 0.1\ \text{Ti}$$
$$+ 0.05\ \text{S} + \text{trace amounts of more than 15}$$
$$\text{other elements.}$$

The removal (scrubbing) of sulfur dioxide (SO_2) gas from flue gases produces large quantities of flue gas desulfurization wastes, which consists largely of calcium carbonates, sulfates, and sulfites. These wastes may also contain trace quantities of some of the elements in fly ash, but the concentration of these elements depends on the source of the coal and the type of scrubbing systems used. Because flue gas desulfurization products are usually more than 70% water, these wastes are disposed of in drying ponds and are often treated along with power-plant wastewaters. This waste mixing may add significant amounts of soluble salts (e.g., NaCl) that increase the salinity of sludges.

Despite new gas scrubbing technology and stricter emission standards, sulfur dioxide and nitrous oxide have been reduced but not completely eliminated. For example, current emissions of these two acid-forming gases still exceed 10 millions tons/year. However, significant reductions (>60%) are mandated by the U.S. EPA in the next 16 years via a new *Clean Air Interstate Rule* (CAIR), which affects 28 eastern U.S. States.

Mercury metal emissions from coal-burning electric power plants have also been a controversial issue. For the first time, reductions in Hg emissions from coal-burning power plants are being mandated under the new March 2005 *Clean Air Mercury Rule*. Under this rule, by 2020, reductions of 70% Hg emissions are expected form coal-burning power plants.

Industrial Wastes High in Organic Chemicals

Most industrial wastes contain varying amounts of organic chemicals. With few exceptions, carbon-based chemicals reagents, solvents, feedstocks, and raw materials are extensively used in most phases of industrial processing. Exceptions to this rule may include mine tailings and metal-plating wastes. Wastes high in organic chemicals include those originating from oil refineries, as well as petrochemical, chemical, pharmaceutical, and food-processing industries, and paper mills. However, in recent years, these industries have reduced their polluting waste streams by applying aggressive pollution prevention strategies such as wastewater treatment process before discharge, the implementation of water reduction techniques that include recycling, and changes in industrial process with emphasis on waste minimization processes.

Invasive Species

Invasive species are an environmental problem of growing concern worldwide. Invasive species are organisms that have been introduced to a new ecosystem that have a severe, often irreversible effect on agriculture and natural ecosystems. Any organism can become an invasive species, including microorganisms, invertebrates, insects, fish, plants and animals. Invasive organisms often find few enemies (predators and diseases) in their new locations, allowing them, at least initially, to grow and reproduce relatively easily.

It is important to note that a key component of this is sue is that humans typically introduce the invasive species. Species can gradually spread into new areas as a natural process; this process is usually slow and involves adjustments by all members of the ecosystems. Conversely, human introductions are usually relatively fast, often resulting in large disruptions of the ecosystems.

In most cases, invasive species take advantage of opportunities in ecosystems that are disturbed by human activity. Disturbances can be flow control of rivers, disturbed soil along roadways and agricultural areas, human structures (e.g., pigeons and sparrows are better adapted to cities than many native birds), water temperature change due to power plant outflows, and so on.

Some invasive species were introduced to provide erosion control, such as kudzu and salt cedar. Other, such as Lehman lovegrass and red brome, were repeatedly introduced over large areas of the Western U.S. as forage grasses for cattle and sheep. These grasses have radically altered the fire ecology of western ranges, which in turn has changed plant populations, wildlife distribution, and nutrient cycling. Other invasive species escaped from gardens. A widely known example is purple loosestrife, which is a colorful perennial plant that is prized in gardens. Purple loosestrife has spread widely in the eastern and northern U.S., choking waterways and supplanting native riparian species. Animals released as hunting stock have caused problems. Examples include opossums in the northwestern U.S., rabbits in Australia, and red deer in New Zealand. Invasive Zebra mussels in the Great Lakes have caused millions of dollars worth of damage to water intake systems, while simultaneously decreasing like biodiversity. Fire ants (*Solenopsis invicta*) decrease biodiversity while causing major economic damage.

Kudzu

Kudzu (*Pueraria montana* var. *lobata*) is a well-known, highly visible example of an invasive plant species. Kudzu is a broad leaved, fast growing perennial vine from Japan that was deliberately introduced in the early 1900s to control erosion and provide forage in the southern U.S. Kudzu grows rapidly and stabilizes loose soil with large, fleshy roots. In the U.S., kudzu has few serious checks on its growth by insects or disease, which allows it to grow as much as 20 m (60 feet) per season. This growth tends to completely cover existing vegetation, and can break branches and block sunlight form the native plants, eventually greatly weakening or killing them. Kudzu can also cover cars and entire buildings. Once it is well established, kudzu is difficult to remove. In addition, there is some evidence that kudzu is becoming more cold tolerant, extending its range to the north. It is estimated that kudzu covers about 25,000 square kilometers (10,000 square miles) in the U.S. and that it costs somewhere between $100 million to $500 million dollars a year in lost cropland and control costs.

Salt Cedar

Kudzu is quite obvious, even to the untrained eye, and causes visible damage as it smothers other plants and buildings with its extremely rapid growth. Many invasive species do not cause such obvious problems. Salt cedar (*Tamarix* spp.) has rapidly colonized riparian areas throughout the western U.S., causing major changes in this habitat. These changes are not obvious to the casual observer and yet are causing profound changes in riparian ecosystems.

Multiple species of salt cedar were originally introduced more than 100 years ago for erosion control and ornamental use. Salt cedar is tolerant of drought and saline and alkaline soils, grows quickly if there is sufficient water, has high seed production, and resprouts easily after fire. In addition, salt cedar has been implicated in lowering water tables at the expense of native species and also of salinizing soil. It is generally thought that these characteristic have enabled them to supplant native stands of cottonwood (*Populus* spp.) and willow (*Salix* spp.) That provide wildlife habitat, while producing little useful habitat of their own. As a result, land mangers consider salt cedar a prime example of a detrimental invasive species.

Salt cedar is now found throughout the western U.S., thriving in response to human disturbances related to dams and diversion projects along large drainages. Research indicates that salt cedar changes the species composition of riparian communities and reduces their biodiversity. Thickets of salt cedar tend to replace native shrubs and trees such as willow and cottonwood, generally without replacing their usefulness as nesting sites and food sources. This may be due in part to the control of floods by dams, as willows and cottonwoods tend to establish new seedlings after flood events. In addition, regulation of river flow in general is causing many riparian areas to become drier and more saline. Recent research indicates that salt cedar may be better adapted to these new growing conditions, which allows them to outcompete the native species.

Slat cedar is also widely regarded as a cause of salinization of soil, which is thought to prevent or diminish the growth of many native species. Salt cedar is very tolerant of salinity and is able to use low-quality surface and ground-water sources that many native cannot. The plants store excess salts in salt glands in the leaves and also excrete salt onto the surface of the leaves themselves. Since salt cedar is deciduous, the leaves eventually fall to the soil surface and build up a salt-rich litter.

In areas with floods or sufficient rain, this salt is moved out of the root zone, but salt cedar usually grows in arid areas with low rainfall and along regulated waterways (preventing regular floods), thus allowing some salt buildup. Recent research indicates that there may not be salt buildup over a period of years, as rains and occasional floods may leach the salt out of the root zone. Other research indicates that the salt buildup is small enough that it does not affect some of the more salt-tolerant native species.

There is no doubt that salt cedar is an invasive species. Land managers are finding it difficult to remove salt cedar and re-establish native populations, and have blamed salt cedar for drier conditions and more saline soil. However, salt cedar may instead be able to adapt more readily than some native species to human-caused ecosystem disturbances.

Invasive species have caused major ecosystem changes throughout the world, resulting in billions of dollars of damage to agriculture, forestry, power plants, and the like each year. They are almost impossible to eradicate and difficult to control once established.

INDEX